EX ITENT ER

EX ITENT ER

ENCOUNTERS AROUND TAROT
VOLUME TWO

ENRIQUE ENRIQUEZ

EyeCorner Press

© ENRIQUE ENRIQUEZ & EyeCorner Press | 2012

EX ITENT ER
Encounters around Tarot
Volume 2

The interviews are reprinted with the permission of the authors.

Published by EYECORNER PRESS
December 2012
Roskilde

ISBN: 978-87-92633-21-7

Editorial, cover design and layout: Camelia Elias
Image: Fabrizio Chiesa

Printed in the US and UK

To the letter V that slips
with me.

CONTENTS

BENT SØRENSEN: TAR O TAR T / 9

encounters with

JOHN RIGGS / 16
GINNY HUNT / 27
ART ROSENGARTEN / 43
DAN PELLETIER / 56
MARCUS KATZ / 81
ARON PRICE / 98
TANYA JOYCE / 106
REECE HENDLEY / 120
ERIK DAVIS / 136
VALENTINA BURTON / 142
STEPHEN SCHWARTZ / 148
JAMES RICKLEF / 156
DOUG DYMENT / 164
DEAN MONTALBANO / 171
DONNALEIGH DE LAROSE / 177
EMILY CARDING / 189
ANGELO NASIOS / 196
RICK MAUE / 206
STORM SCESTAVANI / 220
KATRINA WYNNE / 227
JAMES WELLS / 236
YVES REYNAUD / 245
WILFRIED HOUDOUIN / 253
PABLO ROBLEDO / 269
YOAV BEN-DOV / 274
ENRIQUE ENRIQUEZ / 281

TAR O TAR T
THE ENTRIES AND EXITS OF ENRIQUE ENRIQUEZ

Bent Sørensen, professor of English

In this second batch of extended e-mail interviews or encounters with stars of the Tarot firmament, Enrique Enriquez (EE) discusses matters of art, performance, visual and verbal punning, rhyming and poetics with 25 artists, magicians, hypnotists, deck designers, card historians, occultists, philosophers and practitioners of Tarot (as) Art. We thus get both Tarot as Tar + O and Tarot as Tar + T, but regardless of the fact that we live in a modern world about to run into overtime/OT, we are invited in this volume to wallow in EE's tar(ot) pit of words that is about to change our perception of what one can do with cards, in a manner as profound as the change a giant sloth would experience as it sank forever in the tar pits of La Brea near the end of the Pleistocene Epoch. One enters tarOT and the sticky hot pit of concepts within entirely at one's own risk...

Every encounter in this book takes as its starting point an enquiry into the uses of Tarot in these end times. Traditionally Tarot was used for fortune-telling purposes, but over the last three decades the language of therapy has invaded more and more the vocabulary of the Tarot professional community. Latterly fortune-telling has fallen on hard times and gotten a bad rep, in a world that represses its desires for mystery in the name of rationality and cost-benefit analyses. At the same time the desire for the unknowable has not disappeared but rather been displaced into the worship of new icons and deities – ranging from Angelina Jolie to Donald Trump. We do not truly live in a secularized world, but perhaps rather in a post-secular one where our needs for the sublime, for metaphysics, and for the liminal force us to attempt to rationalize away all that threatens our stability and our superego's vice-like grip on things.

EE's unique contribution to the world of Tarot is to seek to go beyond the two spheres of fortunetelling and therapy – and ask of the card professionals whether there might be more uses of Tarot than we tend to realize today. EE is happy to live and let live, and in his gentle manner he never casts aspersions on fellow practitioners who insist strongly on the occult significance of Tarot as guideline in our material world, or on those who venture to combine therapeutic techniques with cartomancy. However, it is very clear that what EE wants from the Tarot is something else entirely: art and poetry. In his enquiry he turns both to the earliest known roots of Tarot and to some of the most recent developments in art and poetics.

EE repeatedly returns to the ancient tradition of the *tarocchi appropriati* where courtiers would give the object of their affection a Tarot card (or several) and improvise a sequence of verses in her honor inspired by the card(s). This practice of cards inspiring a text or a specimen of literature is of great significance to EE who also has uncovered numerous other instances of similar practices. For instance, the best-known 20th c. writer to be obsessed with Tarot, Italo Calvino, used his Tarot deck as a story-generating machine (best expressed in his Boccaccio-like sequence of tales, *The Castle of Crossed Destinies*). André Breton, the French Surrealist poet and novelist, used self-designed Tarot cards as a springboard for quasi-automatic writing akin to prose poetry, for instance in his book *Arcane 17*, inspired by The Star card. Many of American post-WW II non-conformist poets, such as those of the Black Mountain and Beat literary movements, were also more or less openly inspired by the Tarot and sometimes other occult practices: Robert Duncan, Jack Spicer, Philip Whalen and Charles Olson, to name but a few central figures, wrote and published Tarot-inspired works, or occasionally straight-forward ekphrastic poems, describing the cards as images. All of these predecessors point forward to EE's practice of describing the cards whenever he sits down with a client, a practice he humbly describes as "looking at the cards with people", or simply "talking about the cards." Doing exactly that – describing in full, through the use of words, a pictorial element – is in fact the textbook definition of *ekphrasis*.

Dadaist forerunners to Surrealism, such as Alfred Jarry, the creator of *Ubu Roi* and founder of the science of imaginary solutions (which he named 'pataphysics) also figure prominently in EE's pantheon of honorary tarologists. The (predominantly French) OuLiPo writers are particularly near to EE's heart, as he sees their insistence on the potentiality of literature, born out of the absurdest of constraints (George Perec once wrote a whole novel eschewing the use of the letter 'e') as akin to what the Tarot contains of potential for unlocking not just a plot or story world (as Calvino discovered) but a whole new language that is purely mimetic and metonymic, as opposed to symbolic or metaphorical.

The small number of recurring pictorial elements in a *Tarot de Marseille* deck is close to the small number of letters in our alphabet, or sounds in our spoken language, and yet they generate rich multitudes of signification chains when regarded as structures of rhymes (visual or auditory), mirrorings and parallels. EE borrows the French term *la langue des oiseaux* for this new mode of expression that is founded in seeing images, breaking them down into their constituent parts, and reassembling them in words and sounds (with all the potential this creates for punning double or triple meanings) that one can share in a reading, or more accurately, a seeing/telling/hearing event with the tarologist and his client as co-practitioners of 'the language of the birds'.

Many other, more contemporary poets, such as bpNichol, Jen Bervin and Michael Stewart, resonate with EE's practice of punning and dividing words and phrases into new constellations that create a *Verfremdung*, or alienation effect in the reader or auditor, who suddenly sees new meanings emerge out of tired everyday language or dead metaphors. A typical poem by Canadian conceptual writer, bpNichol, is the one that reads:

A

LAKE

A

LANE

A

LINE

A

LONE

This poem is carved into the pavement near the place where bpNichol lives. A friend and fan of his diligently waters the line that spells the word LAKE, neatly keeping its signification afloat. One immediately sees the similarities with the new type of language game EE has devised under the name of 'tongue exercises', one of which runs:

TAROT

TO RAT

THORAX

HO AX

The permutations of the word TAROT leads to a new and wholly unexpected constellation of elements – but of course do not do so until they have literally taken a trip through the speaker's THORAX. For many more examples of 'tongue exercises' see the last encounter in the book, the collaborative interview between EE and Paul Nagy.

It is not exclusively art and poetry that inspires EE's work. He is a well-read person, pursuing studies in many arcane academic fields. He states in the conversation with Dan Pelletier: "To me, the Tarot has been fundamental for understanding how our brains work, and why we do art." A surprise to me, at least, is that in the field of metaphor theory, EE is particularly enamored of Lakoff and Johnson's work on a universal grammar of master metaphors that according to them structure not just our language but also our entire thinking of and behavior in the world. In my academic everyday practice as a scholar of American literature, I have seen too much universalist abuse of Lakoff and Johnson's work, along the lines of reducing every mention of vertical and horizontal orientation to either good (up!) or bad (being horizontal equals 'sick' or 'dead'). Such oversimplification is, however, in counterpoint to EE's otherwise clear preference for the contradictory, or outright subversive, so one wonders if the flirt he conducts with these theories is completely in earnest. At least I am confident that EE is occasionally very comfortable while horizontal, asleep and dreaming in the language of the birds, and that he would concur that growth is not universally a good thing when applied for instance to cancer tumors, nor that it is a good sign, say, when one's blood pressure is up…

The conceptual art of performers such as Joseph Beuys who once did an ekphrastic piece, entitled *How to Explain Pictures to a Dead Hare* (a phrase that might resonate with some Tarot readers when faced with a particularly annoying client), is another crucial strand in EE's approach to the Tarot. As he says "The art of the Tarot is in the performance of the Tarot", just as "Poetry is language happening", and this emphasis on the action of reading and the agency of language in interaction aligns EE with the thinking and theories of the Fluxus movement in art and the Situationist movement in theory and performance (from which EE borrows the term *détournement* in one of the encounters). To EE the deck of cards is just pieces of card-board with crude images imprinted upon them, until the moment the tarologist opens the pack by looking at the pictures and talking about them with the client. Only in the act of 'tarotizing' does the art of the Tarot come about. Only the live interaction between the cards and the human hands, eyes and tongues create an event that has meaning.

Of course EE is not blind to the profound effect of a Tarot experience on the client, and he does not fully reject either the potential therapeutic or religious aspect of such encounter. His language often betrays the presence of such insight, despite his occasionally vocal denouncement of especially the 'woo-woo' aspects of the Tarot profession.

When EE aphoristically cites "the idea of Tarot as a visual sermon", he clearly realizes that a sermon is delivered under very specific circumstances and in settings that are never non-institutional and casual – and, particularly, that sermons are not for just everyone to deliver. While EE would abhor the full implications of seeing himself as a reverend speaking from a pulpit to a congregation, he knows that he is a facilitator of insight, a teacher by example, and a man privy to confessions whether he wants to or not.

When he throws out a phrase such as "I think that the Tarot's main function is to heal language", he comes very close to admitting the therapeutic value of the cards, the reader, and the reading as event. He may displace the 'problem' from within the client to being located outside, in language itself, but if language suffers from a virus (rather than, as William Burroughs would have it, IS a virus), it still follows that whatever ails language is contagious and spread via linguistic practices themselves. As with any homeopathic cure, the way in which Tarot heals language is by poisoning it a little bit further, as EE does *par excellence* with his 'tongue exercises'.

Thus, when EE says with a wink: "I assume that a person comes for a Tarot reading because she ran out of reasonable options", he knows that whether the reader likes it or not, the client will seek out the Tarot for her personal motivations, and that her agenda may well include more or less conscious desires and longings for the sacred or for the gift of healing, i.e. the exact things neither reverend nor therapist (the reasonable options) could offer her. EE knows that his option (the Tarot) is utterly unreasonable, and he will not hesitate to point this out to the client, yet he also says: "I became a Tarot reader because there was nothing else I wanted to be, or perhaps, because there was nothing else this city [New York] was willing to accept from me."

This unreasonable claim, affording agency to the city of New York, and allowing for what truly sounds like fate to play its part, indicates again his sincere humility, but also reflects a man speaking at the height of his considerable powers to re-enchant the profanest of American urban spaces. EE's love affair with the space of NYC is movingly told in the closing encounter where Paul Nagy coaxes some autobiographical analyses out of EE, who concludes: "I made myself a Tarot reader because I needed to survive [...] I needed to relocate myself within the world of images, a world outside which I don't know how to live."

In the process of becoming a reader of images on cardboard pieces, EE became much, much more. I see him as a great visual, conceptual poet and wordsmith on a par with the best American practitioners coming out of the melting pots of New York, San Francisco and many more cities and small towns across the land. While EE perhaps prefers Allen Ginsberg for his open mind and bravery to speak unpopular truths, always at the wrong time, I am reminded both typographically and in terms of spirit and presence of that other – albeit non-capitalized – ee who went before EE in challenging both our eyes and ears with his pages of exercises of our imagination. To quote cummings:

```
        the
           sky
                was
        can   dy   lu
        minous
                edible
        spry
             pinks shy
        lemons
        greens   coo   l choc
        olate
        s.

          un   der,
           a    lo
          co
          mo
                tive   s   pout
                            ing
                              vi
                              o
                            lets
```

To ee the train contained already in its own name the rhyming syllables tooting out of its smokestack: LO CO MO, as well as the hissing consonant S, both pouting and spouting forth the steamy cloud shape that the poem itself inhabits.

To EE it is the Tarot that contains multitudes, both of images and words, which ultimately to him are one and the same thing: image-words or word-images (to coin two mirroring specimens of EE's favorite things, conjoined words). Thus, now that we have newly sensitized eyes to see and ears to hear with, it should no longer surprise us in the least to hear-see that TAROT already contains within itself the TAR as well as the TART, the ROT as well as the TROT, the OAR and – not least – the ART that we need to survive into overtime.

"We watch movies about mythical beings instead of owning our own cast of real-life super-heroes, simply because Magicians have chosen to surrender their power."

A conversation with JOHN RIGGS, magician, mentalist

In his 'Homo Ludens', historian Johan Huizinga wrote: "Whether one is sorcerer or sorcerized one is always knower and duped at once". We are used to the idea of suspending our disbelief in contexts like the theater, the movies, and presentations of secular magic, but how much suspension of disbelief do you think is involved in the expression of faith? In which way do you think a reader is duped by his own reading?

This is a very interesting question, and one I've contemplated much over the years. Many readers have total belief in their oracle, or in their psychic ability. At the other end of the pole, there are those who do not, and who practice a form of reading that's completely illusory. We have terms for these two kinds of readers, "Shut-eyes' and "Open" readers. Ford Kross and I have discussed what he calls "Wink-eyes," and what I call "Winkies," that is, people who are a mixture of shut-eye and open eye. In other words, they have one eye open and the other eye closed. I would describe myself as a Winky.

What this means is that while recognizing there can be a degree of deduction and analysis involved in a reading, there can also be an almost-magical process involving intuition, insight and even clairvoyance, which defies logical explanation. Plus, as many people have learned, some of whom were skeptical at first, the oracles seem to work on their own without assistance from the techniques of cold-reading.

I used to do a lot of work at psychic fairs, and some of the older, hipper readers began to strike me as Wink-eyes. It seemed to me some of them understood, or figured out on their own, that what they did was to utilize knowledge of human nature and observation as much as some inner gift. As I came to know them and developed trust I engaged a few of them in conversation about this, and we discussed these issues. One woman, a Tarot reader, admitted to me that a lot of what she told people from her cards was pretty vague. When a card indicated a person was "stubborn," for example, she said, "What does that mean? Anyone can be stubborn. You can say that about anyone." So I know that at least some of those we consider Shut-eyes are aware of "shotgun," boilerplate, or Barnum statements; call them what you will: those general statements that fit most people – cultural archetypes. Don't get me wrong. I'm not saying psychic readers are frauds. While I'm sure most psychic readers believe in their gift or oracle, and a percentage of them realize there are other more mundane aspects to their work while recognizing their gifts. But it's only mentalists who make a big deal over the distinction. Sometimes I think mentalists are more naive than those we call "Shut-eyes," at least the more experienced ones.

There's another aspect of this work that's not been discussed much. I think hypnotism and readings have a lot in common, at least there's some overlap. The power of suggestion is very much at play. Both the reader and the subject can become caught up in a mutual spell of suggestion where both believe something truly magical is happening, and each will reinforce the other's perception of this miraculous happening. For example, the reader can instill false memories in the sitter; the sitter will agree with whatever the reader says; a sort of back-and-forth role playing. A truly powerful personality can create hallucinations, amnesia, summon spirits, you name it. I'll confess I've deliberately used covert suggestion in the context of readings to create desired effects, but for beneficial purposes. I intend to discuss this at length in the near future.

I'm not saying this happens a lot, but it happens, and depending on the personal power and charisma of the reader, it can happen a great deal. You can convince people you're a miracle worker if you understand suggestion. We all know people often remember "miracles" we've performed we could never have accomplished. Multiply this principle by ten and you begin to grasp the scope. The problem is when the reader becomes caught up in the spell too, and believes he or she really is producing these miracles. Unless, of course, he or she really is, a possibility I do not discount. I've lived long enough, and have seen enough things, to where I don't say anything is impossible. I've been proven wrong too many times.

One possible bottom line could be that, in order to give a convincing performance, you must believe in yourself as a true psychic, otherwise you'll project internal conflict to your clients. Furthermore, you'll wrestle with all kinds of guilt and moral issues which will only cripple your efficiency and facility as a healer and entertainer. If you're going to do this thing, you must go all the way, I'm afraid; it isn't something with which people will allow you to just dabble.

You are touching on something I am very interested in: the connection between readings and hypnosis. I avoid talking too much about it in public, since it is a very complex subject and I fear one may be giving idiots permission to play with fire; but talking to you feels like a great opportunity to elaborate on it a little bit. I tend to suspect that readings run through hypnotic patterns. From the moment you put a deck of tarots on the table, you are working with the suggestions the tool itself carries: "this is an old oracle", "it gives us messages", "it talks about you!" the credibility of the tool precedes, and contextualizes whatever is said in a reading. I have mentioned elsewhere that most of these suggestions don't even come from the tarot's connection to the occult, but from the tarot's origin as a game of chance. Gaming has taught us that the cards we are dealt define our fortune.

Shuffling, cutting, mixing the deck... All these actions are designed to suggest a connection between the cards and the client, and therefore, to validate as relevant any cards the client may get. Those are "her cards". Asking the person to think of a question is part of this process. The question narrows down the semantic field from where the client will map analogies to the cards she got, rendering meaning-making easier. Then we have the actual act of reading the cards. Most readers I know place the cards on the table facing themselves, which is a misuse of the tool. Even so, I have seen lots of readers who will say something to a client, whatever it is, while tapping on a card, as if signifying they are getting the information from there. This may or may not be the case, but using the cards as convincers is extremely effective. Building up on that, I do my best at having whatever I say mirroring the images on the table. I do place the images facing my clients, because I intend to use these images on them. When a client can visually confirm what you are telling her, the likelihood of her accepting it is higher. At the same time, describing the cards is a way of pacing the client, by pointing to them 'facts' they can corroborate, so you can lead them into accepting some other points you need to make. Just as this process works within one single card, a sequence of cards is also a pace and leading structure: "if you got such and such cards, followed by such and such cards, then this final cards means this". Again, you give the person something she can corroborate visually, then something else she can verify, and then you use that verifiability to suggest a third notion that may not be verifiable, but is what you really need to impress upon the person.

I believe that all readers, consciously or unconsciously, do something like this. But the real suggestive work doesn't stop there. When you describe the body posture of a character in a card, you are eliciting meaning from the client who has an experiential knowledge of that posture and a set of memories associated to it. Any literal description you make of an image has a metaphorical innuendo for the client. Then, you can work the same process in reverse, and anchor some suggestions to an image so the client, by remembering it, can elicit these memories again, or reenact certain attitudes. That is what I call "prescribing a symbol". I guess that the 'desired effects' you mentioned are part of this kind of work. I tend to suspect that what readers call predictions are more likely to be post-reading suggestions. The amount of suggestions built into this process makes readings a very delicate thing. Readings can be potentially beneficial, in the same way a symphony or a movie can be potentially beneficial, if the response they elicit gives people strength. But they can be harmful, and haunting, if these responses are disempowering. To me, the key of a reading is not what you tell the client, but how you make her feel. You can give a person permission to fail, to dismiss reality, or to be the best they can be. What scares me are those readers who are unaware of these processes and therefore are unaware of the imprint they leave on the people they work with. An image can haunt a person for years, so I try not to leave any lose ends attached to it.

I would love to know any thoughts on the matter you feel comfortable sharing. Now, with all that potential for harm as well as for good, and without feeling predestined by a divine whim, what gives us the right to do readings? What do you think gives you that right?

Enrique, the hypnosis discussion could go on for volumes, so I'll address your next question: What gives us the right to do readings? This is another issue I've wrestled with, as I'm sure many of us have, at least those of us with a germ of conscience. For a long time I couldn't answer this question. There seems to be a great amount of hubris in the heart of an individual who takes upon himself the mantle of the oracle. However, the responsibility is also humbling if you give it any thought at all. I know when I was a very young person I didn't consider the responsibility very much – I don't think any young person can – but as I grew older, and experienced the pains and heartbreaks of life, and healed from those heartbreaks, I gained the experience I needed to understand exactly what those other people, our clients, were bringing to my table. So over the years, my approach became gentler and more compassionate. I set aside my own agendas and answered the call of all those people who needed something I could give them: a sympathetic ear.

So what I realized eventually was that doing readings is a calling, so it really isn't a question of having the right to do it, but for some of us it's something we cannot avoid. For a while, I tried not to do readings, and people wouldn't let me. After my shows, even when I was just minding my business at home, people would hear of me and ask me for advice. So it is a calling; like the Hero's Calling; you can run from it but you cannot hide. If that sounds like an exaggeration or ego-tripping I'm sorry, but if you're truly meant to be a reader it will find you. Joseph Campbell said: "The adventure is always and everywhere a passage beyond the veil of the known into the unknown; powers that watch at the boundary are dangerous; to deal with them is risky; yet for anyone with competence and courage the danger fades." The danger of doing readings is knowing where the boundaries lie and who the guardians of those boundaries are: are you the guardian or is it your clients? Because their expectations can be so demanding you would kill yourself trying to meet them; but on the other hand they're nothing compared to your own expectations of yourself. You can ask more of yourself than anybody else in the world, and burn yourself up. If you're not careful, you expect omniscience and inerrancy. And only a deity can deliver that, and so far we haven't even seen that from any of our deities. So ultimately, the only right we should ask of ourselves is the right to be fallible and human.

I used to think I got into readings to get back at pain. Not my pain, but pain. I thought so until I had this woman coming to see me. She had some sort of cognitive impairment, so, besides the fact that she couldn't really focus on what I was telling her, she drooled all the time. She brought a coffee with her, so she had this little river of coffee-stained saliva running down her chin, on my table. We sat in silence for 45 minutes, then she left. I understood then that I am no Mother Teresa. I need the other person to meet me half way. I guess what I am trying to say is that I understand what you are saying about understanding pain as we grow old, and about becoming more sympathetic to the pain of others through our own experience of pain. But I also understand my limits, and the limits of what I can give to others.

Now, if we take fortunetelling away from readings. What are we left with?

If by fortunetelling you mean making prognostications about the future, we're left with a great deal. Mainly, we're left with our own, and our sitter's, delusions. As I turned your question over and over in my mind, I kept coming back to this. I came up with all sorts of facile and charming responses, but all roads returned to this: we're left with our delusions. We think we have some sort of control over our actions and our fate; that we even make our own decisions, but deep, deep down, far beneath the surface of conscious thought, wheels turn and strings are pulled about which we're completely unaware of. We all have an agenda; a list of priorities, fears and dreams, things we think motivate us, but before we even begin to make that list there are several items before our visible list that drive us even harder than the ones of which we're aware. Harpies and Furies from our Dark Mind that whip us on.

This is what I mean when I say we're left with our delusions. People come to a reader for two reasons: desperation or curiosity, and there's very little middle ground. Yet, they are wrong. People think they know why they come, and I believe they are wrong, completely wrong about the reasons they come. They come because they must, but the true reasons are hidden in the darkness of delusion. Knowing this, I nevertheless address these delusional reasons with delusional answers and delusional responses of my own. My delusions communicate with theirs, and there is an illusion of communication. Yet, I hope with all my heart that those Dark Furies and Hell-Hounds within both of us are listening, and perhaps learn something, and pause in their torments.

A Reading is therefore a shared fantasy between Reader and Sitter. Even if the Oracle is true, if Psi exists, and there are moments of true clairvoyance – and I think there are; because it was in such a moment of Clear Seeing I saw this truth of delusion – prognostication is neither necessary nor even desirable in most cases. Many people expect it, however. They feel cheated if you don't include at least some Fortune-Telling. Now here is the shocking part: Once one realizes the delusional nature of a thing, the delusion has no power. It's only when you mistake the dream for reality that it can harm you or deceive you. Once you realize you're dreamwalking, then you can control the dream toward your ends, and now we're beginning to understand how the reading, though a shared fantasy, can conjure real magickal experiences. Anything – ANYTHING – is possible in a dream. If I can tap into my sitter's dream state, his delusional power, and make it work for him or her and me, then there is no limit to what can be achieved.

John, yours is probably one of the most brutally honest, and interesting, answers I have gotten so far in this series of conversations. Something I have alluded to in my series of articles on the tarot's 'pataphysics is the idea of a reading being an exchange of delusions that usually take us "two degrees" away from reality. A person brings her imaginary problems, we give them imaginary solutions, an emotional exchange takes place, but still, we are weaving the rug on which we stand.

Your answer reminded me of something I often think about in this 'world' of ours: we live in a world of sanitized shamans. There is an enormous need of the Trickster, who comes around in the context of magic, and pokes, and provokes, and threatens everybody's stability so things can actually shift and change. Not everything can be sugared with purple, silver stars and rainbows.

We all are limited by our delusions, and I wonder if we should know the limits of our delusions. I would say that this is the 'magic man's' duty: To look under the rug, but more precisely, to know we are all standing on a rug, and to know where the rug ends, so he can lift it up if needed. But to me, this realization always takes me to one question: How can one be a trickster without being a charlatan?

This is easy enough. A charlatan is a self-serving deceiver. He practices deception for profit or for the thrill of tricking people. He fools you only for the sake of fooling, or for money. There is little or no benefit for anyone other than the Charlatan. Usually, in fact, the other person may wind up feeling used or poorer for the experience. Many magicians call themselves "Charlatans" in jest, but I wonder if they truly realize the full implication of the word. Charlatan implies "Con artist."

Now, the trickster is another story. He is archetypal. The Trickster helps people along their quest for knowledge and growth. His deceptions are toward an end. He tricks us because we're often too stubborn or too stupid to know what's for our own good. He is the wake-up call. He uses Zen-like methods to open our awareness to higher truths. He works with metaphors and similes; fashions sense from chaos. Yes, he may take something from you, but he gives you something in return: usually a lesson; and if you're wary, you may gain far more than you give up. The Trickster is more than a deceiver, he is a teacher and a motivator. Often he sets up a puzzle you must solve in order to move on to the next step along your path toward Enlightenment; as in the story of the Buddha's vigil under the Bodhi Tree. Mara tempted the fledgling Prince Gautama three times. Once with his three beautiful daughters, once with worldly fame, once with wealth unimaginable. Prince Gautama placed his hand on the Earth and asked it to bear witness to his resolve, and gained the title of Samasambuddha: the Perfectly Enlightened One. We see this theme repeated quite often; in the Three Temptations of Christ, the Riddles of the Sphinx, the Trials of Hercules. Puzzles to solve, tasks to master, labyrinths to navigate. Bluebeard gave his wife keys to all the doors, but told her not to open just one. And of course when you tell a person not to open a locked door you've made it the most desirable thing in the world. Bluebeard basically handed his new wife a death sentence, as we learned he did seven wives before.

When I watch a magician, I often ask myself why I like a certain effect. When I was a child, I had different reasons. I loved a trick that told a story. Sometimes all it took was the magician wearing a colorful robe and the props having dragons on them. This sparked my childish imagination into thinking I was witnessing some exotic miracle from a faraway land. Then when I became a magician, I liked tricks with clever methods. Now I've returned to my childhood and I like effects that I can turn into a story, especially if it can be woven into something archetypal.

I think most Magicians are Charlatans. They have no desire to ennoble the craft of deception. They want the thrill of fooling the audience, of pulling one over on them. And to tell the truth, most audiences ask no more from their magicians. And yet, audiences respond strongly to an archetypal Mage. They sense they've seen something different and somehow more mature, which is why mentalism has been called a more adult form of entertainment than magic. Yet magic, properly performed, can be extremely powerful too, if the magician will look at it from a different perspective; that of the Trickster.

In which way could our contemporary world benefit from an "ennobled craft of deception"?

In the absence of the Noble Trickster, Hollywood has taken over the role of the fantasy-merchant. We watch movies about mythical beings instead of owning our own cast of real-life super-heroes, simply because Magicians have chosen to surrender their power. We used to conjure the Elements; now we twist balloon doggies and make weak jokes out of what used to be an Art which subjugated Pharoes and entranced Emperors. Furthermore, whenever someone is bold enough to answer the call of the Trickster, to graduate from Charlatan to Shaman, to attempt to adopt the Ancient Mantle, his own brothers will fall upon him like a pack of wolves and rend him. It's a dangerous thing to be a visionary, more dangerous still to be truly talented and unique. The lesser hoard will not have it. This is true in all things. Great artists in all fields have had to deal with the inertia of the mediocre. Many do not survive.

It's beyond comprehension that people would accept the Trickster in cinema but not in real life. I don't believe it. We face despair and depression on an epidemic level. People seek redemption from the frightening and uninspiring world in which they feel trapped. Only magic can help us escape. Rationality has failed. Science can give us medicines and gadgets but falls short when the spirit cries out for healing. For this task, we need the Magician. But if the merchants of magic don't take their own craft seriously, if the best we can offer is corny tricks with no context presented by mumbling geeks, then where is the redemption? There has to be context, meaning, depth, soul. The audience must feel transformed by the experience; uplifted and inspired. Even if they're not sure why, they must feel as if the magus has evoked something deep and primal within them. Otherwise, they'll feel they've been touched by a Charlatan, and reactions to a Charlatan range from contempt to amusement, but seldom involve transformation.

One last question: what role do readings play within that "ennobled craft of deception", and how can we actually ennoble it?

That's the easiest question you've asked. Imagine a wounded person, not wounded physically, but wounded emotionally, psychologically and spiritually. This person damages himself and others. Perhaps not even intentionally, though many people, in their agony, strike out at others. Maybe his or her pain leaks poison, like the recent BP oil leak poisoned the oceans. These people have extreme Darkness in their Dark Mind. Like all of us Their Dark Mind seeks salvation. Not many people know this, because the Christians have co-opted the word, but the root of the word "salvation" is not "to save," but "to heal." So they are driven to cry out for help, and their actions speak of this need. Society itself is poisoned. We see it everywhere, in its obsession with sex, fleeting pleasures, the decline in intellectual and cultural values, the increase in depression and despair. People are trying to run from this sense of oppression, not realizing that it isn't something OUT THERE causing this sense of oppression but our own inner self screaming for release. We can't escape something we carry with us all the time. We have to stand still and listen to what it wants. And our own souls are leaking poisons.

A Charlatan sees this sickness and turns it to his advantage. When a person in pain comes to him for help, the Charlatan sees a dollar amount on the person's forehead representing the amount of money the Charlatan thinks he can get out of the person. So he encourages the illness, providing some small relief for the symptoms, but never treating the root cause of the suffering. By the way, in case you haven't noticed, I just described the fundamental dynamic of most organized religions: to provide superficial solace, promises of a happier state eventually, and keep coming back.

However, the Ennobled Practitioner — and have we coined a term here — may actually try for a cure. He shows a person the alchemical means for transforming dung into gold. How to take the poisons of daily life and turn them into golden talismans. Meister Eckhart said it isn't of itself a work is sacred, but by our attitudes we make it so. So even washing dishes can be noble work. They say the same thing in Zen: "After Enlightenment – the dishes!" Which means that life itself is sacred and holy, and even though the world is at times a truly awful place, life itself is a wonderful thing, and this realization is the lesson of the Mage. The realization that Life is good can turn that leaking poison into a flow of the most delicious honey, and when life is good there is no such thing as boredom. Even washing your dishes and scrubbing the bath tub brings us joy because we are ALIVE and AWARE. So our job is to catch people's attention and make them aware, if even for a moment, of LIFE. Because most of us walk around half asleep.

But first, the Mage must heal himself, and in the old, ancient traditions, Shamanistic and Hermetic, there were grueling rituals to ensure this. A poisoned Mage will only poison others, and this cannot be allowed. The rituals were designed to separate the flawed from the pure, like separating gemstones from rocks, and the weak sometimes did not survive these rituals. In the Parsifal legend, the sorcerer Klingsor was cast out of the Brotherhood over a shameful act – he castrated himself – because he could not control his lust. Dominance of the Higher Self over the Animal Self is the necessary ingredient for the Healer-Mage, isn't it? If all you think about is using the rest of the world for sex and money, you can never heal, and by extension the world will never heal. I'm not saying sex and money aren't good things, but they aren't everything nor are they the most important things. Moral strength and personal integrity are contagious, and people respect these qualities. One person in a community who's honest, noble, courageous, and wise sets a standard to which other people wish to live.

Lacking an Hermetic tradition, the modern Mage must heal himself. He must confront his own Dark Mind, go inward, and be brutally honest with himself. He has to peek under his own rug. What are his limits? Are there limits? He can't be afraid to experiment, fail, try again. The advice of others will be of mixed value because very few people have done what he is setting forth to do. Most work within safe boundaries. To forge new territory you have to go into the Unknown. Not somewhere Out There, but inside yourself. And when you look at yourself, you'll see things you won't like. If you look hard enough and are honest, you'll experience agonies. But you'll rise from those ashes renewed. You'll be something different. People won't recognize you. Some will think you're crazy. The world will never be the same again. The opinions of others can't touch you. And in this madness you may find true sanity for the first time in your life. This is what the Mages of old claimed. When you gain mastery of yourself, they say, mastering the Elements is a breeze.

New York / Bloomington Indiana, July 2010

> "I think the way we create that art, the art of the tarot reading, can inspire others to view the art in tarot in a way they had not seen before."

A conversation with GINNY HUNT, tarot reader

What is the absurdest thing a client ever asked you? My top two are:

Am I allergic to this? (this after producing a can of prune juice from her purse!)

There is a certified letter waiting for me at the post office. What does it says? (I felt like Kreskin)

Which ones you remember?

When doing an online reading a client asked me, "Can you feel my energy from there?" I'm not an electrical cord, I'm a tarot reader, so the short answer is no. (I understand the reservation about long-distance reading, but this just struck me as funny.) "Am I going to die?" Again, short answer, yes. We all do eventually. Finally, after detailing a long, drawn out story about an internet "romance" that never consummated into a real-life meeting, and after not hearing from the "beloved" for over six years the client asked me, "Will we get married?" One more: "Who is prettier, me or my boyfriend's ex?" Oy.

I was looking into some research done by Jennifer Whitson at the University of Texas. Her findings suggest that when people experience a loss of control in their lives, they are more likely to detect patterns where there are none, or to engage in superstitious rituals. I guess that the good news for us readers is that our clients, who often come to us precisely to fend off their lack of control over certain situations in their lives, are coming somehow conditioned to find meaning in our words. The downside of that may be that we are always talking to people whose minds are in 'survival mode'. I wonder if that accounts for the unreasonableness of some expectations they bring. What do you have to offer to a person coming to you for a reading? What do you expect from the tarot's images?

From personal experience, that research could be simply be phrased as "grasping at straws." Anything can become a life preserver in those times, and sadly, I have had clients who, though I caution them otherwise, seem to cling desperately to the one bit of evidence for their own foregone conclusion that comes through in the reading. In those instances, I hope they got their money's worth, but it's not a particularly satisfying experience for me. I know the reading isn't about me but I feel it was an opportunity wasted.

I prefer readings where the client doesn't feel an immediate need for an answer. It helps that I often have a waiting list and truly cannot read for a client's query right away. It serves to dampen the expectation that the reading is going to magically or immediately solve their problem. Therefore I don't do "emergency" readings. I don't feel tarot is best used in that way and I'm not on call anyway. What I hope to offer someone coming to me for a tarot reading is perspective and insight. I'd like to use some of that desperation to the querent's advantage. A friend once quipped, "It's kind of hard to see the picture when you're inside the frame." A tarot reading can facilitate taking a step back and, with a measure of objectivity, observe one's situation from a different vantage point. I prefer a reading where we can examine not only the past, present, and likely future, but specifically what the client can actively do to mitigate those feelings of helplessness in the face of chaos or the uncontrollable. I'm a big fan of the Advice card. It places your future right into your hands now and is no longer completely at the whim of Fortuna. What sucks is when the Advice card is rubbish, but that's another story.

The images in the tarot are so… I hate to use the word but it's the only suitable one… archetypal that everyone can relate to them. They can be tailored to anyone's experience in any given situation. This is, in fact, one of the objections I've heard to counter the validity of tarot reading, that the card meanings are so broad and generalized to the human experience that they cannot help but deliver an accurate but cold reading. Point taken. But that doesn't account for the eerie detailed accuracy that the skilled tailoring of those messages can and do deliver in the course of most of the tarot readings I've done. Because while the Two of Swords, for example, portrays a time of indecision or deciding not to decide, something we've all experienced, how that card is specifically applied to the client's question and situation, including which precise words are chosen to describe the dilemma at hand, falls outside the realm of generalities. It often then lands right in the province of woo woo — the paranormal.

At one time I expected nothing from tarot's images. I only expected the tarot reader to extract what I needed to hear from them. Then I bought my own deck and for a while the images sat mutely before me like a picture book of disorderly portraits and scenes that didn't seem to connect to each other. But as I looked deeper into the symbolism that was "hidden in plain sight" within the cards, I started to notice a conversation began between me, my self, and the cards. When I dared to share this conversation with others was when I realized the language of the cards seemed more than general musing on the human condition but very specific to one's direct questions, often with answers I myself wouldn't think to give. I try not to hold expectation of a tarot deck, though. It is, after all, only pictures and symbols. What gives them life and meaning are what we have ascribed to those symbols. They do fascinate me in many ways. They are history, art, archeology, sociology, spiritual, religious, playful, fantasy, stark, rude, truth-telling, but above all, evidence of the connectedness of being human.

You are touching on several things there that I would like to comment on. Let's start with the first one that caught my attention: "the reading isn't about me". I know that we all say that. I understand it to mean that we don't read to satisfy our ego, or say things to the effect, to make ourselves look good. But I would also like to challenge that idea. As soon as we are engaged with someone else in conversation, the event becomes a relationship, and relationships are about "you and me" not about "you". We are not ATM machines. We don't produce a standardized output on command. Sometimes we are more engaged, sometimes we are less engaged, and that certainly depends on several factors, the most important being: who is the other person? What does it takes for the experience of a reading you do for another person to be "satisfying"?

Well, the reading is about me in that I am the reader of the cards. It's not even so much about entering into a relationship, although you're right about that. It's more that, by necessity, it is MY reading of the tarot cards, my unique view of them. No one else is going to see exactly what I see in a particular configuration of tarot cards and no one else is going to communicate that in just the same way. In that sense, the reading is "mine" but it isn't about me. It's not my question, it's my client's. The messages portrayed are not for me but for them. Which isn't to say I don't also benefit many times from the truths, advice, wisdom and humor that comes through. But the focus of the reading is my client. I have to be ever cognizant of that because it is tempting to put my own personal "spin" on the reading if I allow myself to be concerned about myself in the reading. If I become too concerned about my reputation, for example, or how the client will perceive me, I might soften a message or dilute it to something completely off the mark. If I worry about whether or not they will become a returning client, or if I think they will think I'm crazy, or even if I think tarot is crazy and giving bad advice, I am focusing on me. There is a kind of schizophrenic duality that has to happen, where I am fully present with the cards and my client, but also distant and emptied of self enough to be a proper messenger. It's not like a normal conversation between friends where I am fully engaged, being myself, sharing my opinions, advice, questions and thoughts. I have to take my self out of the equation while still allowing my talents and gifts to play. While my readings often do take on a "conversational tone," a lot of what is being conveyed is not of me....but it is coming through me and therefore colored and shaped in form by me. I don't want to veer off too much in this direction as it begins to sound like I am some kind of "spirit channel" which I do not believe I am. I do not vacate my self in order to allow some other entity to use my faculties in my stead. My readings definitely bear my personality imprint. But honestly I do not know where some of the information I share comes from. There are things that I've seen in tarot cards about the other person that I had no earthly way of knowing and simply by telling them what the card means to me in that particular reading, this information hits the mark precisely. How I saw that, I don't know. To me it seems as simple as describing the image on the card and how it relates to the others, and at the time I have no idea how specific and accurate the explanation is until later when the client writes back and is utterly astonished that I described something so unknown to me so precisely. How can that be "about me" when I had no idea at the time? I was just blabbing about the cards, or so it seemed to me.

I am sure this doesn't happen in every reading with every client. What I have noticed, though, is I can be completely engaged with the person and the reading seems dull and lifeless to me. Likewise, the opposite can happen. I don't necessarily have to feel a personal connection in order to give a spot on reading. Other times I feel disappointed that the reading wasn't more exciting because I really, really like the person and, well, honestly, probably wanted to impress them or at least give a great reading because I like them. While I'm sure there are many reasons for this, all very individual and circumstantial, it has further bolstered my belief that I don't really have control while reading tarot. The random-ass cards have more control than I do!

As for a "satisfying reading," well, it's definitely a subjective thing. Sometimes the words just flow, I get full sentences, impressions, whole ideas that I can translate into coherency for the client. I just know. Clair-audience, I think it's called. I actually "hear" words in my head, not from a disembodied voice or anything creepy like that, but phrases and full thoughts suddenly "speak" in my mind in reference to certain cards. I still have to work to relate them all together, but those clairaudient phrases hold the key to a satisfying reading for me. If I don't get them, I can still read satisfactorily, but I don't feel the buzz or get energized. And again, I have no control over when or if these sensed words and phrases will come. They either do or they don't. It's also very satisfying to know that a reading I've done has helped someone sort some significant thing out. I feel I've earned my silver.

I would like to jump forward, and pick on something you said towards the end of your response: "It is, after all, only pictures and symbols". I have heard that very same thing from several other readers. I am not sure I understand what it means. I am reminded of a discussion I had with a friend, years ago, about a certain episode in the life of painter Henri Matisse. Being as poor as only a painter in the early 20th century could have been, Matisse fell in love with a drawing by Van Gogh. He finally scrapped the money for a downpayment, and went to see the art dealer who had the drawing. But the dealer had placed the drawing at the back of his shop, and while he went to look for it, Matisse saw this little painting by Paul Cezanne hanging on a wall. He liked it so much that changed his mind and took that painting home where it stayed for about 40 years. At some point, when Matisse was considered a great French master, his wife suggested he should donate that Cezanne to a French museum, which he did. In the speech he gave that day he acknowledged how, all along his career, looking at that painting had provided him with all the reassurance and the encouragement he had needed to overcome any moment of doubt about himself. Wouldn't it be great if we could say the same thing about the tarot?

My friend told me the story was absurd, since a painting is only a "material object". It was an 'aha' moment for me, as I realized some people are immune to images. It never occurred to me this was even possible!

I think I agree with what you are saying, in that images are a repository of knowledge. They bring back ideas that are both collective and individual. But to me it is also very important to acknowledge that artwork isn't only about what we wanted to say with it. It is also what it is. It is color, and shape, and pattern, 'speaking' to the brain. An image is a physical experience that is meaningful in itself, in the same way T.S. Elliot said that "Genuine poetry can communicate before it is understood" What would you say is the principal obstacle for our clients to experience images in such way?

I loved your story about Matisse. I have several pieces of art that I've stumbled upon over the years and felt them "call" to me from where they hung. I found one beautiful oil painting at a flea market once that I brought home and literally gazed at for hours. I've found, too, that these same pieces will not always have the same impact on me in a different time of my life. What struck me to the core of my soul when I was 30 does not have the same effect on me at 40, yet I am still fond of them, like an old friend. These tarot images are art. Some are very good art and some very bad art, but art nevertheless. Art being expression and communication, evoking response through symbols, defies definition and there is much ongoing argument about that. The dictionary defines art as "a visual object or experience consciously created through an expression of skill or imagination." However, today art is defined by the artist as New York Times art critic Roberta Smith's guiding dictum says, "If an artist says it's art, it's art." We might quibble when we approach a piece that looks neither imaginative nor skillful in its creation, not to mention aesthetically lacking, but as beauty is in the eye of the beholder, so is art. I've seen tarot decks that I thought were hideous but somehow the artwork speaks poignantly to many readers who love them. To each their own.

What I mean when I say "tarot is only pictures and symbols" is that they themselves don't mean anything until the viewer, or in this case, reader, ascribes meaning to them. Who decided that red was a symbol of passion or water symbolizes emotion? We did, collectively, as humans. In my forays into the study of symbolism I have been particularly struck by the commonality of nations and people-groups ascribing the same or very similar meanings to colors, shapes, numbers, animals, elements, and so forth. Before people were able to travel very far and share knowledge among cultures they separately designated meaning to symbols and so many of those meanings are the same, cross-culturally. I find that fascinating. I'm also very interested in how meanings come to be formed over time and how they evolve and change. In my writing I share how, for example, the position of the Hanged Man can be found in Christian frescoes depicting torture in Hell well before the tarot was painted. The image of Strength wrestling a lion is evident hundreds of years before the first tarot deck. I think people who used the first tarot decks knew precisely what those images were meant to portray just as easily as we, today, understand a red octagon means "Stop." They seem mysterious to us today only because we have lost the connection to that common understanding of that time. The timelessness of art, however, allows us to ascribe new meanings to those same images that may or may not bear resemblance to the "traditional" or "historical" meanings. Personally, I prefer to research the origins and allow those meanings to play into what I see in the art, mixed with modern ideas. A kind of cross-centuries translation. I also like to read the books that come with modern tarot decks that include the artist's intentions. I want to know what the artist was trying to portray. But we don't have to know.

A photographer friend of mine, attending one of her own shows, is always very surprised at the varied responses and reactions she gets from those who view her work. She used to get indignant, "That's NOT what I meant at all!" But then she realized that when she releases her art to the world, she releases it to all the world's interpretations and that process enlarges her art and it becomes so many different things and expressions rather than her own limited one. Once she realized that – and it's not easy to do, to separate oneself from one's soul work and allow others free reign with it – it set her free to create without concern for how it will be received. It's like this verse by Anna Nalik, songwriter:

> "2 AM and I'm still awake, writing a song
>
> If I get it all down on paper, it's no longer inside of me,
>
> Threatening the life it belongs to
>
> And I feel like I'm naked in front of the crowd
>
> Cause these words are my diary, screaming out loud
>
> And I know that you'll use them, however you want to."

A tarot reading is like that. To give what is inside of you, based on what you see and feel and ascribe meaning to from pictures and symbols, relating it to another person's life you don't even know, also knowing they may take something entirely different from what you've said, using it however they want to.

Tarot reading is... art, in that sense. Is it not? A dance rests on music, another art form, but the dance is art, too. I think the way we create that art, the art of the tarot reading, can inspire others to view the art in tarot in a way they had not seen before. As a young dancer, I remember often hearing music in a new and exciting way by either imagining choreography or watching a dance performed to an unfamiliar piece of music. The dance had a way of showing me the music in an entirely different light. So, too, a good reader can bring the images in the cards to life in such a way that the client sees the images in a new way. A reading then becomes both art itself and interpreter of art, much like a dance.

You are making a very apt analogy: the reader as an artist. I agree in that readings could reach the level of art, and for that reason I don't think just anybody can do it. There is some talent that is needed, although I won't define that talent as any kind of psychic ability, in the same way I won't define the ability to craft a good song as paranormal. I often like to think of myself as a musician. I have an instrument I carry around with me, and when the time is right I take it out of its case and play it. We play these images like a violinist plays his notes. Perhaps I like the music metaphor because music is a mood enhancer and that is what I think I am as a tarot reader: a mood enhancer. I say it while accepting all the limitations, and possibilities it implies. As long as the person who sits with me leaves my table feeling invigorated, I did my job.

Back to the readings-as-art analogy. What we call 'talent' is not enough to make a good artist. I know that artists don't simply play by ear. There is craftsmanship, and there is a constant nourishment of some sort of formal investigation the artist is doing that will take that artist through an evolution of style, or through successive formal incarnations. In which way can you see that happening with your work as a reader? How do you expand your craft? How does a reader improve, set new directions for what he or she is doing, or change reading styles? I am not talking only about techniques, as for example when I understood that all communication in a reading circulates through hypnotic patterns – and I studied hypnosis – or when I looked into short-term therapy, metaphor therapy, cognitive therapy etc, as a way to understand the mechanics of helping someone in a brief period of time, or when I looked into homiletics to see if there were some specific techniques about how to talk to people in an inspiring way. These are just different aspects of what I would call craftsmanship. I am asking in terms of aesthetic goals. Do you have any aesthetic goals in regards of your readings? Have those changed along the years?

I agree that more than talent is needed to be an artist. Anyone can read tarot with a deck and a book of meanings, but being a true tarot reader brings more than that to the table. Anyone can draw, but one must have talent and desire first and then hone that talent with skills. I'm not sure how I would define the talents needed to be a tarot reader. Certainly one must be rather visually inclined, the images must cause a reaction in the reader. But also one must be verbally able to communicate those impressions and reactions into words that effectively tell the story, the message. One must be a bit of a storyteller, then, able to weave the pictures into a coherent, meaningful dialogue with the cards, the reader, and the client. It's not something everyone can do well.

In order to expand my craft as a tarot reader, I have to find new and fascinating things about the cards themselves to prod me to deeper and broader understanding that I can then use in my readings. That's why I tend to dig deep into history and art symbolism when I research and write about the cards. I need those discoveries that excite me and push me to higher levels. So I tend to find external connections and study more inspiring than internal. Some people meditate on a card. I've tried that and it doesn't do much for me. I'm an intellectual at heart so I get a thrill when I find out something new. I'm not so much a scholar, though, like our prominent tarot historians.

Experimentation is always a great way to hone one's craft. Trying out different methods, researching other systems that some people use with tarot, such as Kabbalah or astrology, or numerology, interacting with other readers, exchanging ideas and musings on various cards, and teaching. Teaching is always a win-win because I always learn something new while teaching others. Teaching forces me to really make sure what I am saying is correct, so I dig in and do the proof-texting and research so I am sure I am not spreading bullshit. There's enough of that in the tarot world. Along the way I always uncover some beautiful gem I had not found before. But the best way to evolve one's craft is by doing it over and over and over. I am a much better reader now than I was when I started. I'm better now than I was a year ago. The repetition can get tiring, but it is also necessary to good reading.

As I do primarily email readings, I have had to hone my writing skills, become more precise and less wordy. I love to write but I have a tendency to over-explain. I would spend hours on a reading and realize it just wasn't worth all that time and effort. So I've been forced to become more direct and yet clearer and more precise in my words without losing my distinct style and "voice." But honestly, the greatest inspiration to delve deeper into tarot waters has been my own solitary studies that I share with others on my blog.

Poet Anna Kamienska wrote: "The experience of faith, so like poetic inspiration, is self-sufficient. It needs no expression beyond the experience itself, it needs no words. What wants and seeks for words is the uncertainty of our faith".

I often long for that moment when a person looks at a card on the table, and she doesn't need me to know what that image is. I don't mean what the image means from a historical, or iconographic perspective, or its name, but what that image is to her. Only rarely a moment of truth needs words. Do you think it is true what Kamienska is saying, are words that thing we use to fill the void we call 'doubts'?

Oh Enrique, you speak blasphemy! To a writer, words express the spiritual experience and truth within. If I but experience something but cannot express that in some way, it remains an ephemeral moment that has but a momentary impact. If I express that experience, and for me it usually means through words, either speaking it or writing it, but for others it may mean painting it, or singing it, living it somehow, that experience becomes integrated into one's self. I do not believe we were meant to be hermits all our lives, even though solitude is necessary to our growth. Human beings are social creatures and as such we need to process our solitary experiences by sharing them with others. The expression of our soul journeys becomes art. Art is meant to be shared. Which leads me to the question: are our spiritual experiences meant for us alone or for us to share with others in some art form?

That moment you speak of, when someone experiences a tarot card and understands its message without any interpreter is wonderful, but I wouldn't place it as any better than one who receives the same understanding through interpretation. We can look at a painting, listen to music, or read a poem and receive that which we were meant to. It doesn't seem to matter which delivery service is used, only that we get the message. It's all so circumstantial, really. I've been changed by poems, struck deep by paintings, and moved beyond words by music. I was never forewarned when one of these experiences was going to happen. The poetry leapt off the page into my soul, the painting held me spellbound, the music carried me away, and I wasn't told it was going to happen. It just happens. So, too, I think, that moment you speak of can happen. It's a spontaneous direct spiritual experience. As such, I feel it is completely out of anyone's control. In those moments, words are unnecessary and clutter the experience. It's just that we can't really plan those moments or facilitate them. On the other hand, I would love tarot cards to be so "readable" to anyone that no one feels they need a tarot reader. But as it is a skill, I think readers should always be desired. Just like I can massage my own aching neck and it helps a bit, a 30-minute session on a professional massage therapist's table is going to help a lot more.

Just yesterday I was thinking on the importance of giving a horizontal emphasis to any spiritual practice. In my readings, I have met countless clients who define themselves as 'seekers' and whose lives, sadly, are interrupted in any direction other than the one that will take them back to their own navels. Many of them live under the illusion of potential: they have "lots to give" but they are awaiting "higher instructions" on how to give it. I am always reminded on Mother Teresa. When someone asked her "what got you started?" she said: "I saw a kid on the street and I took him with me. Then I saw another one and I took him with me too". We don't need a PhD to be useful. We don't need a direct line with any 'higher' power to be meaningful. We only need the willingness to engage with others. What I find in most of these 'seekers' is lots of self-indulgence. They spend a whole hour talking about how they have always been special, yet they cannot keep a friend or find their place in reality. But then again, the whole point of Western esotericism seems to be to harness some sort of natural potential, so an individual can use it for his or her own benefit, 'on' others, not 'with' others. It is said that the shortest path between two points is a straight line. I suspect that may be true in every single case, except when it comes to what we call the 'Self'. The most direct path to find love is to love, then, the most direct path to find fulfillment is to be fulfilling.

The problem of spirituality is the problem of beauty. Recently, a writer friend of mine told me that, for him, looking at a beautiful woman was half awe inspiring, half terrifying. I understand what he is saying. I once met this woman at a radio interview. She was so beautiful that I called her a "monster". She was a monster in the etymological sense of the Latin word 'monstrare' which is "to reveal". Beauty is a revelation. When a man sees a beautiful woman he thrusts his elbow between his friend's ribs to share his discovery with him: "look at that woman!" That moment is a fundamental moment. If the friend sees the same beauty, their friendship gets strengthened, but if the friend fails to acknowledge the beauty his friend is sharing with him, they suffer an epistemological rupture. I am using the example of a woman because finding physical beauty in people is something we all have experienced. But the same thing holds true for all realms of human experience. That friend of mine, the one I told the story about Matisse, failed to see the beauty in the story. He thought it was silly to get so engaged with "material objects". I knew right then that our friendship was doomed, for one of the attributes of friendship is the possibility of coinciding with someone 'in' beauty, and to be lifted up by it. I am not saying we ought to end all friendships if our friends don't share our same sense of beauty, but having a similar taste, a similar sense of beauty than our loved ones, is something we always find comforting. We even take it as a sign suggesting we belong together with these people!

The person who experiences a spiritual revelation is also experiencing beauty, and he also wants to share that beauty with those he loves. That is the main compulsion behind religious proselytism. When we share that beauty with someone who fails to see it, we feel a little bit betrayed. That is an important component of fundamentalism. The fundamentalist understands the world in terms of "either with me, or against me". Either you accept the truth the fundamentalist is offering you, or you are embracing a world of lies and therefore deserve no mercy. I still don't know what the connection between truth and beauty is. Do you? I suspect those are two names for the same thing. But we tend to be more respectful of other people's idea of beauty than we are of other people's idea of truth. At the very least, I fail to recall any war fought in the name of beauty!

It is often repeated that artists shouldn't work for others, that they need to be true to themselves. But you cannot develop your voice if you never speak aloud. In a conversation with John Riggs, he told me that being a reader is a 'calling'. Do you agree with him?

You touch on a couple of things here. The horizontal spiritual experience or practice. Absolutely! This is what I strive for in my tarot writing. I want to bring tarot out of the ethers and into the real, to make it reachable and useful to others, to share that which I have found growth-producing and enriching with others. Tarot reading means nothing but navel gazing unless we can use it and apply it to real and material lives. I've done my time in spiritual ivory towers being too heavenly minded to be of any earthly good. I found the more I learned, the more "spiritual" I became, the less I connected with others that didn't share my exact worldview. I became isolated and totally out of touch with the rest of the world. It wasn't until I realized that this stuff wasn't meant for my understanding, wasn't meant just for "enlightenment" but to actively change my life and by extension the lives of others I come into contact with, that I understood the complete irrelevance of a spiritual study or practice that didn't help anyone but myself. My first lesson coming out of that ivory tower was tough – I had to learn to love without any agenda, without self-seeking, with utter respect and compassion, and without expectation. Love is primarily a verb. Without love, we can't share a thing. Without respect, you can't love.

Beauty being in the eye of the beholder is definitely a subjective experience. I agree that we are generally more accepting of other people's idea of beauty than we are about their spiritual ideas. Because there's this fallacy that abounds that says there can't be more than one truth, that if what I believe is truth and what you believe is different and also believe it is truth, one of us must be wrong. Why must one of us be wrong? I know there are some conflicting ideas, but it doesn't mean they aren't each true because when we are speaking about spiritual things we aren't speaking about measurable, concrete facts. We are speaking about things that are bought on faith. Belief. If one believes it, it is true for you. That's truth, but it isn't truth for everyone. Of course we feel more affinity with people who share our ideas, whether they be on beauty or on truth. The challenge is then not to demonize people who radically differ in their perspectives, their "truth." In this sense, then, beauty is a visceral response to something experienced and so is truth also experienced that way. It is a perspective, a belief, and the basis of one's actions. Our ideas about what is beautiful provokes us to try and create that beauty in our world and share that with others. But if someone else doesn't share your idea of beauty then your "beautiful world" would be hell to them. So there is a reason, I think, why we feel so much more attraction to those that share our idea of beauty. It's so we can share our world with them in a way that enriches both of us.

The tarot is based on the idea that there are universal truths that all of us believe because we have experienced them. The expression of those truths in art form is often better received when the art itself aligns with the person's concept of beauty. If the pictures aren't enough to provoke the response, then maybe the reader's art – the words that convey the meaning – may be beautiful to them, in that they resonate and evoke a spiritual response. If neither is the case then it would probably be perceived as a "waste of time" even if the statements given were factual. So a lot of it is about perception and ideas.

Reading tarot being a "calling?" Hmmm… well, I think of a calling as something one feels meant to do and would do it whether they are compensated for it or not. It tends to be something that serves others, but it is definitely something we feel a great sense of purpose about and is fulfilling. In that sense, yes, tarot reading is a calling. People who do things as a "calling" tend to have inborn traits or gifts that draw them to their vocation. So there do need to be some natural abilities to be a tarot reader. But if it means that being a reader is a "higher calling" in that we are to be somehow more spiritual or more responsible for benefiting others with our gifts, no. I don't think being a good tarot reader means you are any more or less responsible to others than you should be in any other relationship or vocation. I think one has to be grounded in love in every area of your life and that will express itself through everything you do, in your vocation as well. Being a tarot reader doesn't come with a mantle of spirituality or sets anyone apart any more than being good at carpentry.

Whom do you write for? Why is that so important?

I had to really think about this question. I have always written, I can't remember I time I did not write. It has always been "for me" that I write. But writing, by its very nature, is communicative. It needs a reader. My online tarot journal began because I couldn't seem to develop the discipline needed to keep an active tarot journal. I made it public in order to prod myself into writing about tarot more often. If I believed there were others who read what I wrote and who wanted to read more, I would write more because "they" were expecting more. I am tired of talking to myself, so I imagined an audience that I could talk to and with. So, yes, I write for "them" too. But it's a blog, so I write what I want and don't feel obligated to write anything expected. It's MY journal, after all. So it's for me and for anyone who cares to read my meanderings and soul babble.

One of the coolest things, to me, is to write something that prompts someone to comment, and then someone else comments, and I comment and then we have a conversation going. On the one hand, I would write whether anyone commented or not. I would write into the air, it doesn't matter, because the very process of writing my thoughts helps me clarify them and process through the internal disorganization. I have had many startling revelations through my own writing. It's as if I don't quite know exactly what I think or feel until I write it. So it's an internal process made external. But if it connects with another individual in some way, I love that, too. It's like howling until you find your pack, or until they find you.

I have a final question for you: what is the role of tarot readers in Western contemporary society? Are we a relic from another time, catering to the ignorant? Are we bringing something worthy to the table? Are we evolving? Should we?

It's funny that you ask if we are a "relic from another time." If so, which time? I think fortune-tellers and mystics have been around since humans have formed communities. We've always had a place in our societies, at times more elevated than others. In our modern age where science is the prevailing religion, where people feel they must justify their every act by proven research, tarot readers offer an opportunity to explore or just experience the unexplainable, the mysterious. I think our human souls and minds are deeper and more vast than we want them to be, deeper than most people are comfortable with. We like the concrete explanations that science gives us. Those explanations comfort the modern person just like myths about the gods used to comfort the ancients. Science tells us that if we can figure out how it works, we can eventually find a way to control it. We are terrified by chaos outside our ability to control – weather, natural disasters, accidents. We work tirelessly to come up with ways to protect ourselves and avert these things. When science isn't enough, we look to other ways. If we can see it coming, we think we can at least prepare for it. So seeing a fortune-teller combines our need to control the uncontrollable and the need to explore the areas of our soul and mind that science cannot explain or reach.

However, the flip side to dark chaos being uncontrollable is the fortunate uncontrollable. We hear stories about finding a magic lamp with a genie inside, winning the lottery, unforeseen happenings of tremendous good luck. There's a part of us that wants to be able to control those things too, in order to create happiness in our lives. So even if it isn't fear-based, we still have a compelling drive to know what is unknowable. In an age that disparages myth and magic, we still love to watch the street magician levitate and perform illusions. We are captivated and both want to know and don't want to know how he does that. I really don't think we want to eradicate life of all its mystery and unknowns. We want to believe magic still exists so that we might stumble upon that leprechaun's pot of gold ourselves. I know that I have, at times, felt embarrassed at my vocation as tarot reader. For an intelligent, well educated woman to read tarot in this day and age is, well, suspect. Why on earth would I rely on such superstition? Still, some of the brightest minds read tarot. All I know is that I am drawn to the mystery, the wonderful feelings of awe and astonishment when a reading is so directly insightful and accurate when you know, logically, it shouldn't be.

Tarot reading naturally evolves within the society it is placed. As readers, we can't help but be informed and conditioned by the culture in which we live. I've noticed readers attempting to be more logical and scientific with the cards, more "psychological" and therapeutic in their approach and I can't help but think that is more a reaction to our culture's dismissal of anything that is not based on scientific research. In the end, none of us can explain how tarot reading "works." All of us have experienced those moments of stunned awe where we are entirely without any rational explanation how these random cards answered so specifically. If it only happened half the time, we could say it's simple chance, like flipping a coin. But we know by experience that the ratio is much higher and we have no explanation for that. In the end, we fall back on mystery. If we, as readers, fully accept and embrace that there will always be mysteries in life, we can help others feel more comfortable with the unknowable as well.

So yes, I think we do bring something worthy to the table. We bring a sense of the possibility of being in control of the uncontrollable, even if it is, in the end, an illusion. Like many other tarot readers, I prefer to try and help my clients find areas of a situation that they can act on and therefore control, to empower them in their life dilemmas so they don't feel like helpless pawns of fate. The irony is that I am using a completely randomized deck of pictures to help them achieve that. I am using chaos to bring a sense of order.

New York / Hagerstown, Maryland, 2010

"If you are sincere in participating with the tarot method, it will always be relevant. I stand by that."

A conversation with ART ROSENGARTEN, psychotherapist, deck creator

A couple of weeks ago, that extraordinary sculptor, Louise Bourgeois, passed away. There is a piece of hers, a 'cell' as she calls it, consisting of a room in whose center there is a table. On top of the table there are two hands, clasped, carved in marble or some other solid material. The table and the hands are surrounded by several large glass spheres. Bourgeois said somewhere that the hands represent a teacher, and the glass spheres, a group of students. She also said that we are all like glass spheres: if someone tries to put something inside of a glass sphere, or opening it up to fill it, the sphere just breaks. I found that metaphor quite intriguing. Who would be more likely to shatter the glass sphere, the therapist or the tarot reader?

The therapist is more likely to shatter the glass sphere due to the clumsy fingers of intervention which have previously been his friend. His job, by any ethical means, is the repair of ailing hearts and minds. His versatility, as such, is his great virtue. The work of the therapist is not really meant for the cell, but rather the supportive walls of the antechamber. The reader, by contrast, is indeed trained to participate inside the cell. Her job is to facilitate the journey. She understands that transmission occurs when no one is doing anything. This, of course, is true for the therapist as well, but not the *sine qua non* of his profession.

The reader melds into the querent, the room itself, and the cards themselves, becoming parts of the surrounding glass spheres. They contain the alchemical table upon which the journey emanates. The hands on the table – the teacher – draws unique delicate patterns of light and symbol into this dense, simultaneous, holographic mind-moment. This intelligence IS "the fingerprints" of the hands, always unique, indelible, non-replicable.

The therapist operates by a different contract; one that is also useful, but more limited and preliminary. He was likely consulted previously, before the cell was entered. He is like the physician to the astronaut, consulted before undergoing his advanced training for space travel. The mission could be aborted or compromised without this precaution; not just anyone is ready to be an astronaut.

Glass-shatterings no doubt had occurred previously for this candidate, and repaired naturally or with help. But the rigors of space travel necessitate proper readiness: genuine openness and curiosity. The reader, however, belongs aboard the starship, melding herself with the querent, the cards, and the table joining with the open spheres of glass; her job is but one: to facilitate the journey so that the teacher can again stamp his omniscent fingerprint anew.

Do you remember the first time you encountered the tarot?

The very first impression of tarot cards was in mid '70s. I was living with a girlfriend in a shared house high up in the Oakland hills, above Skyline Blvd.. . I believe I had just taken the est training. One of my girlfriend's housemates, an attractive, petite, and somewhat intense woman named Chris had taken out a deck of Rider Waite Smith in the communal kitchen and was reading them for another male housemate. I thought they were interesting, a little weird and edgy, and didn't give another thought to it. I was a Master's student in Eastern Philosophy at the California Institute of Asian Studies at the time. The tarots were a little too Egyptian for my taste initially. About 18 months afterwards, however, in an amazing weekend seminar on The Tarot at CIAS offered by a fairly young, very cool redhead named Dr. Hillary Anderson, herself a graduate of the program and now a professor of Integral Psychology and a Sri Aurobindo scholar, I was now officially introduced to the tarot seriously. I was hooked immediately, and decided I would focus my doctoral studies around the psychological possibilities for the unbelievably rich and untapped deck of archetypal symbols. Which, of course, I did and then some. I know because it's all written in my journal of that year, in red ink. It was some months, as I recall, before the first *Star Wars* movie came out (which of course I saw in San Francisco on opening night). The visual arts were very powerful then to us New Age intellectual-types in the Bay Area.

As a tarot reader, a big part of my work consists of making room. I sit at my table, waiting, but to me waiting isn't a passive act. My waiting is an active invitation to a space where a person can enter. Even so, it is the client who chooses to sit with me, and even when they may be the ones making that choice, not all of them can benefit from what I have to give. I am not clear as to whether tarot forms part of your therapy practice, or if you keep both works separate. If so, how do you deter-

mine which person could benefit from it and who couldn't? Do you find any resistance towards the tarot from the people you work with?

It is an important question – how tarot can weave into psychotherapy. I've learned that you cannot plan it ahead, but like the divination itself, it unfolds organically without pushing anything. As you say, a big part of the works consists of making room, or what we might call "creating a clearing." This could arise naturally in the first session, or after three years of weekly talk therapy, but when the clearing occurs it seems totally obvious and feels unusually safe to experiment with wisdom tools. Elvis has entered the room so to speak, and therapist and client alike can feel the vibe in wonderment.

The point is this doesn't take place in time, or work well as a planned strategy, but rather it occurs naturally in the shared field of consciousness. I've grown to recognize these moments when they occur – when therapy naturally invites divination. Synchronicities have uncannily underscored this spiritual awareness, perhaps from something the therapist contributed in a previous session or the client discovered on their own from the unmasking process. No longer is it about their "problems" or my psychological knowledge per say. Rather, we've opened something extraordinary together at this moment, call it transpersonal awareness, and turning to a great oracle – say the tarot – for deeper mirroring of this awareness feels like an excellent thing to explore. Why not?

Perhaps, the most polemical topics about tarot readings are predictions. Some people think the tarot is about making predictions. Period. Some other see predictions as something that detracts from the spiritually elevated messages the tarot offers. Some people see the tarot as a Rorschach test in which predictions have no place. Some people say "the tarot is about the present, not about the future". I have to confess I am still forming my own opinion about all this. I like to think that, by doing all these interviews, I have embarked on some sort of virtual companionage, to use a notion from my friend Jean-Claude Flornoy. It is just that, instead of traveling from town to town to learn and share my craft with other craftsmen, I send e-mails! The most important thing I have learnt through all these conversations I am having with people is that I have faith in images. By this I don't mean religious faith, but faith in the fact that images can connect me with a sense of beauty that can have me experience truth. The second, quite obvious, most important thing I have learnt from my conversations is that what you get from images depends on what you expect from them. I was trained in visual communication. In objective terms, I am not trained to expect images to tell me the future. My faith in images won't take me there. I tend to believe images are useful to remind us of things. We use images to give ideas a memorable shape. At one level, the tarot can remind us of intimate information, as in a form of anamnesis. Whomever works with the tarot will experience that, daily. At another level, the things the tarot reminds us of could have a cultural relevance. Since I am interested in the iconography of the tarot, I am aware that the historical evidence links the tarot with the European Danse macabre, the De Casibus Virorum Illustribus and the De remediis utriusque fortunae. So, from a iconographical point of view, the hierarchy of trumps seems to remind us that the practice of Virtue would have us triumphing over all the vicissitudes of life. Recently, and unexpectedly, I found this quote from George Lakoff: "Virtue is about character. An ethics of virtue is based on developing a strong, wise, even-tempered moral character that will lead you to choose what is best and to act morally [...] Morality is about growth, about the person developing his or her own capacities and exercising them to the fullest extent in order to realize what is best in them". I wrote that quote down because I thought: "Ah! This sounds like the kind of stuff I expect from these images!" I even like how the three moral virtues present in the tarot are included in the first half of the quote!

Let me give you an example: Yesterday a woman came to see me. As she sat, I asked her what was she expecting from my reading. She told me she wanted to know what her co-workers were thinking. I have to confess the question put me down. I suspect I am not the same tarot reader every day. Any other day I may have just gone along with this. But yesterday I wasn't there. So I asked her to look at the cards and find herself in the deck. No randomness, no Chance. Just a conscious choice. This obviously put her off, as she was expecting to be a passive participant and be told about all these plots and confabulations against her. She didn't even look at the whole deck. I pride myself at being good at creating rapport with people, and this was going wrong. She stopped half way through it and told me she didn't know what she was doing because didn't even know what the cards meant. She ended up giving me Le Bateleur, The Magician, probably because it was the card that was first on top of the deck.

When we go to a restaurant, a bakery, or a deli, we look at the offering. Sometimes we already have a craving in mind. Some other times we don't know what we want. We only know we are hungry. But a menu, a shelf full of pastries, those are invitations to dance. Sometimes our body responds to the invitation by realizing that it needs a milkshake instead of coffee, or fish instead of a hamburger. When I ask a person to openly (I don't trust the term 'conscioulsly' here) choose a card from the deck, I am hoping for the person to tell me her story in images instead of words, but also, for the person's body to manifest an inclination, a craving. There is a silent script going on in this transaction that says: "Pick what you need. Show me what you want".

She chose The Bateleur, and I told her: "There is a message here for you: Know your place. Stand by it. Do your work." In other words, since I don't expect from the images to be a crystal ball (I definitively expect that from crystal balls), I won't see a conspiracy displayed in my cards. What I can see is an attitude, a quality of character my client can enact, so she can develop "her own capacities and exercising them to the fullest extent in order to realize what is best in her". That would be consistent with what I see as the purpose of readings: to give people strength. I often think reading the tarot is just a mood-enhancer. Notice that I am not saying I can't see a conspiracy. We can obviously map such things from the person's question into the images, especially if we are primed by the client's question. I could have seen Le Bateleur as 'Deception'. But that is a game that, yesterday, I couldn't play. The "I see a dark-haired woman plotting against you" storyline is quite emblematic, yet I rarely see a point of feeding people's fear of other people.

Even so, this woman wasn't happy with that. She said she felt "discouraged" by my reading. I found that choice of words fascinating, as it accounts for exactly the opposite effect I hope to achieve in my readings. (I am a big fan of failure. I learn lots through failing). Obviously, I thought I was giving her the tools to face her problem, yet the tools she needed were of a different nature, and she left my reading feeling naked, not armed. But still, I feel I have an ethical responsibility of not putting words in the mouth of people who aren't even present at my reading. Since I don't expect for my tarot cards to be a crystal ball, I cannot, in good conscious, tell my client what other people are thinking about her. If anything, what comes up in the cards would always be a projection of what my client thinks of herself, expressed through the eyes of her co-workers. Where I may have failed yesterday is in that I could have explored why my client felt jeopardized by her co-workers. By telling her to keep to herself and do her job the best she could, I was failing to acknowledge her feelings of lack of control. She obviously doesn't feel her wellness depends on being a good worker, alone. The reason why I didn't pursue that route yesterday was *because a few cards later in our reading made it clear that this woman was not only unhappy at that place, but was planning to leave. "If you are going to leave, let's talk about where you want to go" was my suggestion. This line of inquiry wasn't useful to my client. The other reason why I didn't explore that route is that I am not a therapist. I am a tarot reader. While describing the contents of another person's mind is not a prediction, both "what is she thinking of me?" and "what is going to happen?" are questions that belong to the realm of 'seeing what is hidden', and both correspond with a common expectation people have about the tarot. I usually try to understand the question behind that question to avoid giving a prediction. But I have also come to understand that predictions have a therapeutic value. I suspect that most predictions are suggestions: they set a whole array of conscious and unconscious mechanisms in play, so a person can be more or less inclined to produce a certain outcome. For that reason I don't think so much of readers as making predictions as I think of them giving, or prescribing, predictions. This is a fascinating topic, but also, I am afraid, a slippery slope. So, my question to you, and I apologize for the long-winded set up, is this: do you think predictions can serve a therapeutic purpose? In that case, who is entitled to give such predictions?*

Whether there is a good rationale for predictive tarot, of course, depends upon your belief system. Let me respond from my own and simply say, "no." Prediction, I believe, is a linear process that implies someone (or something) is going somewhere. These are dubious assumptions I think, which certainly from the Buddhist perspective cannot be found to exist. Rather, we are nobody, going nowhere, doing nothing in the ultimate reality. The future is assumed in predictive practices. I don't know that it really exists beyond a construction of time. Also, an ability to assess "accuracy" – whether an actual event matches a "predicted outcome" implies a fundamental subject/object dichotomy, and challenges the observer effect proved by quantum physics. Can there be objectivity? The fantasy of prediction incorporates core linear and dualistic assumptions that don't really resonate with my own worldview. I believe the future is a construct (of time) much like the past that exists solely in thought-processes. The popular *Power of Now* books by Eckhardt Tolle have beautifully distinguished this perspective, and I think it is totally relevant to the fantasy of prediction.

Presence, or simply "awareness" points closer to the goal I set for both therapy clients and tarot querents. In fact, that is the goal I set for everything. This means getting closer and deeper to the present moment (without remainders – nondual awareness – meaning the timeless/formless dimension of reality. Well then you ask, "how to measure presence?" and I think the answer comes not by way of conceptual/philosophical thinking, magical invocations, or scientific instrumentation, but rather intuitively and energetically. We know IT to greater or smaller degrees via our intuitive faculties. I like the psycho-theorist Eugene Gendlin's phrase "felt sense" to describe this intuitive/energetic faculty which tells us immediately when we have greater or lesser, deeper or less deep, "presence" operating in the present moment.

OK so do tarot readings predict things, or operate effectively as predictors? Conceivably yes, they might, but only insofar as a "deepening of presence" can be experienced in the felt sense of the moment. However, talking about "the future" or connecting the dots of causation are very reductive and seem secondary in this worldview, only because one must engage in conceptualization and interpretation which, I'm afraid, actually lowers the energetic pitch. Given that such conceptualizations ultimately mean nothing, I prefer to keep the gaze present-centered. But I'm sure there are many tarot types who will see things very differently.

These days I have been reflecting on how often the meanings we assign to The Fool seem to be founded in what George Lakoff and Mark Johnson define as a 'complex metaphor', namely, that A PURPOSEFUL LIFE IS A JOURNEY. It is interesting how Lakoff and Johnson propose that these complex metaphors are built by combination of primary metaphors plus commonplace knowledge. I am bringing this up here because The Fool seems to be 'someone' going 'somewhere', so we see in him a depiction of what is a common superstition of the Western world: people are supposed to have goals in life. I am not even going to wonder if that is a verifiable iconographical meaning for The Fool, that is, if that Fool we see in the card actually has any goals. What is clear to me is that we tend to see The Fool that way because our cultural bias have us assuming, by default, that life is a journey and we are actually supposed to get somewhere. I think this idea may be useful sometimes, but some other times it is good to understand that this is a superstition, and we may very well be 'no one' going 'nowhere', as you pointed out.

The metaphorical line, A PURPOSEFUL LIFE IS A JOURNEY, includes several analogies that are interesting to analyze under the light of the narratives we commonly associate to the tarot:

> *The person leading a life is a traveler.*
>
> *His purposes are destinations.*
>
> *The means for achieving purposes are routes.*
>
> *Difficulties in life are impediments to travel.*
>
> *Counselors are guides.*
>
> *Progress is the distance traveled.*
>
> *Things you measure your progress by are landmarks.*
>
> *Choices in life are crossroads.*
>
> *Material resources and talents are provisions.*

The list resonates with many of the tarot's images, not only The Fool. If we assume that A PURPOSEFUL LIFE IS A JOURNEY metaphor is actually embedded in the way we think about ourselves and about our lives, it is easy to see why an a priori reading of the trumps would produce narratives such as The Fool's Journey, for example. I like to think images are gatherings, water holes we can all drink from. But it seems that images don't quench the same thirsts in everybody, nor offer a standardized beverage to all of us. How do you approach meaning-making in your practice? Do you start with a predefined set of meanings for the cards? Do you take into account the meanings people project on the cards? Is there a departure point and a destination, or is the 'journey' its own purpose?

The questions you raise are at the heart of my new deck *Tarot of the Nine Paths: Advanced Tarot for the Spiritual Traveler.* My system very much uses the language of becoming which takes place in time, and is clearly about being "someone going somewhere doing something!" The mover I indeed call "the spiritual traveler" and the various archetypal "stations" on the journey I conceptualize as "departures, transitions, and arrivals." Very much in the process model of Jungian individuation and the classic tarot mythologem of "The Fool's Journey." So far so good from a Western, linear, dualistic paradigm from which the making of meaning is part and parcel, but here is where it deconstructs on the nondual superhighway: the essential wisdom of paradox! From the nondual tantric schools of Buddhism stemming from The Heart Sutra, as well as the nondual subtext of Taoism, I Ching, and of course, Zen we widen the viewpoint to account for obvious, inbuilt contradictions of the more Western subject/object dichotomy. We see two-sided coins of possibility, the "both/and" such as "we are BOTH someone AND no one," "we are BOTH going somewhere (ostensibly, our spiritual journey etc.) AND going nowhere (as in Heidgger's "Beingness", for example) because there's nowhere to go and because we've already arrived." Finally, in this example of fundamental paradox, "we are BOTH doing something AND doing nothing" as we fuddle our ways through the metazones.

So far I have pointed to one-half of the paradoxical possibilities before us in the "LIFE IS A JOURNEY' paradigm. Before I get any further, however, I just want to underscore the point here: because of essential paradoxical nature of human consciousness, and more specifically tarot symbols and archetypes, we are facing a BOTH/AND situation here and by the way that's only the real situation by half. Once this is clarified, I'd like to show you how I have solved this riddle in TNP. The solution is quite obvious really, do you see it?

What comes to mind is one of Italo Calvino's readings for the Ace of Coins: a man flips a coin to avoid choosing his path on his own, and the coin falls vertically on a bush: it is neither heads nor tails! I didn't know you were working on a deck. Please, tell me...

Yes my deck was published last October by Paragon House – *Tarot of the Nine Paths* (or TNP) – which includes a 50 pg booklet "The Travel Guide" summary of my personal vision for the expansion (and reduction) of the deck[1]. In all modesty, I believe I've discovered the first significant structural change in tarot since Waite (1909). This is explained in The Travel Guide. The deck is the culmination of my many years meditating and puzzling over the obvious incompletion of the existent Major Arcana (as descended down through Marseille/Waite/Crowley); a deficit is particularly apparent when you study constellations à la Angeles Arrien and Mary Greer and compute so-called "Soul and Personality" cards numerologically via mystic addition. The canon is badly asymmetrical I'm afraid, particularly as a matrix of higher consciousness from the vantage point of dialectical change and psychospiritual growth. I have thus carefully "completed" the edifice without disturbing the sacred architecture. How? By using a secret number code embedded in the canon itself, which after a long, creative and intuitive journey

---

1   See http://tarot9paths.wordpress.com/

of my own, has yielded the addition of five new inferred trumps – which I believe now finalizes (Jung) the inner teachings of the psychologically-whole perspective based on the magical properties of number 9. The new cards, Trumps XXII-XXVI, are respectively titled: The Well (Renewal), The River (Flow), The Ring (Wholeness), The Dragon (Initiation), and The Great Web (Interbeing). Nine, by the way, is a magnificent nondual number (as is the zero) because it always returns to itself.

But now back to the paradox: you see tarot, and really the entire archetypal/imaginal dimension of the human mind itself, is a rainbow. Impermanent, precious, multi-colored, supramundane, seen by multiple observers, though also intangible, short-lived, and fantastic! I call this region 'The Intermediate Territory.' Now we see relativity at work. Tarot is BOTH real AND non-real, simultaneously. Tarot is BOTH meaningful AND meaningless, simultaneously! Therefore, half of the paradox is solved. But what of the other half? I think the Calvino example is apt, but what really clears it is the dharmic teachings of THE FOUR RANGES. Capesh?

I like the rainbow metaphor. It has an illusory quality I am always tempted to assign, or find, in images. I am very interested in the notion of meaning being an illusion (although I suspect that it is also an illusion). But not only the meaning of an image can be an illusion. Mimesis, the foundation of all all pictorial representation, is also a form of illusionism. One of the most interesting notions brought forward by the recent publication of Understanding the Tarot, *by Caldwell, Depaulis and Ponzi, is the notion of "moralizing". In a conversation with two of these authors, Ross Caldwell defined moralizing like this:*

> A morality is when a game is explained as reflecting the human condition, human customs and society, or some aspect of them (like war). It can be both diagnostic (describing society or the particular part the morality is concerned with) and prescriptive (how to live in society, or behave in war, and the purpose of life). Since the world was seen as the center of the universe, and man was the center of the world, and everything was united in a chain of being from God through the stars and planets down to the elements and living things, then a morality can sometimes include both cosmogony and human society. Both the play and the objects used in the game can be moralized.

Would you say that your tarot is a new moralizing?

Is my deck a new moralizing of tarot? If moralizing is defined as "when a game is explained as reflecting the human condition etc.," I would answer with a qualified: YES! (Dammit it...) My qualification however is this: TNP's presupposition of morality – that it reflects the universal (meta) condition of humanity – must be tempered by the fact that TNP is ALSO consciously self-aware of its own "rainbow existence" in the human condition. It knows that tarot is an intermediate journey, not an ultimate one. As merely a rainbow this phantom presence points to reality like in Plato's caves as shadow projections on the walls. Its function is to facilitate your liberation from the cave. TNP embraces its own paradoxical role in the larger scheme of of non-things. It understands its true nature as a "spectrum of possibility" residing universally in the deep human imagination, and that its highest mandate in no more than a transitional object, or (as the former Governor of Alaska would have it), "a bridge to nowhere." In this case, however, "sometimes nowhere, nirvana, the unconditioned mind etc. is a mighty cool place." Can you think of another tarot system that so transparently makes this claim?

By talking to tarotists around the world I have realized that there is an economy of words linked to the idea of 'predicting the future' that goes out of the window as soon as we take fortunetelling out of the equation. Faced with the need to explain what we do, if what we do is not telling the future, we need way more than three words to explain ourselves. Things really can get messy there! My own suspicion is that, if we eliminate the idea of giving predictions (and if we are in no position of offering therapy), what we do becomes a homily. The tarot becomes a visual sermon we read aloud, hoping to achieve an edifying effect in the other person. Homiletics is the art and craft of interpreting a sacred text. Would you say that defines what you do? When you activate your own moralization of your own tarot, are you giving homilies to people? I know that words like 'moralization', 'sermon' or 'homily' aren't 'cool', and they certainly don't feel up-to-date, but please, bear with me. I guess my question also includes another question: to what extent do you think these images can be considered 'sacred'?

About the glorious claims... I like to say that tarot no more "tells the future" than therapy "fixes personalities." Old wives tales, in both instances. Both tarot and therapy are imperfect, intuitive, healing arts with tools that can open a clearing for awareness, self-understanding, skillful actions, and behavioral change. But, always there's no panacea, no guarantee!

I also like to say (with one caveat) that "Tarot is always accurate". However, "accurate" is really inaccurate in this usage. (Accurate) in terms of what? The receiver's own self-narrative, expectations set, interpretations and self-explanations, projected onto a pattern of images from the deck of human possibility? I don't think so! The problem is there's no independent, objective validation-criterion from which to assess a reading's "accuracy" when most of what takes place in oracular experiences is highly subjective, experiential, symbolically-condensed, directly and non-verbally absorbed. (Note, the same problem exists in psychology and has spear-headed the clumsy "evidence-based" methodology surge in the psychotherapeutic world).

Accordingly, what I prefer to say is that "a tarot reading is always RELEVANT!" And by "relevant" I mean: meaningful, helpful, and personally deepening. By the way, that single caveat I mentioned in the first paragraph above? It centers around the issue of sincerity. That is, if you are sincere in participating with the tarot method, it will always be relevant. I stand by that. (If you are merely going through the motions, having a laugh, disguising your true motives), shame on you (and tread not on the tarot gods for they may tread on you!).

I like your precision and the distinction you are making between 'accuracy' and 'relevance'. I tend to believe that any magic operator (I am using the word 'magic' cautiously) has the 'shamanic duty' of assessing the true value of superstitions. In general terms, superstitions are an integral part of how we interact with the world. Superstitions are psychological techniques. We have the urge to be in control of all events relative to our lives, and when we can't directly control a situation, we create a symbolic counterpart we then control, or affect. But in specific terms, while it may be a part of that shamanic duty to acknowledge when a superstition is just being used as a stress-management technique without affecting the way we function in life, it is, I believe, very important to defuse those superstitions that are paralyzing. What made you think it was so important to reinforce the non-dualistic aspect of our relationship with images by creating a new deck? Was it something you found along your interactions with the people you work with?

Why I felt it important to reinforce "the nondual aspect" in my deck? Well, because duality is killing us and we don't quite get it yet. It's the insanity of our age and condition, "either/or ness" à la right or left, positive or negative, predictive or reflective, good or bad, Waite or Crowley etc. Like I've been saying, the wiser view sees "both/and" (which marks the first half of the central paradox of the nondual). I wanted to create a deck where endless conceptualization is abandoned quickly, where possibility is presented inter-connectedly via a particular spectrum or combination of spectrums, where resting in the openness of nothingness (i.e. "The result level") could be easily attained via cartomancy. (I love the portability and image-transmission that can bring people here almost instantly).

In the chapter on Synchronicity in my book *Tarot and Psychology* (2000), I wrote about "habitual causality" modernism's kneejerk need to construct a causal explanation for everything. Why has this happened? What does this mean? What if it were different? Who is at fault? etc. This thick and destructive mental habit fuels the fires of linear explanation over direct perception, conceptual analysis over deeper intuition born of contemplation, reduction of receptivity into "this means THAT" over the direct seeing of "this means THIS." Dualism is always about becoming someone, going somewhere, over being no one, going nowhere. My experience is that the nondual approach is far more immediate, nonconceptual, direct, transparent, accessible, interesting, and transformational.

Wow! You are like Batman. I wasn't expecting an answer from you the night of July 4th! William Carlos Williams wrote: "A poem is a small (or large) machine made out of words". I like the way the phrase applies to the tarot. Do you think the tarot can be accurately described as "a machine made our of images"?

Well, Enrique... Perhaps I'm like Batman. Neither of us have a life beyond our work, and though I have a wife...he had Robin. As far Dr. William Carlos W's suggestion that "a poem is a machine made of words" I would say absolutely sure, "tarot is a machine made of images." But I'd probably be a little more specific. Tarot is a magical machine made of mysterious parts and origins; it can be used for higher contemplation, problem-solving, creativity, and awareness. As a "monumental and singular work as strong as the architecture of the pyramids" (Eliphas Levi) Tarot, I would add, reveals a template of final ends within the initial seed of all human consciousness.

Holy matrix Batman! Dr. Rosengarten is really The Joker...

New York / Encinitas, California, July 2010

"It is incumbent upon us to share the beauty of the art, the underlying philosophies, and the art of reading to the public at large. The only way to remove the limits of current perception is by live participation in the art."

A conversation with DAN PELLETIER, owner of Tarot Garden

Let me start by sharing with you a passage from Don Quixote. Maybe you know it already:

> Don Quixote was about to reply to Sancho Panza, but he was prevented by a cart crossing the road full of the most diverse and strange personages and figures that could be imagined. He who led the mules and acted as carter was a hideous demon; the cart was open to the sky, without a tilt or cane roof, and the first figure that presented itself to Don Quixote's eyes was that of Death itself with a human face; next to it was an angel with large painted wings, and at one side an emperor, with a crown, to all appearance of gold, on his head. At the feet of Death was the god called Cupid, without his bandage, but with his bow, quiver, and arrows; there was also a knight in full armour, except that he had no morion or helmet, but only a hat decked with plumes of divers colours; and along with these there were others with a variety of costumes and faces. All this, unexpectedly encountered, took Don Quixote somewhat aback, and struck terror into the heart of Sancho; but the next instant Don Quixote was glad of it, believing that some new perilous adventure was presenting itself to him, and under this impression, and with a spirit prepared to face any danger, he planted himself in front of the cart, and in a loud and menacing tone, exclaimed, "Carter, or coachman, or devil, or whatever thou art, tell me at once who thou art, whither thou art going, and who these folk are thou carriest in thy wagon, which looks more like Charon's boat than an ordinary cart."

To which the devil, stopping the cart, answered quietly:

> Senor, we are players of Angulo el Malo's company; we have been acting the play of "The Cortes of Death" this morning, which is the octave of Corpus Christi, in a village behind that hill, and we have to act it this afternoon in that village which you can see from this; and as it is so near, and to save the trouble of undressing and dressing again, we go in the costumes in which we perform. That lad there appears as Death, that other as an angel, that woman, the manager's wife, plays the queen, this one the soldier, that the emperor, and I the devil; and I am one of the principal characters of the play, for in this company I take the leading parts. If

you want to know anything more about us, ask me and I will answer with the utmost exactitude, for as I am a devil I am up to everything.

By the faith of a knight-errant, [replied Don Quixote,] when I saw this cart I fancied some great adventure was presenting itself to me; but I declare one must touch with the hand what appears to the eye, if illusions are to be avoided. God speed you, good people; keep your festival, and remember, if you demand of me ought wherein I can render you a service, I will do it gladly and willingly, for from a child I was fond of the play, and in my youth a keen lover of the actor's art.

I like the way this passage evokes a common attitude we, tarotists, all share: while looking at the tarot we all fancy "some great adventure". When, or to what extent, do you think we should "touch with the hand what appears to the eye" as to "avoid" illusions?

Well it's tough to eat with a helmet on. There is a clue in the statement, "…and in my youth a keen lover of the actor's art." I've often wondered at his ability to see through some illusions and not through others. Right before he enjoys a sumptuous feast of moldy bread (with his helmet on), Don Quixote tells the 'damsels', "Modesty becomes the fair, and moreover laughter that has little cause is great silliness; this, however, I say not to pain or anger you, for my desire is none other than to serve you." For my desire is none other to serve…

There are a ton of illusions about the Tarot and the world of Tarot, that can be touched, or peeled back. But avoid? There's the New York City Neon $10 introductory offer reader, there's the mysteries of the hermeticism in the Kabbalistic Klezmer Karnival Kitties Tarot, there's the whole study of the evolution of linguistic morphing of meanings through time – how language usage and translations have gotten us to where we are now. We could discuss the Jungian approach, a therapeutic approach, a witchy-woo-woo approach, a cowboy cowbella approach… perhaps how approaches are related to the actors' arts. A continuance of specific illusions. And I believe perhaps there is a touch of theatre or RP present in some readings. Further, some degree may even be necessary. I'm not sure I'd avoid any of it.

I remember one night in San Francisco, I heard one of the most freeing things when Holly Voley looked through a cloud of smoke and said, "The biggest secret of the Occult is that, over a period of time, a bunch of guys, made up a bunch of stuff." Now that doesn't say or mean it doesn't work. In *Liber O vel Manus et Sagittae*, Aleister Crowley wrote, "In this book it is spoken of the Sephiroth, and the Paths, of Spirits and Conjurations; of Gods, Spheres, Planes and many other things which may or may not exist. It is immaterial whether they exist or not. By doing certain things certain results follow; students are most earnestly warned against attributing objective reality or philosophic validity to any of them." But none of it means a ding-dang when there's a sitter in front of you. If you cannot take off the helmet and see the meal for what it is, how can we tell giants from windmills? Learning to differentiate is important.

After the last Readers Studio (2010), Jeannette Roth (my partner at The Tarot Garden) and I were at a local bar in West Des Moines, enjoying a glass of wine and studying a deck. One of the locals came over (a member of the softball team that is sponsored by the adjoining restaurant) and asked what we were doing, I told him we were studying tarot cards. He asked Jeannette if he could get a reading from her. She answered that he could get a reading from me, and I like an idiot said, "I could if I had the right deck," and the guy goes kind of ballistic, with the "Why can't you read with this deck?" Jeannette asks, "which deck?" I tell her, and she bolts out the door, "I'll be back in 15 minutes." His friends are wantin' to go, and he stalling, going to get his 'tarot reading with a special deck'. It's all fun and games. Jeannette comes back with the Baseball Tarot. I take the guy to a back table. He says in all seriousness, "I've never had this done. So this is gonna be spooky and all..." I said, "Just think of me as a coach." I used Rachel Pollack's 'Dr. Apollo General All Purpose Spread' but arranged the cards as 1st, 2nd, 3rd bases, home plate and pitchers mound. When we were finished (and it weren't purty) he looked at me and said, "I just had the same conversation with my therapist earlier today..." Some illusions have their place, others are fun. Sometimes it's more fun to wiggle the curtains, rather than draw them all the way back. Like dropping game origin of Tarot onto a group of newly minted mall witches. "Game... WHAT Game???" We can enjoy so much more with our helmets off. And I can be of better service... The Great Adventure is more fun, when you know you're part of it.

In his work with metaphor therapy, Richard Kopp talks about the importance of working with the metaphors the client brings to the dialogue. Using a baseball-based deck fits beautifully into that strategy. Something the tarot has implicit, at least since Court De Gebelin, the idea of communicating through images. I am not just talking about expressing an idea, or documenting some memories, but about the possibility of crafting a dialogue through images. I know that is one of the things that attracted me to the tarot. What about you? What brought you to the tarot?

Working with the sitters, metaphor is something I love, but it's not always possible. A while back I had a corporate gig where I was reading for clients in an upscale clothing store (Armani is their 'low' end), so I used *Le Calzature Fantastiche*. That deck would not have 'gone over' as well at a Pub reading, but in that place at that time – it matched the contextual needs of the sitters as a group. However, it is not always possible to have THE deck when you need it. Sometimes we have to use the tools we have on hand.

I feel that crafting a conversation around and through the images, and how those images resonate with us today at this exact moment in time, lies at the core of what a good reading is about. In a round about way, I began reading Tarot as a methodology for improving my ability to communicate (how to talk to girls 101), and ended up over the years discovering that reading is more dance-like than formulaic. Formulas are a snap to teach. Dance is more difficult. That has, in my opinion, been the main issues of Magicians and Cold-Readers when they watch us; thinking it is formulaic as they try to 'figure out how we do it' and duplicate our success. But as a reader, I'm a dancer – and I don't always lead. I just keep the rhythm and accentuate the tempo. The sitter provides the music (subject), and the cards are the orchestral inspiration, and dictates the waltz, foxtrot, or the tango. Building rapport to me is the key of that crafted conversation. I want to build rapport, as the sitter provides context, and the images of the Tarot guide us and our conversation to the answers the sitter needs. So that is sort of kind of what brought me to Tarot. But that's not what keeps me at Tarot.

If I'm sitting with you, reading, conversing, dancing, building... I'm the least important thing there. I may be doing 90% of the talking, but I'm the least important thing. One of the beautiful things about the Amberstone's Readers Studio, is that each of the presenters has the attendees do exercises, they read face to face with each other. It moves interpreting symbols to experiential practical applications – a dance. Two people, and the Tarot providing the steps. I feel this lies at the very core of Tarot.

It's my opinion that *tarocchi appropriati* was a methodology or practice to encourage correct and civilized courtly conversation during *Tarocchi* play as opposed to "You trumped my wands trick and now you play Le Fou? You rotten sheep's bladder! You dung sodden trollop!" I think conversation through symbols has always been the true heart of Tarot. Yeah, crafting a dialogue through images. I like that. That's what keeps me in the dance...

I think there is something profoundly magical in the moment a person chooses a card and places it on the table, as if saying: "here, this is me".

What makes it difficult for some magicians, or cold readers, to get the gist of the dynamic behind readings is a problem of mindset. A magician is understandably trained to see a magic effect as a linear narrative with one single possible outcome. As magician Jimmy Ian Swiss said to a dear friend of mine who is also a magician: "confusion isn't magic". There is an extraordinary clip on YouTube titled "the non-ambitious card trick explained," or something like that. Usually, magicians perform the 'Ambitious Card', an effect in which you choose a card, put it back in the middle of a deck, and with a snap of the magician's fingers it pops on top of the deck, over and over. In the YouTube clip, everything happens as in the usual trick with one exception: the card never gets to the top of the deck. It simply ends up lost among all the other cards, whenever you put it in. There is a very interesting moment of puzzlement we experience when we watch the effect performed for the first time, and at the revelation we find that the card on top is not our card. But the whole thing is truly a joke, of course. There is no awe in it.

A magician is trained to be in control of the sense of awe he creates in his audience. A reader is trained to detect awe whenever it appears, to accept its manifestation and go with it. I would actually say a reader is trained to seek for awe together with his client, so both can experience it at once. Magic is something you do for a person. A reading is something you give to a person. But there are exceptions, of course. As a matter of fact, a fake reading can be as effective as a real one, although, perhaps, those are not fake readings but readings given by fake readers. What do you think?

Holy Poopsky! I didn't realize the fuses were lit! Let me just say, Ricky Jay is God. A Magician may or may not create awe in his audience. A Magician juggles reality. Often tricking the senses to suspend disbelief that the usual laws of reality are suspended, and during that time regardless of whether awe is inspired, the audience is meant to be entertained. Magic is an art form that gave us both Uri Geller and James Randi. However the function of Penn and Teller with their clear cups and balls, or you or I doing a reading, even without a visible deck, is quite different. One is *Le Bateleur* (a comic juggler or street busker), the raconteur who entertains with the apparent suspension of the laws of reality, and the other is an active intimate social intercourse built around the random appearance of symbols for the purpose of providing another member of the event answers and/or guidance based upon the chosen or selected symbols. The reader... Don Quixote recognized the occupants of the wagon as symbols, rather than actively being what they represented. So he allowed them to pass. A reader is also a symbol. But quite different than *Le Bateleur*. The key difference between the two active symbols is intent.

Certainly the reader may be a raconteur, and *Le Bateleur* may enlighten... but sometimes intent may become confused. Ego can justify all kinds of crimes. Mr. Geller may have set true psychic research back decades. When the tools of the magician are brought into the reading, lines blur. If I'm bird dog catting my sitters I'm not providing a reading, I'm pretending. So even if I provide 'correct' guidance, my intent has polluted it. Likewise, if I augment the message of the symbols with an RP aspect, I've elevated myself into a place of importance above that of the symbols we're discussing.

In a proper dance, there's a triad of music, steps, and dancers. Or you could have dancer A & B, and the music. However you want to slice it, there's an equality between participants and music. I may lead, but you can always snap me back to rhythm should I get out of step; one dancer's sense of importance can disrupt the delicate balance. It's the balance... the sense of service. Regardless of whether the sitter recognizes it or not, they too have become a symbol as they slide their face down cards singly, out from a ribbon spread before them. It has already begun – the event. Nothing turned over yet.

I refer to the event that we call a reading as The Process (it was also the obvious title for my audio book). A reading does not consist of turning over cards and reciting memorized meanings. A reading should unfold, blossoming like a rose. And some roses (like a Rio Samba) change color as they open. I learned long ago that each reading is singular – and most never end up how we imagine, when we started. As we reveal the cards slowly, unfold the story – real magic can and may occur. Fake reading fake reader... it all comes down to intent. Scam money or provide a service. I also think it is necessary for the illusions to exist. But as a reader, I never juggle reality, or the illusion of reality. I partake in an unfolding event that exists for the benefit of the sitter. I just thought of something... Sancho Panza... Panza... La Pances. I love this stuff! Now, have you your air-filled bladder ready? See the bumpkin with the dappled mule? Let's go have some fun!

I obviously agree with you: Ricky Jay IS god! My contention comes from the fact that illusions seem to define a boundary: you are either in or out. Either you believe there is something profoundly magical in what you are doing, or you don't. Perhaps a distinction could be made between the nature of a reading as an event, and the nature of the processes at play in that event. In the course of these conversations I have found many people to whom the tarot has opened a door towards the occult, the transcendent, or god. To me, the tarot has been fundamental for understanding how our brains work, and why we need art. There is a whole difference there in terms of belief systems! Maybe we all believe there is profound magic in readings, but we don't necessarily agree on why readings are magical.

One could say that *The Baseball Tarot* is about as far away from Tarot as one could get. It contains none of the symbols that one expects from Tarot. No Star with her footsie in the water, no Magician in the pose of a FC Mason, no guy hanging from his feet. However, the sitter came to the reading holding expectations. *The Baseball Tarot* (loosely based on the Crowley Thoth) served to bridge the gap between his expectations and the message. For him to have the Tarot tell him the same message as his therapist had told him hours before, to him that was magic.

Sometimes even *Kabalistic Poodles of the Viennese Mermaids Tarot* can have merit – if it helps bridge the gap between sitter and reader. Sometimes ya just gotta fly with it. But you do wonder what the mechanism is, what's the trigger... Few years back I'm reading in Portland Oregon and Robin Ator (creator of the *International Icon Tarot*) walks up and asks if he could buy a reading for a friend of his (turns out he hadn't seen this guy in 20 years), I say sure, and do the reading. The guy leans back and goes, "Wow...that was strange." I asked what was strange about it. He says, "I had Robin read for me before I sat down with you." "...And..." "Completely different cards, and you both told me the same thing." The guy was blown away and Robin and I both chuckled. We (Robin and I) trust in the message, and the medium, and we do not confuse the two.

There's a difference between dance and choreography. It's that linear approach you talked about... like calling a score – music. I think the message is the magic. And it's a beautiful thing to be part of. Belief systems can limit. Belief systems may hold us back... There's that one Tarot Forum (the purple one) where week after week there's a tread about 'cleansing' your cards of their negative energies, and prior readings. Perhaps we should set up a professional tarot card cleansing service? Some folks believe that one should knock the deck on the table to 'knock out the negative energies'. I was once told that one should not shuffle a Tarot deck like a poker deck because it "Flaps the magic out" (of the deck). These are in my opinion limiting beliefs.

I believe that growth – be it spiritual, intellectual, or emotional – is not about becoming more. Our goal is not to be more spiritual, more intellectual, or more emotional (As Tom Robbins wrote, "It is what it is. You are what you it. There are no mistakes"). Growth, is never a matter of growing more... it is always of matter of limiting less. Perhaps if each day we limit less, one day we'll awaken to find we've have become limitless. Tarot may transcend belief systems in the hands of a competent reader. A purist may cry for the One True Tarot, but the sitter may need a more Freemasonic approach (as provided with some decks like the now OOP Knapp-Hall) before he climbs back into his rig and drives through to Tonopah. Some decks, like the Crowley Thoth, carry tons of 'baggage' along with them. That baggage may act as a benefit or a hindrance depending on the sitter, and the reader. It may be difficult to leave the house with the One True Tarot in our pocket at all times, so we usually make do with something that suits a more moderate presentation. Sure *The Tarot and the Mysteries of Love and Sex* may not be the best deck for general readings, but it too can serve as a bridge given the correct time and place.

Belief systems rarely differentiate between the event and the process that takes place during the event, or a Tarot facilitated journey to the center of self. Both, may open doors for the participants. Both may lead us towards becoming limitless. Or with limiting beliefs, Tarot can serve as a barbed wire fence, prohibiting growth and understanding. The mind behind the eye that beholds makes the distinction – for good or ill. But the helmet that limits our vision is only held on with green ties…

I guess the problem I have with these superstitions about putting diapers to your tarot deck and taking it to McDonald's for a Happy Meal is that they aren't conducive to an understanding of the tool. I am especially aware of that since I want to speak to those who have no interest in the occult and shudder when they hear the word 'magic'. I am interested in those guys because I am one of them. The reasons why I got into the tarot are so far removed from the common reasons other people usually share with me! I was telling to a friend that, through the tarot, I haven't found the occult, nor the 'other' world, nor a spiritual life, nor god. What the tarot has given me is a reason to believe in art, and through art, a reason to believe we carry the means of our own healing, our own empowerment, and our own change. If we can make an image that can make ourselves cry, we can change anything. But again, the magic of the artist is the magic of the trickster: chiaroscuro, perspective, slow-motion, close ups, sound… things you learn by practice and by accepting what materials and tools can do and what they cannot.

Dylan Thomas used to say that poets should work "'out of' words, not 'towards them'." I think I am interested in working 'towards the image', not 'out of image'. When you think about the tarot in terms of images, the whole thing takes a different dimension, since you can only expect so much from images. Poet Seamus Heaney put it beautifully: "That is one of the functions of the doing of any art and one of the benefits of putting yourself into the contemplative, receptive and transporting presence of art. It makes you a bit better than yourself for the moment; it doesn't mean that you won't relapse or fail yourself". What have you found through the tarot?

The Welsh poet Gwen Thomas said, "The joy is in the walking; we are deluded by the destination." What have I found? I often ask folks, "If River Tam (character from Firefly/Serenity) had a Tarot deck, what would it look like?" Tarot is a tool, it's an artifact of the fifteenth sixteenth seventeenth eighteenth nineteenth twentieth twentyfirst century. It's been added to, edited, created, recreated… They added on a geocentric model to a heliocentric paradigm and called it good. They added the letters of the Hebrew alphabet when they didn't even have the knowledge to translate grade-school French (and 'they' were anti-Semitic to boot). Layers and layers added to an ancient artifact.

Wassily Kandinsky wrote: "...and art is not vague production, transitory and isolated, but a power which must be directed to the improvement and refinement of the human soul to, in fact, the raising of the spiritual triangle." If art refrains from doing this work, a chasm remains unbridged, for no other power can take the place of art in this activity. And at times when the human soul is gaining greater strength, art will also grow in power, for the two are inextricably connected and complementary one to the other. Conversely, at those times when the soul tends to be choked by material disbelief, art becomes purposeless and talk is heard that art exists for art's sake alone. There is a bond between art and the soul, as it were, drugged into unconsciousness. The artist and the spectator drift apart, till finally the latter turns his back on the former or regards him as a juggler whose skill and dexterity are worthy of applause. "The artist must have something to say, for master over form is not his goal but rather adapting form to its inner meaning."

The artist evolves. We remove limits. We evolve. We are culturally quite different than we were seven hundred years ago. Kandinsky also said: "This art which has no power for the future, which is only a child of the age and cannot become a mother of the future, is a barren art. She is transitory and to all intent dies at the moment the atmosphere alters which nourished her." Baggage added to the Tarot, may at the time have 'meaning' for the baggage handler. Later it becomes a dead weight. Riccardo Minetti (of Lo Scarabeo) once said, "While the Rider-Waite is probably still the best single deck one may work with, it is working like an anchor, slowing down any evolution of the concept of Tarot. Every time a deck tries to go in a different direction, it is labeled as "wrong." You would be surprised to learn how many complaints we receive from North America, from people saying: "that deck is printed wrong, as Justice is 8 and Strength is 11. I want a copy that is printed right".

River Tam would be lost attempting to find meaning with the fallacy of a geocentric representation of a heliocentric reality, that vanishes completely upon changes in the point of reference of the viewer (participant). The Tarot deck itself has served as a repository of esoteric thought for awhile. Lévi added his bits, Papus his, Waite plagiarized and added his twists, Crowley added his constructs (and told folks they were constructs)... and development ceased.

Tarot has developed in the last two hundred years an entire mythos of its own. The cards have theirs, and the practice of reading Tarot has developed its own mythos also. Take for example the practice of allowing a sitter to choose a deck for their reading. I have to ask, "Why?" Does the average sitter appreciate the variances between a Flornoy Dodal, and a Grimaud Marteau? A Crowley Thoth and a Liber T? Most readers even think the Thoth deck correlates to Crowley and have never studied an Etteilla Thoth! Should I take 10 minutes of a readers' time to deliver a history lesson? As soon as I request a sitter 'choose', I've ceded control of the reading to them... Let's say you're going to choose a 'volunteer' from the audience. Whom do you choose? The belligerent drunk or the ditzy blonde – depends... the latter will not work for a pick pocket routine, the former as a mind reading subject. Allowing a sitter to choose a deck is a practice, based on an erroneous mythos. And we must differentiate between Myths and Development. One has become dynamic while the latter remains static. Ooops. That's wrong. See it's really fun to listen to contemporary 'experts' pontificate about Tarot – as though this Eurocentric artifact has remained Eurocentric.

Riccardo Minetti once stated, "In continental Europe, I think people started using the 78 card decks in the seventies, when the influence from USA came to Europe." So even as a European construct, it's now been USA'd into something else. Experts continue to pontificate, ignoring Europe. A Tarot deck has 78-cards. At The Tarot Garden, we often get emails: "I bought a deck from you guys, and you only sent 22 cards. I want the whole deck thank you very much." People over here have no idea that, until recently, reading with Majors Only was the norm in many places in Europe. Cool. But now Tarot has exploded in Asia. Asian Tarot has taken on whole new avenues based on European Tarot, based on Etteilla/Lévi 22-card systems, so the market is not ignored. 'Experts' pretend it does not exist!

You once mentioned:

> Every time we blink the tarot suffers another mutilation. It has become whatever an editor wants it to be. This process has evolved as one might expect, starting in the 18th century as a concoction whose main ingredient was the ego of several successive authors, and by the 20th century becoming a set of inventions motivated by pure financial interest. The market basically needs something new to sell every month: 'If we already sold the Kabbala, and the mermaids, now we can sell the Mermaid's Kabala'. 'Some people like poodles and some people like Vienna, so, let's give them the Viennese Poodles' Tarot. And then, the Kabbalistic Poodles of

the Viennese Mermaids Tarot!' The tarot is a Rorschach test that, in the 18th, 19th and early 20th centuries, said more about the ego of those who projected their theories onto it, than about the tarot itself. Now, in the 21st century, the tarot is saying more about what the market allegedly wants than about itself.

However that statement only addresses one aspect of Tarot. The United States market of the Tarot deck. It ignored the global market of the deck, the practice of reading, the myths of reading and the deck itself. Perhaps that Tarot can never be a 'mother of the future', having 'died at the moment the atmosphere which nourished her altered'. The Victorian era is long gone. Perhaps that deck is now impotent.

I like to move Tarot out of the market. Like River Tam – take Tarot off planet. What survives? What gets lost in the black of space? The interpersonal communication, regardless of whether it is via *tarocchi appropriati,* or an insightful life changing conversation, the interpersonal communication crafted over the images... A qabalist might say, 'The way to achieve joy and fulfillment, is to become a being of sharing', I have found that the true Art of Tarot, is the deep level of communication and sharing that may develop between two people and the music of the imagery.

I am with you: "the true Art of Tarot, is the deep level of communication and sharing that may develop between two people and the music of the imagery." I am right there with you, 100%. Now, how does that art dialogue, conceptually, and aesthetically, with the 21st century? It can't just all be about the reader's intuition, but there has to be some formal pursuits. If the art is in the telling, the elements of "The telling"are the formal constraints a tarot artist should explore and expand. This is not the same as learning methods. How do we do that? Who is doing that?"

That was exactly my impetus for writing "The Process". You know, the 'experts' love to preach Tarot and Archetypes. Then – they proceed to become dogmatic about the whole affair and publish tome after tome on 'meanings'. If the images of the Tarot were true archetypes, we'd already know what they mean! Which means the tomes are proof that either the experts don't trust the archetypes or they are not archetypes; or perhaps the experts don't understand the language they use. An archetype by definition is universally understood. Which means we don't need books telling us what they mean. A formal approach consists of a book or a person telling us what we should think, what we should know, what is factual that we can build a foundation upon. Jung stated about his knowledge of Tarot, "Yes, I know of the Tarot. It is, as far as I know, the pack of cards originally used by the Spanish gypsies, the oldest cards historically known. They are still used for divinatory purposes."

Okay, so perhaps he's not the best source for Tarot information since he states historically incorrect opinion. But folks love to 'quote' Jung because it provides a valid justification for our art (believing that it needs justifying). The foundations upon which we base our current education on Tarot is fallacious. I began Tarot with no formal foundation. I believe in and trust the Archetypal Imagery of Tarot. I understand that when a person is presented with a triangle above a square (or a triangle within a square), it is not archetypal. It's a set of symbols.

Three Rabbis went to visit God. One died, the second came back insane, and the third returned enlightened. Same here. Some will never question the square and the triangle. Some will invent their own meaning, or parrot what they were told by another. The third will seek out and study and find the varied meanings of confluence of the two symbols. Perhaps even find deeper meaning in the Mason's apron and the Waite Temperance.

Intuit? Back when James Randi unmasked Uri Geller, some readers saw the handwriting on the wall and dropped the 'psychic' from their sales literature. They became 'intuitive'. Intuitive is a function of logic. The word means that one went from A to D, and skipped the steps in-between; "That Karmann Ghia has a loose number three intake valve," I say as it drives by. That's intuition. I know it has a loose valve without getting down and pulling out my feeler gauge. Psychic is, "Hey, let's wait here on this corner, a Karmann Ghia is about to come by with a loose number three intake valve." Intuitive essentially means that we're human. We think, we ponder, we reason – we are cognitive beings. Any reader who uses the word, is essentially saying: I'm human. Well bully for you. It's a term used as a label to elevate themselves above others, to appear special. Intuitive reader is a marketing term not entirely dissimilar to fire sale. One may prove a person is not psychic – but one cannot prove that a person is not intuitive. Because they are, after all, human. But its bullshit. They are simply readers. Nothing wrong with that, until you try to tell me you're 'Oh So Special'. Bullshit. You're human just like me and the guy in the seed cap over there.

I used to work in the world of finance. I'd have clients come to me who'd brag about all the books they'd read on the market. My boss was upset one day because I refused to open a 6 million dollar account for a guy. He told me he had six live news feeds and had read all them books... Well, I'd seen the movie before. He was going to trade on news, and blow out his account in a matter of weeks (the quickest blowout I've ever seen was a three million dollar account that blew out in 45 minutes), and then sue me as a result. Positive turnover equals negative returns. Formal education only goes so far in the real world.

The self importance of educators is over-stated in my opinion. Experience backed by curiosity and a personal drive is still the best teacher. Educators in our schools currently teach that the Wright Brothers were the first to fly an engine powered aircraft — even though they were second; that Marconi invented the radio (his patent was reversed in 1943 – but that's forgotten in the schools), and that Columbus discovered the new world, or that J.C. was born in December, somewhere around year zero. Fallacious syllogisms all. Our current New World 'meaning' for the Six of Pentacles revolves around gifts and presents. Some authors go off on tangents about the 'motives' of the giver blah blah blah. What really happened is that when Mathers was, er, uh...'translating' Etteilla's works, he could not differentiate between the French words for 'present tense' and 'gifts'. Well *toda bevaukasha,* I bet his Hebrew was... never mind. But it is taught as fact, by folks, the marketers parade as 'experts'.

Reading Tarot for others is an Art. Not all artists must attend art school. Look around, we have a TV that runs when nobody's watching, a radio blares in the background, IPods clamor for attention over the sounds of life. Plugged in, good to go, got the tunes... Music is art only when it's live. A recording is a copy. Nowadays it's nothing but ones and zeros. Ones and zeros are not art. What you're listening to is not art anymore than sheet music is art. A score is a recipe ("follow these directions and you may come close to what I had in mind," says the composer).

When I was a child, my parents took me to the World's Fair in Seattle (1962). I was dragged around and forced to look at stuff. Then we entered the Hall of Modern Art. My family was aghast, they laughed and pointed. Then I saw it. A Kinetic Sculpture – it was huge – perhaps a hundred long flexible arms with stuff attached, like a willow tree of junk. And if you pressed the button, an electric motor made it jump and sway (and stuff would clang together and make noise). It was wonderful. When you pushed the button – it was never the same twice! It was different each and every time! I was in love! My family laughed. But that was art. It was dynamic. Not static bits of something stuck in somebody else's time.

John Cage (1912-1992) was a brilliant composer, and attended The Cornish School of Arts here in Seattle. My favorite work is entitled 4'33". He once told the story of going into a sound-proof (or sound absorbing) room at Harvard one day. He entered the room expecting silence. Later he said that he "heard two sounds, one high and one low. When I described them to the engineer in charge, he informed me that the high one was my nervous system in operation, the low one my blood in circulation." Cage had gone to a place where he expected there to be no sound, and yet... 4'33" is a performance piece (sort of). The performer enters, opens the key board lid on the Piano, and appears to sit doing nothing for four minutes and thirty three seconds, then closes the lid and exits. It's freaking brilliant! The performer is not the music, nor is the piano the instrument that's being played. The instrument is the audience and the hall; the cough from the man two rows in front of you, and the woman who whispers behind you, the pneumatic door closer, a far siren out in the street, the singing of rain on the windows... these are the instruments.

Nobody listens to silence anymore – we're wired for sound... and we experience no art, no music. We listen instead to math... ones and zeroes. We've turned ourselves into spectators on our own stage of life. I am talking about Tarot Reading by the way... walking around Kandinsky's gallery with our Tarot programs (LWB's & informative tomes) in hand, "Oh, I love the way he's bent over his work – being diligent, I wonder what the program says? Oh... he's bent over his work being diligent. Sure glad I bought the book. These experts know so much!" Art exists in the moment. That's it. Then it's gone. Painting and sculpture are dead. They don't move. Sure Mona Lisa's lovely, but she's dead. At best, I can be a spectator. Yeah, Jackson Pollack may have expressed himself well – but the paint's dry – it's over, done, that was then, this is now. Art should move me to become a participant. Art should make me be a participant. I don't want to be in the past tense, I live in the present tense.

So there's this question I like to ask folks..."Why do you read Tarot for others?"

The answer defines your intent. You may care about history, artwork, and tradition; but what we care about is unimportant. Being a Tarot reader has nothing to do with us. There's a person sitting across from you. They don't give a fig about what that little symbol means. They care about their life. We may be way over in the 'hearing voices' psychic crowd, or way over in the psycho-therapeutic Jungian aspect of Tarot and discovery – but what do we do to re-gear ourselves for their needs? See – we have to be in the moment – we have to show up. We have to get out of our own way. What we think (about Tarot) has zip all to do with how to reach them, the sitters.

Now, what does this have to do with art? Real art, is in the moment. Listening to a recording of an opera, and being there are two different things. Walking around wired for sound... you're a spectator. Listening to a recording, watching TV, you're a spectator. Sitting at the opera – you get carried away. Music, when live, forces you to become a participant. There is a connection between the artist, and the audience. That connection – that's the key... There was a world of difference between listening to a recording of *The Grateful Dead,* and being there...

However to specifically answer your question, I've been trying. And as far as I know, *The Process: The Way of the Reader* is the only Tarot based work that addresses the artistic view of reading and the reader. Because I tend not to parrot what's gone before, newer approaches have come to me. I was in treatment for a bit for PTSD after my first trip to NYC (business trip, WTC 2 61st floor. I had just stepped out for a cigarette when all hell broke loose). After a few weeks I sat down with my psychiatrist and showed him how the Tarot Majors (from a non-WCS deck) show correlation between the archetypal images and the 12-Step Programs, which extend out to a 22-Step Map (of Change). My psychiatrist looked at me and said, "I think anything further would be a waste of our time..."

I talked about the 22-Steps briefly at the Amberstone's Readers Studio 2010. I had one woman come to me in tears. She'd been sober for two decades and had never heard anything so empowering; two other folks had just been discussing they needed to hunt down a meeting and then listened to my presentation – they loved it. All of this is illogical – but sometimes logic doesn't provide the best path for growth.

Ah! You are touching on a point that interests me a lot! I am very fond of John Cage. He famously said "I have nothing to say and I am saying it!" I often think that is the reality of 99% of the tarot books out there! It is only that all those guys don't have the genius nor the charm John Cage had. But your comment touches on two things I would like to address. One is silence. I think silence is a very important part of a reading. When you pour cement on a sidewalk the sidewalk has to remain quiet for a while. You cannot let people walk on top of it until it hardens, or the work is ruined. Sometimes, silence is to words what time is to cement. You cannot just trample all your words with more words. One has to let the high points of any communication breathe. That takes me to the second thing I want to address: I cannot sit in front of a paying client, slip a card through the table, and say nothing, not for four minutes and thirty three seconds, not for half an hour. Clients like to buy tarot by the pound. They want to see lots of cards on the table and hear lots of talking, or they feel short-changed. I think you are addressing something that is fundamental: the reading is always about them. It is their life that is 'on the line' and we are here for them. They don't want to be questioned, provoked or entertained, but to be given answers. Fair enough. The thing is, a craft becomes art, especially contemporary art, when its results transcend function. Duchamp's urinal became art when we weren't allowed to pee in it anymore.

The machine you saw at the museum – I wonder if it was by Jean Tinguely – was fabulous for the same reason it was useless: it moved randomly instead of being precise (like a true bachelor, 'pataphysical, machine). You cannot use that machine to do anything with except experiencing the beauty of mechanical movements. That is a common gesture in art: it reveals the hidden uselessness of something, and by doing so it uncovers a kind of beauty that wasn't present in our original relationship with these objects, or ideas.

A reading doesn't become art just because we are inspiring. That could make readings great therapy, but not necessarily art. To make readings art, one would have to satisfy the client and then give them something more that wasn't present in the original relationship we have with the tarot, or with the event of the reading. Perhaps that is what your projection of the 12-Steps into the Trumps accomplished. This is always hard to do, as anybody who approaches a reader would naturally have the same reaction that those who weren't 'in the know' had in front of John Cage's piece. Painter Oskar Kokoschka wrote: "The natural reaction of people when you present them with something they cannot comprehend is to feel superior, since they consider that you are asking them to waste their attention." John Cage's piece is brilliant, yet his gesture will be wasted on many people. I doubt that speaks about the piece's faults. It speaks about your own limitations. But Cage inhabited a world that supported the production of such art pieces. We, readers, don't inhabit such a world, especially in the sanitized realm of new age magic. I don't want to take much more of your time, but I would like to know your thoughts on how can we, readers, transform our environment so it can support an artistic vision of what we do?

My friend the late Elisa Moscovici, before checking out, as her final post on a Tarot forum, shared the following:

> Take care people, and read, read, read the cards for strangers. It is the only way to really learn and it is fun to do as well. I learned also a lot about myself that way. Oh and I remember a thread about what deck to take with you to heaven or hell. Well, wherever place I go, it'll be my trimmed old Thoth. :) Love, Elisa

I think that about sums it up. We have to be willing to read face-to-face to strangers. We have to be willing to read for both sinners and saints, and the latter rarely come to us seeking redemption. For every reader who won't read for skeptics we have to read for two. For each 'reader' who only reads on the other side of a keyboard we have to read for two. We have to take the art to the street. It is incumbent upon us to share the beauty of the art, the underlying philosophies, and the art of reading to the public at large. The only way to remove limits of current perception is by live participation in the art. The only way we can undo the damage done by the huckster who uses Tarot to bilk the public, is for us to get out and become more experienced. And we may invite derision, laughter, and challenges. Big deal. If we're not challenged we're dead.

I have two other passions besides Tarot. And for me they are all inter-related. One is raising roses, the other is prospecting for gold. They share similar metaphors. When caring for roses, diseased, dead, or dying canes must be removed. To allow them to remain even for a short time invites further disease and insect infestation. You can lose the whole plant. I'd like to close with an essay I wrote once. I hope you enjoy it.

§§§

So I was chatting with Max, buddy of mine the other day, and he was going on about Alchemy of the Human Spirit, and it got to the point where I just couldn't take it anymore.

"You don't know poop."

"What? How can you say..."

"You don't know poop."

"Well then mister big shot know it all, 'splain yerself." He took a sip from the glass in front of him.

"Back in the California gold rush, do you have any idea who really made money?"

"No."

"Didn't think so. Sam Brannan, he made the more money than anybody else during the California gold rush – and he never found a speck of gold."

"You're insane." Max never does mince words.

"Sam Brannan sold shovels. In addition, most of the forty-niners didn't have a clue how to find gold, but they all needed shovels."

"And I suppose you know how to find gold?"

"Listen. The first key is you have to learn how gold acts."

"How gold acts? Are you serious? How gold acts? Tell me how gold acts."

"Depends. Before you can learn how gold acts, you have to understand something about hydraulics. You have to learn how water acts. Then you have to start to learn what happens when water and earth mix. Stuff doesn't just 'go downstream'. It takes a while looking at streams during all stages of a yearly cycle. You want to study how a stream acts during flood stage, you have to listen to huge boulders moving under water, watch how water moves the earth, and how the earth reacts. And you have to learn how water and earth act as floods cease, how earth is deposited."

"Yeah yeah yeah, gold is heavy and it sinks." Max pushed himself back from the bar and signaled the bartender for another round.

"Only when it is no longer in suspension."

"Suspension?"

"Right, it's going to be moving along with heavy boulders during spring floods. And yeah, it's heavy. It will want to sink. It will want drop on down to bedrock as soon as the current allows it. It will hang in crevasses and anyplace the current releases its hold, especially once the hydraulic pressure of current flow begins to abate.

"However when it's suspended, it can hang in moss and grasses along the riverbank. It tumbles and slides to the bottom of a boil. You can study all the geology you want, but if you don't understand how gold acts when it's in suspension, you could be standing on a gold mine and never know it."

"You're telling me you can find gold in moss? I've never heard of such a thing." The Bartender sat glasses of amber swill in front of us and took Max's money.

"That's cuz you never get your head away from them dandy cards of yours to expand your knowledge. If you want to find gold, you have to understand how earth and water act when they mix," I replied.

"Mud-pies. I learned mud-pies in kindergarten."

"But you didn't learn how mud-pies act when they are in motion, combined with another force called gravity."

"Okay, but humor me and tie this back to Tarot." He started rolling one of his hand rolled cigarettes.

"Can't light that here. We have laws. Look – swords are about knowledge, information, learning. In this example, learning how earth and water mix – cups and disks. Cups and disks act differently together than say cups and swords. Cups and disks together move things and produce things – water and earth."

"Dude... what about wands – fire. I guess fire's about refining it all down and melting away the impurities..."

"You really wanna know what wands are about? Just look at gold in the bottom of your pan for longer than fifteen seconds. It will all become clear."

"Dude, you never cease to amaze me." He tucked the cigarette behind his right ear and got up.

"When you come back from enjoying that, we'll discuss square versus round pans."

He paused briefly. "Where does gravity come into it?"

"Ever read what Crowley says about the number five?" He looked at me bug-eyed for a bit before he exited.

After a bit, Max wandered back in, a bit moist. It was raining out...

A few at the bar nodded to him as he tidied himself up in the back-bar mirror. He turned to me, "So tell me about…"

I stopped him mid-sentence, "All I'm talking about are suits. What they really mean, taking them out of some theoretical pie in the sky concept and…"

"We know what suits mean."

"That's the problem."

"What?"

"The problem is, we know what they mean. So we don't think about them. We don't dig beneath the surface. The suits themselves are heavier than we think – we ignore the gold under our feet – and our spirit gets stuck in the suit of swords and we wonder why our lives are 'stuck'. We 'hourglass' and think more information will free us."

Max looked at some mote floating in the air, "More information never set me free. But I've spent my life amongst sword wielders. I always wondered about that 'Live by the sword die by the sword', and 'beating swords into plowshares' thing… could just be information overload."

"Dude, that's precious. You can read all the books you want. You can buy a book from amazon dot bomb, but until you get wet, cold, and miserable, you'll never find real gold."

"Fools gold." Max played with the ring of moisture on the bar top.

"You're startin' to catch on. Like getting' hung up on the shape of yer pans. It's marketing hogwash. Square, round, octagonal… all the same. It's the lips that work as riffles to catch the gold. Not the shape."

"Wait a sec – so it's the riffles that make 'the current abate' inside your pan?" he asked.

"Bingo"

"It's the road bumps in life that make us…"

"Whole – which rhymes with gold."

"I really need to sit on that one a bit… but how does Crowley fit into this?"

"Crowley wrote that fives are what happens when motion is introduced into the stability of the four elements."

"Whoa, that's cool. Like gravity. I know Robert Place once said that fives are what occurs when you move spirit into the stability of the four elements." He finished off his glass of amber goodness and signaled the bartender for another round. "What do you think?"

"I think that fives are about what occurs when you bring consciousness into the stability of the four elements."

"May be the coolest thing ever come out of your mouth my brother. I think I may be catching something here. For years, folks talk alchemy and we end up heading off the the library to read read read."

"And we get nowhere. Mankind is no wiser than we were two thousand years ago. We're just as barbaric, albeit with nifty tools."

"When in reality we should just stop. Go out into the woods, and learn how nature acts – for ourselves – that alchemy should be experiential. When you're cold wet and hungry standing waist deep in muck looking at a pan full of sludge – you begin to set aside the book learning and feel the inward search for truth."

"Sing it."

The bartender dropped off two glasses of golden fluid in front of us.

"You don't find gold in a library." Max continued as he wiped foam off his moustache. "So Tarot is a language. But to learn it, then the Tarot is to be lived, experienced – and fully – or it becomes just another exercise in futility. Finding the gold within begins with swords, but it doesn't stop there. And where some talk of wands being passion, they stop with ardor and never move past it. To find the gold within, you must follow the same paths to find gold in situ in the real world."

Max took a breath and continued.

"Water is always seen as a placid peaceful Walden Pond thing. Where in reality water is a heartless bitch that rips the earth apart, and carries it away, reminds me of the Grand Canyon. Equating water with love is interesting when you learn hydraulics."

The bartender wandered over and stood nearby, Max continued without a pause.

"My father told me once, "Never turn your back on The Mother." At the time he was referring to the Ocean, I think that sometimes things get lost in the meta..." he stopped as I elbowed him harshly. "...what?" He noticed the bartender....

"Sorry to interrupt, I couldn't help but hear most of what you were saying and I have to ask, are you talking about prospecting for gold or Tarot?"

"Both. Alchemy is said to be the father of modern chemistry. However it is also about enriching the spirit, achieving full human potential and becoming closer to God however you envision him her or them. Alchemy is both a metaphor and yet not. Changing dross to gold is a metaphor for pulling ourselves up, enriching our spirit, and becoming whole. Of course, the church way back thought they owned that, that there was one way – their way, or heresy. So everything got wrapped in metaphor and never left. Tarot itself is a metaphor."

Max paused long enough to take a breath and I jumped in.

"I once heard this great quote, don't remember who said it, 'God created man because he likes the stories'. But nowadays, folks just don't. They sit on the butts in front of a computer, TV or book and call that learning, and go out of doors to recreate. Us, we like to go out of doors to learn from nature, and recreate with books or a computer or whatever. You can't tell God the stories if you don't experience them, and as I've said before, everything I know about numerology, I learned from nature."

I took a breath and Max continued, "But there's different kinds of knowledge, some you get from books, and some you get from experience. We all know the story of the monks who one day were told they would 'climb the mountain'. Off they went in the rain, over logs, scrambled up rocks, and hours later arrived at the top to see folks stepping out of a tour bus snapping pictures. One of the monks asked the leader, 'Why'd we have to slog through the muck, when we could have ridden a bus?' The answer was, 'Same Mountain, different path'."

"That's the beauty of metaphors, they layer, and different folks get different messages about the same thing."

"That guy down there," Max indicated one of the patrons, "He's got them octagonal pans. I wonder if he's a Tee Dee Emm user, or if he's ever contemplated the shape of Justice's scales? The suits aren't just air, fire, water, and earth. There are whole other actions going on. Take earth. We grow plants, we make mudpies, and we explore her for minerals. However, she's not static. She's dynamic. She's still forming. Just try to stop tectonic shift."

We both took a swig of cold gold liquid, and he continued. "Back when Mt St Helens blew, them science guys told us the area would be lifeless and dead for years. They were dead wrong. Nature takes care of her own. The area was green in no time."

"Back when the Exxon Valdez grounded and leaked" I injected, "Them smarty pants guys said the waters in the area would be lifeless for years. They was dead wrong. Nature takes care of her own."

"Sometimes you have to pull your head out of…"

"…The books and get your feet wet to really learn how it all works."

The bartender looked back at Max as he picked up my thoughts, "See that gal down there sittin' down there?" He indicated a gal down at the end of the bar.

"The one that looks like she's glowing?" The bartender nodded her head towards her.

"That's the one. She started as a highly depressed individual on the verge of suicide. Was on enough anti-depressants to tranquilize a horse. Her and I worked on Tarot Alchemy for three years. She learned to find gold. Never went to the woods to do it, but she panned the depths of her own soul – and worked the black sand to give up its due. She's now living a life she once thought impossible. True story."

"Black sand?"

"Gold is found in the heavies. Black sand is heavy. It's crushed garnet and heavy minerals so it drops below the overburden along with the gold. When you look at a gold bearing stream, you see rocks and gravel, mud and yuck. That's the overburden. You have to dig down deep, move all that away, to get to the black sand."

"And you guys are saying that this is the same for when a person wishes to grow spiritually, they have to remove the overburden of their minds and soul to find the black sand within?" The bartender asked.

"Told you she was the best bartender in town."

"Now in the Bible, they have the story of Exodus, leaving Egypt. Fact is, we are all born in bondage. Our own private Egypt. And we spend our lives trying to find our way out of the wilderness."

"And that woman? The glowing one? Is that what she did? Journeyed from metaphorical Egypt?"

"No. She journeyed from Berlin. Same same. Long journey, lots of overburden. And she found joy."

"You guys want another round?"

"I'm good, you?"

"I'm good, but I have one last point. Tarot helped her. She found the analogies within the suits, she made the brave choices and took the leaps of faith required. There were times she had to put down the mouse and step away from the keyboard – just look at the results."

"Tarot – is a metaphor, a tool. Study all you want. You have to actually begin using the tool to actuate changes in your life, you have to live the changes. Sometimes you have to fire your guardian angels who resist change, and go ahead and push boundaries like The Fool."

Max looked over at me, "I once heard that your wife once said something like, "Not everybody is here to learn" can you comment on that?"

"Riffles. It's the riffles in the pan and the sluice that traps the gold."

"You're saying that some are here to…"

"Stop. Remember – to others – you can be their riffles."

The bartender held up her hand, "Can I ask you guys a question? Are you twins?"

"Same parents, different families"

"Separated at birth?"

Max looked at me, "Your turn to pay."

What a creep. The bill was paid, and we both left – although only one passed through the door.

(Portions of a rough draft have appeared on Aeclectic Tarot Forum)

New York – 13 miles north of Seattle, Washington, July 2010

"You either speak with honey on your lips from the Book of Clouds, echoing the voice of fire from the living darkness, or you do not. There is no such thing as a half-way Oracle."

A conversation with MARCUS KATZ, tarot teacher, director of Tarot Professionals

Let's start with something simple: why Tarosophy?

Enrique, it is a perfect question and I would preface my response with the same statement I give at any lecture, teaching work or presentation: By our Work we are Changed. Having said that, let us begin. When I commenced my formal teaching work of Tarot, leading to what Naomi Ozaniec has graciously called "the restoration of the spiritual dignity of Tarot", it was necessary to create a temple – a separation – in which this Work could be sealed. So with commercial sensibility and magical intent I looked to secure and register a trademark. I was advised to find a "meaningless word" and so looked to the formulation of Magical Squares to locate a word which would at least have some significance to divination, prophecy and the nature of oracular insight. As I consulted the magical squares in the *Book of the Sacred Magic of Abramelin the Mage* (a work I performed several years ago which after six months of constant practice and seclusion creates a profound mystical fugue in which the Holy Guardian Angel is experienced) I found only pseudo-Hebrew word-jumbles. I was about to switch track when the word TAROSOPHY came into my mind – complete with the O-S-O connecting graphic. I only then realised that the magical square from which I was attempting to derive a word was that of the twelfth chapter, square 2, "To know the secrets of words". On further research, the O-S-O symbol, known to many as that adopted by Jimmy Page of Led Zeppelin, was found to be from a magical grimoire, the Red Dragon, and symbolises Saturn. An astrologer colleague tells me this indicates the nature of tradition, teaching, order and revelation within the word itself. Only then turning to the word, can one see that it is a conflation of Tarot and Sophia, "triumph" and "wisdom". It is now a registered trademark and the title of my book on Tarot, and something very dear to me. Once upon a time, words were magic, and this is a word given through me.

O S O looks like a snake moving from one cave to another one. Perhaps we are looking at the 'footprints' of a snake! The mark a rattlesnake leaves in the sand reads like an invitation to silence: "Sssssssssss..." It is nice to notice how these two letters, the S and the O, can be turned around 180 degrees and still be the same. The letter O, is it full or it is always empty? Maybe both at once? In any case it feels like a centered ego, while the letter S shows a constant flow that goes up and down. Perhaps it is connecting Above and Below.

So, which one it is? Is the letter O full or empty?

The sigil created by the letters O-S-O in Tarosophy could well be taken for a snake passing between two caves, or a loose ladder of ascent between the All and the Nothing. This is why both 'O's are full and empty. In the Western Esoteric Initiatory System (WEIS) I teach, the formula of "0=2" is the primary ontology; Aleister Crowley called it "the unique, the simple, and the necessary solution of the Riddle of the Universe" and I am delighted to see it present in Tarosophy. So the Snake (Wisdom) descends and the Ladder (Intelligence) ascends, but Angels may pass between both eyes. When contemplating the images of Tarot, as the 'footprints' of a snake, we are seeing only the memory of truth. As Umberto Eco remarked, and could have been so eloquently describing the divinatory moment, "truth is brief, the rest is merely commentary".

The letters of the word Tarosophy and the Tarot cards themselves are, I believe, emergent principles arising from the relationship of Self and Universe. They are snapshots in structure of the engagement of Self in Universe and Universe in Self. We see this elegantly posited by the Fool and the World cards. The images of Ciro Marchetti often allude to this relationship, one within the other, more so than other deck designers. I have chosen a particular image of such – the Fool dancing upon the World – for the cover of Tarosophy. But I feel we must be careful not to get overdrawn into graven images. All images and words are pointers only to experience. Even the poet Keats, when he wrote *Hyperion*, lamented that he would not be able to shape into words the tragic nature of the fall that had beset humanity. But there is redemption – and a re-memorising – for whilst Kabbalists talk about the 'shattered shards', the Gnostics the 'sparks' hidden by Sophia until the Archons return, we Oracles have our Tarot cards – like Saturn, in Hyperion, waiting for us to give them voice:

> Sat grey hair'd Saturn quiet as a stone,
> Still as the silence round about his Lair.
> Forest on forest hung above his head,
> Like Cloud on Cloud. No stir of air was there,
> Not so much life as on a summer's day
> Robs not at all the dandelion's fleece:
> But where the dead leaf fell, there did it rest.
> A stream went voiceless by, still deadened more
> By reason of his fallen divinity.

The stream is deadened and even dry, perhaps – whilst Jupiter and the Olympians overthrew Saturn and the Titans, Apollo – the God of Prophesy – would also become stilled, for the last oracle of Delphi is said to have told Julian the Apostate:

> Tell to the king that the carven hall is fallen in decay;
> Apollo has no chapel left, no prophesying bay,
> No talking spring. The stream is dry that had so much to say.

So it is time to recover their voice – the voice of the Oracles. We must ensure the Tarot cards do not become the "monstrous forms" of their images, as Keats alluded often to the Titans becoming as their own statues, fixed and silent. The Oracular Voice is a word, is a speech, is the snake passing between the caves of the known and the unknown. Tarosophy is an attitude that leaves behind it a trial of techniques – diverse spreads, card rituals, oracular mannerisms and esoteric methods. I sometimes teach that Tarosophy is a "Tarot to engage life, not escape it". By this I mean that one could spend a few hours online writing about how many "celebrities" one could 'spot' in Tarot cards (i.e. figures that reminded one of the appearance of others), or rather one could take two Court cards, and say to one's partner, "How do you think these two would make love – show me".

In the former 'exercise', one is being badly trained to learn a psychotic behavior (one I would have to undo with any of my clients in therapy) and in the latter exercise one would generate an experience not otherwise present which would ensure a profound and pleasant discovery to reflect upon for many months. One is an entirely escapist pursuit to fill in time until we become worm-food, and the other at least occurs in generative and creative activity. This is why Tarosophy differs from many other Tarot teachings.

With regard to many of the exercises given in Tarot, I am reminded when I first read as a teenager, in the fantasy epics of Michael Moorcock, the lament of Prince Corum, watching as the forces of chaos destroyed the cities of the civilized world. I have since learnt it was a phrase originally given by a Byzantine noble ruling the destruction of Constantinople by the barbarian hoards; "If only they understood what it was they were destroying, I would despair less". Our community of Oracles must return to the very wellhead of inspiration and draw more from the depths until eventually the stream flows again – blow away the dead leaves of past expectation and light again the torches of innovation in the carven hall of tradition. Otherwise we will become what Keats again mourned of the Titans, "What benefit canst thou, or all thy tribe, to the great world? Thou art a dreaming thing, a fever of thyself".

Why do you think the tarot has acquired such a bad reputation these days?

I covered a lot of this ground, on Tarot and its reputation, in a paper on "Tarot organizations and teaching (1888-present)" which is part of the presently unpublished *Tarot in Culture* anthology edited by Emily Auger. It's also something we cover in our Marketing Guide for Tarot Professionals, in a section provocatively entitled "Half your Market think you are Evil". Whilst all Tarot readers can attest experiences both positive and negative when introducing their Art to those who are "the public" when it comes to Tarot and divination, there have been few proper surveys into the perception of Tarot outside of Tarot readers themselves. The only one I discovered was a fascinating piece of research done on behalf of a media advisory board in the UK. Whilst the survey itself is terribly flawed, it revealed something quite fascinating – and we could perhaps return here to the O-S-O symbol to explore it. In fact, as that sigil embedded in Tarosophy is itself a symbol of Saturn, constraints and tradition, fixed thinking, and the slow passage of time, it is somewhat appropriate.

The survey reveals that whilst a majority of people think of "Astrology" as 'not occult' and therefore 'harmless' (the word 'occult' is used in a pejorative manner in the survey to indicate 'evil') they think of "Satanism" as 'occult' and therefore 'evil'. So far, so good – in a way, unless you know of very charitable Satanists and terribly manipulative Astrologers. The survey also had palmistry and Yoga in the almost random mix of subjects it surveyed! Now the thing is this – the 'evil' and 'occult' end of this spectrum was classified by the surveyed population of 3,000 people as the area which 'messed with your mind' or gave advice other than 'general or positive' information. In effect, the population do not want anything that is directly relevant and may cause change to their life. The fact that Astrology was seen as positive was specifically given as "because it is in the newspapers" and was seen as giving non-specific advice that could be ignored as a "bit of harmless fun". I think this is why Tarot readers degrade their art by stating the often non-required and often illegal in itself "for entertainment purposes only" small-print. Not because it is required by law (we cover this in our legal guide) but because it attracts more customers! If I advertised "Not for entertainment, these readings will change your life forever" (which I feel is the only absolute requirement for a divinatory Tarot reading) my potential market would probably drop by a factor of 90%.

Tarot was placed by this same population right on the threshold between harmless/good and occult/evil. A 50/50 split of opinion, hence "half your market think you are evil". This is reflected in the O-S-O symbol. The Tarot standing as the snake, the connecting principle, between the known and the unknown, the seen and the unseen. Whilst it is the way out of Plato's cave, it is also the shadow. It is utilized as a threshold significator by popular culture in all media forms, accounting also for the fact that the ultimate threshold – Death – is the most commonly depicted and recognized card. So Tarot is our own placeholder of the mysteries. It serves to remind us of the profound depths of the Universe whilst remaining merely a stack of 78 pieces of cardboard. It is true then, that in encountering them, we must tell truth and then hold silence, like the passing of the snake of which we speak. In fact, the snake was seen as sacred to Apollo and connected with the Oracles – as well, of course, as all the other symbolism of the serpent as bringer of knowledge. You either speak with honey on your lips from the Book of Clouds, echoing the voice of fire from the living darkness, or you do not. There is no such thing as a half-way Oracle.

Last night I was watching David Byrne talking about how the music musicians make is constantly evolving to adapt to the architecture where that music is played. The same phenomena can be seen in birds, whose callings adapt to the specificity of the terrain where those birds live. The talk got me thinking on the notion of 'adaptability' and how it seems that the tarot, and the whole Western Esoteric enterprise, seems to have failed to adapt to the 20th century. The survey you mention seems to confirm my own suspicions: it is the link between the tarot and the occult what gives the tarot a bad reputation, because occultism is basically at odds with the way contemporary Western society sees itself. What seems especially interesting to me is that the link between the tarot and the occult can be traced back to a specific point in history. I am referring to the misreading Antoine Court de Gebelin did of the tarot in 1871. While we should be thankful to Court de Gebelin for expanding our understanding of the game of tarot to include divination, we should also acknowledge the absolute lack of validity of his views. Won't it be easier to simply dismiss all that nonsense? From where we stand now, we can see roughly 300 years of tradition of the tarot as a game, in which the images may have had a moralizing intention, and where we even have a well developed connection between the tarot and poetry (all of those are notions that would cause no rejection in our contemporary audiences) and then, another couple of centuries where the tarot has been linked to any possible counter-cultural doctrine, occult model and conspiracy theory.

As a matter of fact, from were we stand today, we even have enough information about how the brain works to understand why we like the second part of the tarot's history better, even if it is not sustained by facts. Can't we just acknowledge the misreading? Even Pope John Paul II apologized for the crusades! When a man gets out of prison on parole he needs to rebuild his reputation. That is why the terms of his release include not seeking the company of crooks. Shouldn't we put the tarot on parole, and keep it away from bad company? I confess I lack the sensibility required to find beauty in the occult. Could you tell me: what do you see in it?

Aplogies for the delay in response – I have been immersed in convoluted research to investigate issues of cybersquatting, typosquatting, trademark law, intellectual property rights, copyright agreements in between countries, etc., for a forthcoming magazine supplement on business practice in Tarot. We are also working with a few publishers of Tarot cards to investigate abuse of images on forums, filesharing sites, etc. At Tarot Professionals Ltd we are looking to ensure that best practice is maintained, so we are issuing a supplement to our magazine in a month or two on legal considerations in Tarot practice. This is part of our remit to professionalize Tarot and raise expectations through education.

So, with that heady commercialism and legal world set to one side – although we are going to return full circle to it – let's discuss Tarot and Esotericism. Although perhaps we can first refer to what you call the "bad company" that Tarot has kept – in your case, intimating this as the esoteric misreading of Tarot. Hmmmmm. I entirely agree. But not in the same way, maybe, as I am a complete apologist for the Western esoteric initiatory system – or WEIS as I abbreviate it – and my next book following *Tarosophy* is a description of this system and its spiritual discipline and goal.

In my paper on "Tarot on the Threshold" for Emily Auger's 2-volume anthology, *Tarot in Popular Culture* (which has now found a new publisher, it seems, so is again "forthcoming" in publication) I researched and reviewed the association of certain motifs with Tarot. These included the symbol of "the pyramids" and the notion of "antiquity" associated with Tarot. This is seen most obviously in the title of the "Ancient" Celtic Cross spread and similar confusions. Whilst we can admit that the conflation of ideas started with the *Book of Thoth* and other esoterica suggested by de Gebelin, it is surprising how the notion was actually rejected (in part) but then deliberately utilised by following occultists. In fact, what few people recognise is the knowingness of popular reception that some occultists utilised. Whilst everyone may have an 'idea' of Aleister Crowley's striking image, they haven't seen the thirty or forty photographs (for example) of the same pose which Crowley then vetted to ensure the best one was released. As ever ahead of his time, Aleister Crowley was fully aware that he was the "brand of the beast" and he used that branding quite knowingly to further his aim to popularise himself and his message.

So in effect, the initial confusion has been promulgated knowingly as a 'shared misunderstanding' or "invalid knowledge" (as seen through the lens of cultural studies) by esotericists, the public, and by the commercial marketeers. Hence we come full circle to commercialism. The early decades of the last century saw many adverts deliberately associating Tarot with antiquity merely to sell the decks. Once that had permeated popular culture, it would be a brave publisher who went against that grain. Many occultists – Waite, Crowley, et. al., had a somewhat knowing 'wink' at such confusion, but of course utilised it to meet popular misconception, hence strengthening it in the meantime. The adaption of Tarot to the 21st century is somewhat akin to the esoteric response. If we see esotericism as merely a "flight from reason" (Webb) or a response against the "disenchantment of the world" (discussed by Owen), or even worse, as one scholar (Gibbons) put it, "a nonsense so palpable [that] mysticism is its best defence" I think we lose something important. A sense of our own mystery, and the potential of the Universe to surprise us. The relationship of the Fool (awareness) and the World (the universe) is always a fundamental mystery, as is the Hermit (time). In fact, each card is its own mystery.

In recently discussing 'Street Tarot' with Ferol Humphrey and talking about introducing Tarot outside its "confines" I remarked that Tarot – as a "threshold artifact" in popular culture – requires a "transition phase", hence the candles, shawl and accoutrements which serve to alert people of the threshold. Otherwise the jump is too big. However, as was suggested by James Rickleff, environment is intrinsic to delivery. So when we look to take Tarot outside of its box – its perceived environment – it is good to work out how we do that. I think using 'Urban Art' is a good bridge (hence Tarot Professionals part-funding of Adam Mcleans "Art of Japanese Tarot" exhibition at the McIntosh gallery, attending as reader-in-residence of the gallery launch of the SPILL photographic deck images at Lancaster University and more recently our promotion of the *Tarot of the Boroughs*) and innovative decks that are not instantly recognised as Tarot (hence our interest in the *Transparent Oracle*). We can also use iApps etc., as Ciro Marchetti and Kat Black have done to deliver Tarot 'within' a recognised 'safe' environment. The fact that Astrology is not seen in the same way as Tarot is – and I quote survey respondents here – because "Astrology is in the newspapers" and so must be acceptable. We certainly have a way to go to 'normalise' Tarot in society, and this is one of the overarching visions of Tarot Professionals Ltd.

On the other hand, the beauty of the esoteric project is that it remains esoteric. Whilst I can talk about the elegance of the initiatory schema, intimate the profound resolutions and experiences it offers, we remain our own workshops. And as it is written in Sufism, "the worker is hidden in the workshop", the Tarot provides a convenient arising of stabilized images projecting into the same unknowable reality as everything else, hence their import in the schema. We might as likely take any other system, or object, such as a grain of sand. Tarot captures the imagination before it shows (and here we turn to your prison analogy) that "the exit door leads in".

What I like about Crowley's anecdote is how, by understanding how important it was to get the picture right, he understood a fundamental premise on the way we perceive the world: we confuse symbols with concepts. The image has to be right because the image is its own message. Oliviero Toscani, the creative force behind all these ad campaigns that put Benetton on the map, used to tell the story of how, instead of marrying his girlfriend, they went into a set dressed up and took dome pictures of them getting married. It was all it took for friends and family to take the union as real.

I think you mention something that is key: the tarot giving us "A sense of our own mystery, and the potential of the Universe to surprise us." But going back again to taking symbols for concepts, why should we assume that esotericism is our best shot at keeping that mystery alive? What seems to be happening is that our culture at large doesn't find a sense of the mysterious in there, and rightfully so, I would add. As you pointed out, the amount of misconceptions, misinformation, misreadings and plain commercial deception is too high to ignore, and any informed reading we make of these things end ups convincing us we are in the realm of conmen and madmen (I often think all these things are fundamental components of esotericism itself), unless the aesthetic pull of these symbols is so strong that we choose to overlook their obvious conceptual pitfalls.

If I want to get a sense of our own mystery, I look into neuroscience. What we are uncovering there in terms of our own nature and potential is both mind-blowing and awe-inspiring. It really gives us a sense of hope. Astronomy, and not astrology, gives us a sense of the potential the universe has to surprise us. The abstractions of physics equal the beauty of the best poetry. We have art to instill in us a sense of transcendence and truth that can be put back where it belongs: within the experience of beauty. When I look at the tarot, that is, when I look at the two verifiable components of the tarot experience: images being seen by a person, I see potential for wonder to be placed right between the realm of neuroscience and art. Not only can we use the tarot to understand these two things better, but since these are manifestations of our own being, we can use it to experience our own wonder.

Today we have way more elegant ways to talk about the tarot than the Golden Dawn had. It is not enough to think that the Western world at large got derailed from the 'olde ways' and should somehow get back on track. The Western world got derailed from the 'olde ways' to discover things like penicillin, so a whole range of diseases could be fought with something more than burnt sage and hope. There is no 'going back to the 'olde ways' unless we experience a rise of irrationality and a decay of critical reasoning. It is actually quite hard for the Western mind to find something in that bargain. I suspect that accepting that as a starting point is fundamental for a healthy tarot practice, and a healthy tarot business.

It seems more appealing to know what Crowley knew about getting photographed than knowing the formulas and incantations he memorized (or made up). After all, I suspect that's where the true craft of the magician lies.

What I have read from you suggests you have a sober business sense and practical acumen. Why do you think there is so little academic interest in the tarot? Why do you think we don't have a Fulbright Award for tarot readers, or a 'tarotist laureate' at the White House, or a 'Divination' category for the Nobel prize? Why aren't we invited to the 'big boys' pool?

I'd quite agree that there is no benefit to be gained in promoting regressive tendencies or superstition in Tarot. I'd also agree in part that neurobiology has much to reveal about the mystery of consciousness and our experience of the world. I particularly refer my own students (both in therapeutic practice and esoteric practice) to Benjamin Libet's work, *Mind-Time,* where it is proposed that so-called conscious intentionality follows unconscious readiness to perform action. Libet later went on to propose consciousness as an emergent field-like property arising from the activity of the brain.

I find these theories fascinating and extremely potent in exploring my experience of Tarot after thirty years. It is interesting that there is no comparative survey of how using Tarot regularly for a great deal of time changes one's perception of time – or indeed, the physical structure of the brain. I address this issue in *Tarosophy* – there are comparative studies that demonstrate that regular meditation changes the physical structure of the brain. I wonder the same about regular practice of divination. There are also many mysteries to explore with regard to quantum science notions of granular time.

I'd also direct people to Julian Jayne's *The Origin of Consciousness in the Breakdown of the Bicameral Mind,* particularly with regard to Theurgy and Divination. He also speaks of the Oracles of Delphi as an example of the 'bicameral paradigm', which has four aspects – the *collective cognitive imperative* (belief system), an *induction* (ritual), *trance* (diminishing of the analogue 'I') and *archaic authorisation*. It is this latter prescription that interests me most – by whose authority do oracles now speak? Our culture does not widely accord to the Apollonian view, and to respond to your question about academic interest, there is little validity given to the contemporary *mantis* (the Greek for the 'freelance' diviner). So without a culturally projected authority, we have little voice. The spring now indeed lies silent, the leaves have fallen and lie still on the floor of the oracular shrine.

Jaynes rightly – in my view – points to the spatialisation of time, a phenomena we see in any Tarot spread where "position 2" or similar "is" the future. This is something that I use in NLP work with clients – re-framing their own representation of their experiences in time which is invariably spatial. We say "I look forward to tomorrow" or "put that behind you now" as if time is a spatial construct. Tarot reflects this tendency in spreads, and hence when we work with such esoteric concepts as the "Cube of Space" we inevitably change our own sense of time through spatial considerations.

You might also be interested – if you haven't read it – in the essay "What is a Concept, That a Person May Grasp It?" by Ray Jackendoff, in his collection, *Languages of the Mind*. I particularly equate his thoughts on percepts as "focal values in a continuous domain" as a Tarot reading. When we consider the multivalency of each symbol, and the several quintillion variations of a 10-card spread using a deck of 78 cards, it is indeed a miracle and a mystery that each of us, with relatively minimal training, can interpret each and every example of the several quintillion patterns.

You are now getting into what I call the 'exciting work'. I believe it was George Lakoff and Mark Johnson who suggested that all of our thoughts are of a metaphorical nature. We understand time because we move through space, we understand that 'up' is good and 'down' is bad because we lie down when we are sick, or dead, and we rise – here is another metaphor! – when we are healthy. Up to very recently, it was thought metaphors were just embellishments of language, when in truth, they are more likely to be the fabric of thought itself. The most interesting, and also challenging aspect of that notion is that the body ends up being the epicenter of our experience of the world. The theory of embodied meaning suggests that we build our more abstract thoughts on top of our bodily experience of the world. We use our experience of what we know to understand what we don't know, from the very basic directions, like up, down, straight, horizontal and vertical, backwards and forward, to the most complex mental operations we are capable of, such as mathematical or philosophical inquiry. Most of the metaphors we use are mapped from the experience of our bodies in space. Life would be described in a very different way if we were given a different body, or no body at all! I wrote a small article on that topic. The Association for Tarot Studies published it last November.

I often think I got into the tarot for the wrong reason: I am actually interested in the images! By getting 'down to the body' we can work out a feasible way of understanding, and utilizing, the way images move us. The mere, literal, description of a tarot card is a more engaging process we could initially suspect. Right there, we are fostering the 'making' of meaning in the client's mind, not only in terms of these memories and associations the cards elicit, but in terms of the physical experience the cards suggest in the person looking at it. Have you seen a client who looks at The Hanged Man and says something to the effect of "I don't want to be like that!"? That very statement implies he already put himself in the Hanged Man position! Staring down at the body allows us to use the client's bodily experiences as a common ground, both to the elicitation of a response (these can take the form of memories, associations, emotions, but also, physiological responses) and to pacing the meaning-making process into more abstract notions. That common ground is also key to leading the client into the prescriptive side of the work: the post-session suggestions people usually call 'predictions'. It all starts with and in the images. One can learn to use an image as one uses a harmonica, or a colored pencil.

Now, you mentioned NLP. I am now conducting a few of these conversations with people within the field of hypnosis. I tend to suspect that tarot readings 'run' through hypnotic patterns. What are your thoughts on that? What has been your experience in that regard?

Yes, we have navigated our course into the beating heart of the body of Tarot. In fact, our next issue of *Tarosophist International* is themed on embodiment in Tarot, so we will talk again on this – we are also featuring articles on wholeness, wellness, healing and being. And of course, Life and Death in the cards. Back to our conversation earlier about neurobiology, I think the mirror neurons of the brain really do respond deeply and profoundly to the constant shocks (as Gurdjieff would call them) of the world. We then have a complex array of psychological buffers ("kundabuffers" in Gurdjieffian terminology) that inure us from the dazzling depth of the Universe – suppression, repression, projection, introjection, depression, etc.

When we encounter the Tarot, we are activating, even by the merest scanning of images, the deepest parts of ourselves that are usually protected by these buffers – the part that wants not to die, the part that wants to keep living, the part that fears, the part that loves. I find on my intermediate Tarot course, where I do a lot of narrative skill-building and exposure to many cards many times in teaching the 'Opening of the Key' method, that after exactly 1.5 days, students stop being able to read the cards at all for an hour or so. It is a curious 'wall' they reach, and always at the same time, no matter their experience – one or forty years. They look at the cards, the images, but their brain can no longer turn them into meaning. I've tested and replicated this phenomena over a range of events over the years, and can safely predict exactly when it will occur with any group. I liken it to the overfilling of the unconscious by archetypal encounters, even those reflected by images. Of course, nowadays that's when I show various videos or we play narrative games with sounds – so no-one notices the gap!

Jung of course spoke of the embodiment of the collective of images:

> These fantasy-images undoubtedly have their closest analogues in mythological types. We must therefore assume that they correspond to certain *collective* (and not personal) structural elements of the human psyche in general, and, like the morphological elements of the human body, are inherited. (CW 9i, 262)

This moves us straight into our conversation on Tarot and hypnosis. As you know, I'm a hypnotherapist and licensed trainer of NLP (Neuro-Linguistic Programming) and Hypnotherapy. I am particularly a therapist who uses the approach of Steven Gilligan (Self-Relations Therapy) and Neo-Ericksonian approaches. Although NLP is relatively disorganised as a modality, I work with it from the postmodern perspective of Neurolinguistic Psychotherapy (see Wake, 2008).

I'm interested in what you quote with regard to metaphors as based on spatial and embodied awareness. I'm far more interested in how this relates to time – a perennial concern of mine and I see it as the philosopher's stone of Magic; the mercurial touchstone that changes all things. Although I read in *New Scientist* magazine only today that "Time does not exist". I'm glad that's resolved then! In

NLP we utilise the natural ability of human beings to represent time as a spatial construct – we've touched on that earlier, with regard to spreads. We might also wonder how and where the clients place themselves in their temporal worldview when they are having a reading. I like to ensure they are taken totally out of their existing time representation, and I use NLP language patterns to ensure this occurs – verb tenses, chunking and a few other confusional language patterns. I aim for the reading to be an atemporal construct. The solution must exist outside of the state.

Whilst I write a lot about my utilisation of NLP in Tarot in *Tarosophy*, I can't talk too much about that here prior to publication, but there's something in Jung I came across that made me think about the usage of "synchronicity" in Tarot books and this phrase is often invoked by readers in an explanatory context. But the thing is that people haven't read Jung in detail, so they don't realise that, at best, a Tarot reading is a "synchronous event" but *not* synchronicity. Jung saw people making this mistake and went at great lengths to write a supplemental piece to explain the difference in layman's terms, even bullet-pointing the elements that compose synchronicity. By Jung's actual definition, if I understand it correctly, *a Tarot reading is only a synchronicity if it carries the elements of what Jung called a "vision"* (in his case, a dream or powerful imaginary incursion into consciousness).

Most experienced readers will know this to be true. There are some readings that take on a certain trance-like quality, time passes in a strange manner, a connection is made between those in the reading, and strange dream-like events may even occur – such as a deer arriving at the window, strange music starting in the apartment next door, a voice yelling a message outside. This is when the reading becomes a synchronicity – not with those events, but with the event in the actual life of the client for whom the reading is being performed. This is the heart of Tarot – when it transports us as a tool into a timeless yet embodied engagement with life.

One of the things that interests me the most about the tarot as a suggestive tool is the fact that such understanding unveils the potential harm a reading can do if the operator is either unaware of being implanting suggestions or deluded by the idea that his or her connection with a 'higher' power entitles him or her to say whatever comes to his mind, no matter how potentially harmful it may be. There is a scary amount of readers, and healers, who dismiss the need of knowing anything about suggestions, hypnosis or NLP. Still, there is not really a choice there. Either you purposefully implant suggestions, or you do it without knowing what you are doing. Not knowing what you do, but doing it anyway, can be seen as irresponsible.

But knowing what you do, in this case, has you constantly walking in the vecinity of manipulation. Milton Erickson was very vocal against demonizing the notion of 'manipulation'. In his view, even when we are walking on a sidewalk and we stop, so another person can pass us by the right, we are manipulating that person. He was a firm promoter of accepting the power that comes with the role of a therapist. I know this makes many contemporary therapists uncomfortable. To some extent, Erickson embodied what now we call the 'trickster', just like another person you just mentioned: Gurdjieff, who was a skilled deceiver. I personally won't put Gurdjieff in the same category with Erickson, but still, both made me think of that quote attributed to John Fire, a.k.a. Lame Deer:

> A medicine man shouldn't be a saint. He should experience and feel all the ups and downs, the despair and joy, the magic and the reality, the courage and the fear, of his people. He should be able to sink as low as a bug, or soar as high as an eagle. Unless he can experience both, he is no good as a medicine man.

The ability we have to acknowledge other people's pain is founded in the pain we have experienced. But the tarot reader is not there to simply share, or validate, the client's pain. This plays a big part on what we do, I would say, but still, the tarot reader's main goals is to affect the client. I guess some readers may have problems with that, but the fact of the matter is that we aren't supposed to leave the client untouched. Some readers would accomplish that by telling a person what is going to happen. Some other readers will give the person tools to deal with whatever happens. Some other readers will make room for the client to find an answer, some give the client strength, and some others will give the client that answer right away. In any scenario, the reader aims to affect his client, so the client doesn't leave the reader's table untouched. Some of these ways to affect a client I just mentioned include a higher degree of manipulation than others, but still, to affect is to manipulate. Are you comfortable with that? Otherwise, what is your rationale to deal with the effects that all of these techniques you use have in your client?

Before I make any presentation, I quote the alchemical saying, "By our Work we are Changed", and to conclude the presentation, I quote the Sufi statement,

"The Worker is hidden in the Workshop". It is the former that touches upon our present discussion, as all communication changes us – and our unconscious patterns, as Erickson so elegantly and powerfully taught, are ever present. As we perform a reading, change is occurring. Communication takes place – a dialogue between reader and cards, reader and intuition, between the reader and the querent, and an often missed dialogue between the querent and the cards. There are even moments of inspiration where another level of dialogue opens between any of these actors (and I deem the cards such also) and the divine. I think any reading that doesn't entirely change a person's life is a wasted opportunity. A successful reading demonstrates to the querent that the world is bound by invisible knots, and their life is part of an unfolding miracle. As I think I have already said, you either speak with honey on your lips from the Book of Clouds, echoing the voice of fire from the living darkness, or you do not. There is no such thing as a half-way Oracle.

You are the epicenter of an incredibly active tarot organization that feels very expansive, both in activities and scope. What do you hope to accomplish?

The work of Tarot Professionals Ltd was described beautifully by Naomi Ozaniec as "restoring the spiritual dignity of Tarot". However, on the grounds that a picture does indeed paint a thousand words, and our time together in dialogue has sadly come to an end, I offer an image. The Video I recently created in honour of my students at The Far Away Centre, which has a song especially written by one student for us, features a series of photographs, one of which is of three women and a young girl. It follows the text caption "The Return of the Oracles". These people are professional individuals, drawn to the study of the Work and are fully engaged in mainstream activities – in their cases, training, psychiatry, and marketing. When this photograph was taken, they were participating in a sacred rite to Apollo, and developing their oracular talents, in a huge cavern in the Lake District. All of them use Tarot in their work and in doing so are returning the oracles to culture – we are answering Keat's question, "What benefit canst thou, or all thy tribe, to the great world?"

The benefit of joining and working with Tarot Professionals Ltd is that we are returning the living oracles to a world which lies dreaming and awakening ourselves in the process. Tarot might be considered a picture of a ladder with 22 rungs, a toolkit of 40 tools and a machine with 16 settings. What you do with it is up to you – we choose to see through our own hearts and into life through it, climbing the ladder, using the tools and switching on the machine.[1]

Poet Arthur Vogelsang wrote: *"Life is uncontrollably sad all the time / Unless we divert ourselves with art objects." Do you think he was right?*

With regard to Vogelsang, I am impressed by his vision above the waves of a "white hole, in which fate doesn't stand a chance" (in the poem, "Character"). I think the delicious terror of life is the joy we find in our ability to envision and reflect upon the whole of creation in such a white hole. There. Even the Tarot cards. Suddenly go still. And we realize all along – they were dancing, and we were not. But it is not too late – you can see them sometimes. There. Beckoning you to dance.

May a full deck of possibilities be yours.

New York / Lake District, England, July 2010

---

[1] http://www.farawaycentre.com, press play on the video and click on the full-screen option.

"Physical tarot has become so refined over the centuries that much of the abstract wonder inherent in the practice has been defined out of it by "experts," the digital form provides an avenue to reinstate some of that wonder by making it more accessible to novices."

A conversation with ARON PRICE, designer of TarotBot

Why don't you start by telling me, in your view: what are the constitutive elements of a tarot reading, those one can translate from the traditional handling of a tarot deck into a computer's screen?

As I approached the design of TarotBot my first analysis was very much what you are asking. What parts of tarot are feeding into the readers' cognition? – cognition being the knowledge processes which occur in the mind. The structure of a tarot reading typically consists of:

- A deck of cards.
- Some interaction with that deck to separate the cards that constitute the reading.
- Some spatial organization of the separated cards into a position template.
- The synthesis of the question, the card images, and the position meanings (generally in a sequential manner).
- In more advanced settings, context is also applied by allowing the surrounding cards to influence how a given card/position is synthesized.

So we have five components, two of which are artifacts of physical cards (i.e. the interaction with the deck and spatial organization) and three are artifacts of tarot itself (i.e. the cards, the synthesis, and the relationships which define influence)

This analysis led me to focus my design efforts on the artifacts of tarot. My initial goals for the new Android interface were to maximize the display of individual cards, design interpretations that enabled synthesis, and flavor the interpretations with the context of the surrounding cards. Android devices really lend themselves to this as you are actually holding a card sized image in the palm of your hand which you interact with. As I played with this new model I realized that the usefulness of the spread display faded quickly when there was no longer a need to recall the meaning of the sequential position.

People often struggle with keeping arbitrary sequences of things in their memory, this leads to the adaptation of memory aids within the sensory environment. A good example of this is with epic poetry: cognitive scientists struggled to come to terms with the fact people were able to recite long poems from memory while their studies showed a working memory limit incapable of such long sequences; but the poems are not simple sequences, they have a structure which makes it easier to anticipate what word comes next – rhyme and meter.

A tarot spread is very similar, especially with more elaborate spreads. When dealing with physical cards these spreads are very helpful in showing a pattern to help recall sequential meanings, with a computing system, however, you do not need this pattern as the positional labels can be provided directly as text. For this reason the TarotBot model de-emphasizes the spread display.

I find very exciting that you are somehow bringing poetry into the mix, since I am mainly interested in the tarot as a poetic device. In fact, I like a lot how a computer could minimize the importance of predestination, or even the person's physical connection with the cards, while emphasizing the role of chance in the selection of these cards. Chance is, in itself, a powerful form of poetry. But just as I like that, I have seen many people, especially those with very invested beliefs, feeling that pressing a button is not 'real'. What are your thoughts about this? Do you think the quality of the experience could be diminished by not having an interaction with the tarot as a physical object?

The distinction between predestination and chance is one of the primary controversies with software tarot. After considering it for some time in the early stages of the TarotBot project I came to see two complimentary perspectives which align much more smoothly on a small touchscreen device than on a desktop or laptop. First you have the view that the mechanism underlying tarot is based on the mingling of the energies of the questioner and the cards. This is a sort of mystical, invisible tie between the act of asking the question and the handling of the cards. From this perspective using a computer to perform a reading should be useless, and for me at best such readings have always felt awkward. This dissonance which was felt when using tarot where you have some intermediary serving as an interface (i.e. a mouse or keyboard) vanished when using a touch screen Android device.

If one logically applies the principles of the mystical tie based on a questioner's energy then it makes perfect sense that such a device would be appropriate for divination. Smart phones such as Android devices are inherently personal items that tend to be saturated in their owners energies having been carried very close to the body for extended periods of time. The fact that you are touching the images of the cards as you do the reading only enhances this effect.

The complimentary side is the random sampling that is dealing a spread. From a cognitive science perspective people anticipate what will happen based on mental models derived from experience and self definition. One of the problems this leads to is the overuse of improper models that lead to incorrect anticipation, often in ways that the person applying the model cannot even recognize as these processes tend to be below the conscious awareness.

This is where TarotBot really got interesting for me. What I found was each tarot card represented a different aspect of life told from a very specific perspective – often including archetypal goals and intentions that everyone experiences in some form. Thus by presenting a random set of perspectives, goals, and intentions tarot is actually helping people see beyond the sleeping self and begin exploring alternative models and potentials. I see the two angles on tarot complimentary in that one deals with the questioner's human will and intention and the other is composed of the same sort of archetypal, universal elements that human will and intention exist within.

There is a French word: dépaysement. *I can't find one single word for it in English. It alludes to a feeling of being spaced-out, out of one's comfort zone. There seems to be a fundamental connection between that state and the experience of wonder. After all, wonder dies out if we take it for granted. A regular tarot deck carries implicit a whole set of suggestions that can take us, by being in contact with it, into that sense of being out of our usual reality, leaving us open to wonder. A computer, and any of our new digital devices, carries also a sense of wonder. I would be interested in your thoughts about how these two kinds of wonder enter into dialogue with each other. Does the computer interface add wonder to the experience of the tarot?*

In some senses I think the digital form enhances the experience, and in other ways it detracts from it. In the end, tarot on a smart phone is a completely different experience to that with physical cards.

In the process of producing the Android Il Meneghello and Flornoy decks I had a feeling of travelling back through time. There was a night not long ago, my family was out of town and I was alone. I was overcome by an intense energy that seemed to be flowing out from my throat. After being entranced by this for sometime I wandered to my bed and laid down, as I did so there was a sense of falling back into myself. Slowly my self perception shifted back through my youth. It was a series of visions where I was able to taste the experience of being 28, 23, 19, 15, 11, etc. There was a trend through this progression. As I went back I found myself increasingly dependent on the environment for my self definition. At the same time everything had a decreasing sense of certainty – leaving everything more susceptible to reinterpretation.

As I explored tarot through history I found a similar (d)evolution. Pamela Coleman Smith's work with the fully illustrated pips brought with it interpretations less dependent on the environment in which the reading occurs – everything is drawn out for you. Step back into *Vacchetta* and you find the semi illustrated pips carry a similar effect, but they are not as completely individuated. The court cards, however, are much more direct here than in prior decks – the king of cups and queen of swords being two of my favorite examples. In the *Soprafino* deck, the details are beginning to tease out – the imagery is distinctly less vague than the earlier *Marseille* style. While in *Dodal* the imagery is much more abstract than these later Italian examples, it has a cultivated feel to it. It is as if the *Noblet* was redesigned to be less raw, less wild. *Noblet* brings an almost animal feel, it has a subtle underlying organization to the design (the word organic feels appropriate). I love how the designs make no effort to separate the human from nature. Then there is *Visconti Sforza*. The dreamlike quality of the paintings provide far less detail. Their nature is entirely dependent upon the readers interpretation providing only simple direction and leaving the rest to you. They carry an almost mythic simplicity. Physical tarot has become so refined over the centuries that much of the abstract wonder inherent in the practice has been defined out of it by "experts", the digital form provides an avenue to reinstate some of that wonder by making it more accessible to novices. At the same time digital presentation has the potential to exaggerate the "concretization" of tarot by providing ever more detail and precise definition. So I guess the short answer would be yes and no!

I like the possibility the screen offers of having us moving towards these images. It is fantastic to be able to zoom in to look at a detail, and have a somehow more invested experience in the tarot as a dream. I enjoyed a lot what you had to say about each one of the decks you have made androids for. Now, how do you decide that a deck is worth working with?

Currently Android has a very low memory limit and weak support for high resolution displays. As it evolves to more high resolution devices like the iPad I hope to expand TarotBot substantially. In my early days with tarot I never got exposure to historical decks. To me tarot was basically whatever they had at Barnes and Noble. A mishmash of different ideas regarding tarot's origins made it hard to understand what it was. At this point whatever images drew my attention sufficed.

When I began working on TarotBot and researching tarot I found it challenging to pick a deck that would be attractive to a wide audience. In addition I had to think about arranging licensing etc. This led me to work initially with Rider-Waite-Smith which was readily available in the public domain and was familiar to many people. As I dug into *tarotforum.net* I discovered discussions about favorite decks. These discussions are where I first encountered Il Meneghello's work. With *Vacchetta* it was love at first sight. I searched around the Internet for a copy and considered using an uncolored version, but Osvaldo Menegazzi's coloring was too nice so I contacted Cristina and made licensing arrangements. After this initial contact I became more familiar with Il Meneghello's catalog and selected what I felt were the best historical reproductions.

I envisioned a series of decks in the market enabling a user to explore the evolution of tarot. Following this I became absorbed by the technical development of TarotBot and the decks dropped to the bottom of the 'to do' list. Once TarotBot began to reach a point of stability, I revisited the decks and realized I was missing a major stage without any *Marseille* edition. Around this time I found Alec Satin's blog post[1], and discovered Flornoy's fantastic work. I had to talk to them so I ordered a copy of each and inquired about licensing. Roxanne was extremely helpful and open to sharing with me.

So from this chain of events I selected the initial Il Meneghello series *Visconti-Sforza*, *Soprafino*, and *Vacchetta* and the Flornoy series of *Noblet* and *Dodal*. With what I feel now is a solid foundation in the roots of tarot, the next step is to launch a series with some more modern visions of Tarot. This is still very much undefined and in brainstorming now – but I plan to continue working with the Flornoy and Il Meneghello studios to spread the availability of historical tarot. TarotBot was designed to have switchable decks and interpretations and eventually I hope to release tools for producing your own.

Now, I tend to believe that every medium brings its own, formal, ideas with it. There are things we can do in painting that we could reproduce in printing, but still, printing offers its own possibilities. All these decks you have chosen belong to a pre-digital era. I would say that any of the Marseille decks you have chosen translates better into the screen than the Visconti, for example, in that the Visconti has the distinctive texture of the hand-painted object. Still, both the Noblet and the Dodal share the quality of printing objects. I don't expect you to be clairvoyant, but I would like to know: what should we be looking for in the future of tarot? Do we need to create a digital tarot that lives up to the possibilities of the digital format? What kind of attributes should it posses?

I would argue that any deck which can display on a printed card can be made to look good on a modern digital display, while my *Visconti* rendition could definitely be improved so that it captures some of the depth of the paintings. Regardless, what you speak of was covered in depth in my cognitive engineering course work – the idea that design falls out of natural constraints on the medium, rather than being created. Essentially what design is comes down to recombining constraints and intention to resolve problems.

The big challenge with software is how few constraints there are, which can make it very hard to tell where to create them to make something useful and interesting.

---

1 http://tarot.alecsatin.com/fool-journey-marseille/

I think the real value of tarot yesterday and today comes from its ability to stimulate alternative perspectives and provide a starting point for revising your models and anticipation. My hope is that people will recognize this value and really apply it to everyday life.

Of course, there are also possibilities with upcoming immersive displays where you could perhaps some day build interactive models of the cards. Tablet and table style computing also presents some fascinating possibilities having a travelling tarot table more able to do multi person readings with, say, a reader and a questioner – or even get into some of the partner style workings discussed by Chris Hyatt and Lon Milo Duquette in their book on sex, magick, and tarot. In my opinion any attempts that focus on tarot as a tool for model revision is moving things in the right direction. What software makers have to look out for is getting too caught up in details relevant to physical cards but unnecessary and awkward on a touch screen.

It can be argued that the general public tends to approach the tarot with fear. Would you say that working from a digital platform could ease these feelings?

The general public tends to approach everything with fear, at least here in the US. I believe this to be the result of monotheism's pretext that there is an absolute truth and anything that disagrees with that absolute truth is evil and must be destroyed. This mental model is then projected by its holders onto all things which disagree with whatever the holder perceives to be authority – equating concepts that disagree with what has been taught through the authorities with fear and hatred. While tarot is derived from a predominately Christian culture, the idea of taking alternative perspectives and considering different approaches to various problems are clearly not strong suits of the general culture in which tarot was born. This is probably the single greatest barrier to people working more with tarot, but I feel it is also tarot's greatest benefit.

What is next? What are you working on now? Are you working with other artist or tarot readers?

I am currently only working with Flornoy and Il Meneghello, but TarotBot was designed to be quickly reconfigured with new artwork and interpretations. My feeling is that much like books, printed tarot cards are (or are going to be) declining in sales as more and more becomes possible in the digital realm.

Eventually I plan on implementing an interface for configuring a custom TarotBot complete with original artwork and text. In fact I am looking for tarot artists and readers to contribute to future premium versions with royalties, of course. I understand the standard rate for tarot deck distributors to pay is around 10% of net, Liberus offers 20% of gross for artwork and another 10% for text all of which is simply required to be packaged in a certain way to produce a new TarotBot.

There are also translations into German, Japanese and Chinese underway. Anyone desiring to port to another language just get in touch with me. Also TarotBot is open source, so any especially ambitious tarot lovers can always compile their own custom version – eventually I'll write up a tutorial on that. The version at Google code is the most recent build with all the latest features and bugs. In the market you have the development build as TarotBot beta and the most recent stable version is just plain old TarotBot.

Poet Christian Bök wrote that this may be the first generation of poets who will write poetry for an audience of intelligent machines. Do you think we could be the first generation of tarot readers having machines for clients?

I have long considered the idea of consciousness equated to activity. If you have a simple wind up toy and you wind it up, it possesses a consciousness – granted a simple one. It is of one mind: release the tension.

Technology such as computers and other machines are merely projections of our models into the world. As we do this we generate feedback as to the validity of the models we are projecting and use this feedback to generate better, more accurate models. As these models have improved, the technology has become smaller, less obtrusive, and more thoroughly integrated into our daily lives.

Some would argue that this is evidence of technology taking us over, but I feel it is us coming to terms with what we are and what is really important to us. We are using technology to better understand ourselves. In this regard I believe that the digital era is providing an opportunity for humanity to internalize the lessons of tarot more thoroughly and completely than ever before, and that's exciting.

New York / Columbus, Ohio, August 2010

"Philosopher and wise man, Jason Lotterhand, told the story that when he was first studying tarot in New York City early in the 20th century, the discussion turned to The Devil. The discussion took place in a home where there was a preschooler. The discussion group decided to ask the young child what he thought of key 15. The little boy looked at the card and said, 'Oooooo!!! A funny bunny!' Then he laughed, and so did the adults."

A conversation with TANYA JOYCE, artist

The first thing I have to ask is: How? How it is possible that the Thursday Night Tarot has been happening for 40 years? Do you have a core group that has been there from the very beginning? If so, would you say the offering has changed to match the evolution all of you have experienced in four decades?

What a fascinating and appropriate question you ask to begin our conversation! First of all, The Thursday Night Tarot is 60 years old this year!

The group was started in 1950 by Jason Lotterhand, author of the book titled, *The Thursday Night Tarot*. The book was compiled by Jason's student and editor, Arisa Victor. Its format of exposition plus questions and answers is a good representation of how the weekly meetings of the group go. When Jason retired in 1992, Arisa Victor led the group until late in 1998, when she asked if I would take on that position so she could work on books she wanted to publish and continue her long standing work with metaphysics for children in the guise of her alter ego, Granny Rainbow.

I began my explorations of metaphysics in the late 1950s and began to study tarot in the late 1980s. I studied with Jason until his retirement and then with Arisa until she asked me to lead the group. I have a strong background in teaching through group facilitation, so it was all a perfect fit. Jason Lotterhand may have been the first person – maybe the first person ever – to open up discussions of *The Spoken Cabala* to everyone – for free with no prerequisites and no obligations. In the Thursday Night Tarot there are no degrees, no examinations, no certificates – except a few for fun that sometimes turn up. There is a rotating group of Thursday Night Tarot participants that number in the hundreds, if you could count them all. It is the archetypal tarot images that hold the group together. As Jason Lotterhand said, the images create an atmosphere in which "we leave our egos at the door." There is no coat check, no receipt, no need to leave a tip to get our egos back. That's just how archetypes work.

Jason also said to Arisa that the group works because whoever is leading it leads it in the way he or she wants to. There have been few changes since Jason's passing. Both Arisa and I have increased the amount of group discussion in the class and we have also tried a variety of strategies for including the minor arcana as well as the major arcana in our weekly discussions. Basically, each week we discuss one card of the major arcana. Why does it work? Because archetypes can suggest a great deal. The High Priestess's scroll includes everything – absolutely everything that ever was, or is, or will be. So we don't need to worry about being repetitive! On the cabalistic Tree of Life, The High Priestess streams straight down The Middle Pillar from the great Unity of all there is, Kether, to our hearts of Beauty, Tipareth. It's the longest path on the Tree and it can keep us busy for quite a while!

60 years! The fact that we have already spent 20 years repeating "Jason Lotterhand did this for 40 years" is uncanny in itself. You mentioned the Spoken Cabala. Could you tell me more? I have great interest in la langue des oiseaux, *the 'language of the birds,' which is often called 'the phonetic cabala'. The Marseille tarot, which is the one that interests me, seems to have a thick 'coat' of sound on top of its images, that one can only experience 'live', traveling through the air, since it dies as soon as you 'cage' it. Are you talking about the same thing?*

The 'language of the birds' is a fascinating study. In the area of conventional academic scholarship, the European Middle Ages is the area of my interest, especially reading English poetry from that period out loud. I just discovered 'the language of the birds' within the past year. Your take on it is exciting and insightful. I might say 'the language of the birds' is part of The Spoken Cabala. The Spoken Cabala is a phrase representing the entire "mouth-to-ear" tradition of oral transmission of what we call esoteric knowledge – that knowledge which is "hidden from" or not generally apparent in our daily life activities. Of course, once the light gets turned on, we see how very much a part of daily life it all is.

I guess my main question about the phonetic Cabala is this one: to what extent are we revealing? To what extent are we creating? When we notice that the French word for 'card' and the French word for 'soul' sound exactly the same, are we revealing a conscious intention, by 'someone' or 'something', behind that homophony or are we creating meaning from a coincidence? I am reminded of Canadian poet bp Nichol, who would take the map of Canada, write down several town names in a row and read them as a whole sentence. The sound of these words put in this new order would take us to new words, or to "concealed meanings". Nichol would then claim that the Canadian landscape is a text, as if by naming/creating the landscape 'someone' (the Manitoban Alphabet Cult) wrote a book.

I can see this as a superb poetic gesture, but I also know Nichol isn't actually claiming this to be a literal fact. We would be safe at intuiting lots of humor in his claim. How do we know when these conflated meanings follow a conscious logic and are not the product of a coincidence? In fact, does it even matter? A gesture like the one proposed by Nichol, 'fake' as it is, opens an awareness in us whose final results have our perception – of the landscape, maps, words, letters – transformed. There is true magic in that, I would say. What do you think?

Are we revealing? Are we creating? What fine questions, Enrique! In what may be called "the big picture," we are creating and revealing all the time, no matter what we do, no matter what we think we are doing. But your questions are much more clearly focused than in a consideration of the overall umbrella under which we live, and breathe, and have our being. "The Spoken Cabala," as The Thursday Night Tarot uses the term, means conversation. This is conversation with others, in the main. This is conversation under the auspices of a tarot card, generally, a card of the major arcana – one a week in our tradition. The cabalistic Tree of Life is also with us in visual form during our discussions, as well as related pictures and words that individuals who have come together for the evening find relevant.

The purpose of the conversation is to learn from those who have also experienced getting to know tarot as "an expression of cabala." Traditionally, this was a discussion between "masters" and "students." Jason Lotterhand was certainly a "master." However, he did not refer to himself as such. He was a philosopher who found conversation stimulating and delightful. For a teacher – or group leader in any discipline – teaching helps with knowing what you know and what you don't. It also helps to hone how you give accurate voice to what you know and, of course, helps you learn from others. This is mainly the "mouth" part of "mouth to ear."

For students, the world becomes expanded. Courage to discuss whatever comes to mind is increased. Wisdom, knowledge, and understanding grow. This is, mainly, the "ear" part of "mouth to ear." But supposed boundaries between teachers and students on occasion disappear. "Whatever comes to mind," is always under the umbrella of the tarot key displayed in large format (currently about 11 inches by 17 inches, so it can been seen easily). These symbolic pictures are universal archetypes, expressed in art styles of whatever time and place in which they were created. They encourage us in such ways that "whatever comes to mind" is, if we focus on it, almost always related to "the subject" of the card displayed.

When we seem to get off the subject, people sometimes ask to return to "talking about the card." Usually, this means a desire to hear traditional meanings, such as Key 4, The Emperor, is associated with the color red, the musical note C natural, the zodiacal sign of Aries, and so forth. That's all fine, except that it is often thought that "the card" (or key) is outside us, that our conversation is not "on track" when the image for the week is not the topic in an intellectual sense. For example, talking about sunspots, auroras, and cell phone disruption during the week of The Emperor may seem "off topic." However, the sun is exalted (finds its strongest expression) in Aries, so how "off topic" is a discussion of solar flares during the time we are "under the umbrella of" The Emperor? It's an open question. My answer is that it is not "off topic " at all, but an example of living the archetype, of realizing the archetype is alive in us.

The quality in which the mouth to ear tradition is different from written material is that it is very fluid. Opinions get modified, questions accompany us home, and so forth, in a way that can seem unnecessarily diffuse if literally transcribed into print. Gertrude Stein said that her prose style (which can seem extremely diffuse and sometimes impossible to comprehend unless you hear her read it) is based on her desire to replicate conversation as she heard it. She was a great reader. Even her most seemingly obscure works are understandable when we listen to recordings of her reading. It is somewhat the same with "mouth to ear." Speaking is a different medium from writing. Gurdjieff is often hard to read. He was a story teller. These are simply a couple of people who come to my mind as being clearer when speaking than they are in writing.

The overall way in which we are not led astray into creations of our personal imaginations that pass for tradition or by personal reveries we may think of as revelation, is as follows. As Jason Lotterhand said, when we come together for our discussions, "we leave our egos at the door." This is not planned or regulated. It is a result of the symbolic images themselves, just as we feel we are living a bit broader than the daily life of calendars and time clocks when we see beautiful architecture or hear music that resonates deeply within us.

There is something else I would like to ask you about. I am aware your group published a book of poems inspired by the tarot. Could you tell me how that project came to be? Was that a one-time event, or do you keep working on these kind of poems? I would also like to know more about how you see poetry fitting within the tarot' scheme.

Here's how the book *Tarot Haiku* came about. After having met for some years at the Ft. Mason Art and Conference Center in San Francisco, The Thursday Night Tarot was looking for a new home: Ft. Mason had become difficult to park at because of crowds at large events. Bus service was also infrequent. Painter and poet Anna Ruth Kipping said we could meet at her house "for a couple of weeks." The weeks stretched into years: we met at her house until she passed to the inner planes in 2006. One of Anna Ruth's passions was haiku. She was very happy about the fact that she had bought her first haiku book from poet Kenneth Rexroth. Musician and healer, Richard Jerome Bennett, suggested that, in Anna Ruth's honor, we all write haiku following our two hour weekly discussion of a tarot key from the major arcana. We used the contemporary definition of haiku – a short poem evoking a distinct impression of a fleeting moment, because not everyone was familiar with traditional haiku. Anna Ruth, who loved the traditional haiku form, explained that form, too, since people were interested. At first, some people were reluctant to participate. "I can't write poetry," some said. Or "I can't write haiku." Relaxation is key to all our studies, so I said, "That's OK. Any time in the future that something comes to you about one of the keys, we'll add it to the poems we have." Some people contributed in this way. The main thing that happened, however, is that people who had felt hesitation saw the quiet focus of the poetry writing that was going on – sometimes all you could hear was literally the sound of pencils on paper – and started writing.

The Thursday Night Tarot operates on the ancient custom of charging no fees. The class is free. We do have a "pass the hat," but with no suggested donation. Since Anna Ruth, as host, had not needed funds from "the hat," we had a nest egg which we used to publish *Tarot Haiku* as a chapbook through fine arts printer and poet David Alpaugh's Small Poetry Press. We printed 200 copies, which are available at poetry events and through the mail. The usual cost is $20 per copy. We are collecting new poems on tarot topics to be part of a new book on a variety of approaches to getting tarot into our daily lives. Components of that book are in progress. David Alpaugh of Small Poetry Press has retired from running the press, though he continues to publish his own work and read poetry at a variety of venues. I'm casually looking for a new publisher while we shape the form of the new book. No dates yet. So that's the story about how the book came to be.

Now to the question of the place of poetry in tarot studies generally. The more I think about it, the farther back in time I go. If we accept the hypothesis that tarot, as an expression of cabala, goes back to ancient times and ideas (I do accept this hypothesis), then we are in a time where the mind was trained to do many things we do in writing today. Poetry is a time tested memory device. Rhyme, meter, alliteration, and other poetic attributes assist memory. There was undoubtedly a high component of poetry in the oral transmission of cabala (which literally means "the reception"). Perhaps the earliest written form we have that directly relates to the transmission of metaphysical practices is the poetry of Gnostic charms. However, the content of many of these charms that survive is vengeful and desirous of retribution, clearly evocative of the same kind of mindset of people today who ask for tarot readings to "get the scoop on other people" or who think they are going to "use the I Ching on someone," having no real idea of the consequences for themselves of "what goes around comes around." So form and content need to be distinguished in this case.

Medieval poetry is full of cabalistic lessons. *Sir Gawain and The Green Knight*, written around the time of the first reference we have to tarot in Europe (last quarter of the 14th century), can be seen as one long lesson on the heart of Beauty on The Tree of Life. The Elizabethans (of either high social rank or participation in art circles) studied tarot and cabala. The Globe Education Center in today's London is full of cabalistic imagery. The stated mission of the center is 50% devoted to performance and 50% to education. A pentacle is above the first small stage you see as you enter the building. On a cabalistic Tree of Life ceiling painting, Kether touches an artificial English "mighty oak" under whose branches people meet for tours. The metaphysics of the Elizabethans is a relatively new study that is taking off like a rocket according to the staff at Field's book store in San Francisco, one of the best sources for information on world wide metaphysical traditions.

The twentieth century drove metaphysics underground as the result of the despondency over the World Wars primarily, it seems to me. Science was god in the first half of the century. Drugs were god in the second half. In this malaise, poetry (and other arts) diverged from metaphysics – at least in many areas presided over by academic scholasticism. Late in life, Picasso said he would have talked about the spiritual elements in his art, "but people would have laughed." Picasso chided Matisse for designing the chapel at Vence. He thought Matisse had "copped out to the establishment" of ossified religion – or so he said. I don't mean poetry or metaphysics was in trouble. Twentieth century poetry is a huge, a rich garden of accomplishment. Twentieth century metaphysics is a flourishing garden, too. It is much more open than ever before, and relatively free of social or legal retribution. However, when poetry events and poetry publishing are run primarily by academics, as is the case currently in the United States, there is a cut off of anything that seems to be genuinely or strongly metaphysical. We read John Donne in literature classes – but only a little. We look down our noses at T. S. Eliot's spirituality, and don't even discuss W.B. Yeats spirituality in English classes. Just as Yeats was told that modern literature was "not a fit subject for tuition" ("tuition" meaning teaching in that case), so today's academics – fearful that "church" and "state" may not be separate enough – shun metaphysics in poetry unless it is so carefully concealed that, through their almost complete inexperience, they miss it altogether.

To be vital, any art needs to be encouraged socially. Today, the Internet helps where traditional champions of poetry often do not. David Alpaugh has a wonderful essay on the Internet about the damage done by book titles such as *The 100 Best Poems*. People think that THOSE 100 are THE poems to read, but usually a professor has picked them. It is one person's opinion and, often, the opinion of one person in an ivory tower.

I have nothing against academic life itself. I grew up in an academic household and learned a great deal from many excellent teachers. At the same time, I can recognize that today the academic attitude toward the arts in general tries to cram what used to be a six month semester into a 9 week quarter (at least in the U.S.). This approach doesn't work for any art (or anything else, in my opinion). The deep, traditional intertwining of the arts and metaphysics is submerged in a world of hype. Tarot meditations can actually clear a lot of the hype out of our minds. Then we need to simply go forward with the courage of our own Key 0, The Life Breath. Paul Foster Case used ancient poetic forms in his *Book of Tokens*. Ann Davies wrote poetry in traditions of tarot and cabala. Probably more people have done that than we know. Poetry moves words from strictly linear and "existing in time" uses of language, into the flowing world of back and forth, up and down, once and future, now and not another time. Poetry is a good example of the text on The High Priestess's scroll in the respect that poems move us into the world of "all there is," seen and unseen, in ways that are closer to music and visual art than they are to rational discourse.

I am mainly interested in the tarot as a poetic device. I don't think so much in terms of using the tarot for writing poems, but as the experience of the tarot being a poetical experience. That said, I am aware of the long-lasting link between the game of tarot and the poetry of tarot via tarocchi appropriati. *In a way, I see all tarot readings as a reenactment of these early poems in which a person would explain in a poetic way why he had given certain a card to a certain lady. That is not far from what we, readers, do, even if we let Chance deal the cards.*

The tarot itself – at least in the case of the Marseille decks I work with – can be seen as a visual poem in that every single element we see in one card 'rhymes' with similar elements in other cards, therefore creating rhythms and patterns whose forms are meaningful in themselves. Then we have the very act of poiesis, the making of meaning, that happens when we see a message in the cards, and when a person who receives that messages transforms it into personal experiences. Moreover, I see poetry as that realm in which language is re-created. With the tarot we transform the words we have to talk about a problem into images that contain themselves many other words, and therefore, can give us new words to name these problems.

Then there is a more debatable link, which I pursue anyway: there is a whole line of French poets who based their work in la langue des oiseaux, which is to say that they used the French proclivity to play with the ambiguity of words that was part of the popular culture as part of their poetic devices. We could say that there is a whole thick layer of sound covering the Marseille tarot images, and that the same puns and double intended meanings that poets used are also used by French cartomancers. (Incidentally, the lore has it that such phonetic approach is only transmitted from "mouth" to "ear"). One thing most of these authors have in common is their relationship, or interest, in Alfred Jarry's 'pataphysics. Perhaps the most outstanding example of that would be OuLiPo, 'Ouvroir de littérature potentielle', a group interested in creating devices for experimental writing, mostly based on rules or constrains, of which Italo Calvino's Castle of Crossed Destinies is an example. (I also take Calvino's book to be a late manifestation of tarocchi appropriati).

The idea of using constraints as alternative to Chance to generate sequences of cards interests me a lot. Something interesting happened to me the other day while I was giving a lecture. I was basically revisiting Calvino's methodology in front of an audience. The main difference was that, instead of having the whole tarot spread on a table, face up, to create horizontal and vertical narratives, I had all the cards facing down, and asked several people to come and turn a few cards over, creating capricious rows in any direction. I read each one of these rows as a story for that person. But when the last person came, the choice was already made for her by all the other participants. She had twelve cards left, and no choice on the matter. Some people even protested this. I read that story anyway. It was the story of a couple who got divorced, and how the woman found a lover she didn't really like but was about to marry anyway, until the last card came: the Chevalier de Coupes, a new man offering love. That was the last story on the table, a story that, as I said, was created by default, almost as if the constraints we applied were "take all the cards off the table except for twelve of them". But that woman told me afterwards that such a default story was actually her story, to the letter, including the late apparition of a handsome 'knight'.

I also think that poetry has been fundamental for my understanding of what to expect from tarot and how it works. I tend to use language, or more precisely, the alphabet, as an example of how can we relate to the cards, but also, to underline the notion of the tarot as a language. Letters are also great to understand how shapes are in themselves meaningful, since they offer a concrete experience we can also get from the tarot images, and because they can trigger all kinds of associations that go beyond, or stand before, the meaning conveyed by words.

I am rambling here, but you have touched too many interesting points. From the mnemonics of rhyme we could go to the mnemonics of visual symmetry, and to the tarot as a series of experiential keys contained in body postures that seem almost like a response to something Thomas Aquinas wrote: "It is necessary in this way to invent similitudes and images because simple and spiritual intentions slip easily from the soul unless they are, as it were, linked to some corporeal similitudes, because human cognition is stronger in regard to the sensibilia. Whence the memorative is placed in the sensitive of the soul". In any case, while reading your response I found myself thinking that you live in a very 'poetic' city, where people still run small publishing companies and there is a whole history of poetic landmarks. Have you met many poets with an interest in tarot, or would you say that's where the academy's stiffness comes forward to keep everything separated and therefore easier to classify?

I am mulling over your view of tarot as a poetic device. As with all interesting things, poetry can mean a great variety of creations and experiences. Yes, tarot itself is a poetic experience and I like the fact that that is a central concern of yours, since both the lyric implications of what you have written and the story telling qualities of tarot are emphasized that way. In my earlier email, I was thinking of poetry in a more narrow, or literal (perhaps) context, a poem that we may see on a printed page or hear someone recite or read aloud. SPEAKING poetry has its own close correlation with tarot from the standpoint that The Fool represents the element of air and the Life Breath, which, in many cultures, is seen as the force that causes things to take on form. Overall, the sense of tarot as poetry seems to me to be similar to what I might call lyric poetry – "characterized by rapture and great enthusiasm" to paraphrase a dictionary entry for "lyrical."

Natica Angilly of Artists Embassy International and Natica Angilly's Poetic Dance Theater, thinks of "poetic" much as Ruth St. Denis conceived of re-evoking movements of Greek dance. To Natica, "poetic" and "lyrical" are nearly synonymous. She enjoys a wide variety of dance forms, but when she is choreographing dances, it is the DeniShawn tradition that is her muse, even though Ruth St. Denis and Ted Shawn created what they called an "Oriental" style. The guiding inspiration of Isadora Duncan is there as well.

I am almost tempted to ask, "What IS poetry?" It is some quality that takes us into the realm of what tarot – and other disciplines – call our Highest Self. Our United Self, shown by winged angels in many tarot decks. Poetry is a land of tremendous power and a land in which we don't fret and worry. We don't dither. We advance and explore, even in the middle of metaphoric night when unfamiliar sounds and sights may be both awesome and terrifying – what the 19th century called the Sublime. We proceed along The Path of Return – or The Yellow Brick Road. You asked if the San Francisco Bay Area is a place of frequent tarot contacts. "Not especially," I was originally tempted to reply, but an experience I had yesterday has changed my point of view. At the moment, I see the Bay Area as FULL of tarot aficionados. A light went off for me yesterday that seems to sparkle in many places on our area maps as I write.

Yesterday mid afternoon, I delivered some paintings to The Pinole Art Gallery, a small gallery in a small community about a twenty minute drive north of Berkeley and Oakland. Pinole is a small town. Pinole Artisans, the gallery's sponsoring organization, is a group of about 85 people. However, it is an exciting group and an unusual one. It is a group in which artists share, work together, and are supportive of one another. We always learn when any 2 or 3 of us are working at the gallery. Paintings, drawings, and poetry are all exhibited. The town of Pinole itself is both calm and energetic in a way that surrounding towns are not. Each town may have its beauty, but the sense of calm and energy is special to Pinole.

After delivering my art work, I went to a local coffee house to get some coffee for the drive home. In the cafe I saw a woman I had met at the gallery. She asked me to join her. Another friend of hers came a bit later. All of a sudden, all three of us were talking about tarot. The woman who asked me to join her had written a tarot column for a New Age publication – now out of print. I had read her column. She and her friend both do tarot readings. I prefer to teach others how they can do readings for themselves (though I do readings for others as well). She said she'd give me a reading – right then and there. It was insightful and enjoyable. Then I realized that another fine tarot reader and metaphysician, Arisa Victor, is currently living in Pinole. I often participate in Monday salons for a mixture of art forms held at a restaurant in San Rafael – a small city a bit north of the Golden Gate Bridge. There is great interest in tarot at these events. Tarot and other disciplines overlap – music and various forms of meditation come to mind at the moment. No one I know is furious or angry (fearful) of tarot, though not everyone is actively interested in it. Many of the interested people I know personally live in San Francisco, Oakland, Berkeley, and the small town between Oakland and Berkeley where I live, Emeryville. Other interested people live down the peninsula near Stanford (Palo Alto) and San Jose – a longer commute. We do not have as much public transportation as in the New York area.

These days I am contemplating these verses from Canadian poet bp Nichol:

consonants as nouns

vowels as verbs

I tend to spend lots of time on very specific ideas, like this one. What I like about it is the notion of sounds that move the words along, and sounds that define the identity of the word. Artist Joseph Beuys said that breath was a material we 'sculpted' with our throat, vocal chords, tongue and mouth. For him, the very act of speaking was a sculptural process, and therefore, a creative act. I think that has to do with that idea of re-creating language through poetry. When I say poetry is a 'space' I mean to say that there is no room in any of the operations we daily do with language, that allow for re-discovering the words we use. These days I am very happy, paying with a little device I concocted: La Conspiration Alphabétique. *I wrote it in such a way that the main idea is a little appendix at the end, and the big joke is at the forefront of the whole thing. The main notion is that we can use the tarot to translate words into images and meditate on them. But I made it appear as a method to find love, inspired by all these early cartomantic manuals that are precisely about romance. I say I am happy because my 'conspiration' has been working beautifully. People engage with the device for the amusement of toying with something romantic-related (after all 'amusing' and 'I'm using' sound alike), but the fact is that they start playing with the attributes of words: homophony, anagrams, analogies, etymology... In other words, they are finding what I truly wanted them to find: language. In that regard, I tend to see all tarot readings as covert poetry acts. We do need to re-create language, but we are too busy to consciously engage in it. I can suggest to people to read poetry, because I truly believe it changes the way you understand the world, but most of them don't understand the reason for such pursuits. Then, one day, they find themselves stuck. There is something bothering them and they cannot think straight enough to find a solution. A tarot reading will expose them to the same kind of process poetry would, but now they see the purpose. It is not 'about language', 'about art' or 'about poetry'. It is about them.*

Now, I don't want to take more of your time, so I will ask you a final question based on something you just brought up: fear. I have been recently persuaded of the fact that fear is the most common emotion people experience when the subject of tarot is mentioned. I would like to know: what have you learned about the fear people feel about the tarot, and how do we combat that fear?

Fear and tarot – or – fear OF tarot. A fascinating topic. What is it all about? I'm sure valuable conversations in response to that question could go on for a very long time and be quite productive. First of all, there's the issue of something new. The more insulated we become from situations and people we don't expect, the more unaccustomed we are to new experiences. We drive in cars with the windows up, air conditioning or heaters on, radio on, etc., etc. Or we walk with ear buds sprouting sound into our minds, not paying attention to ambient anything. As we grow, go to school, get a job, etc., we are also taught what is "good" and "bad." With a low level of experiential time during the day and a high level of isolation, we tend to accept these "goods" and "bads." If we "rebel," we are still accepting what we have been told and reacting to it. We aren't breaking new ground for ourselves.

Tarot is often something new to people, since most of us don't come across it naturally in our homes, schools, churches, libraries, or even Internet chat rooms. When we do come across tarot, we often have in the backs of our minds that it is "fortune telling" ("bad") or "work of the devil" ("bad"). None of this is a natural state of curiosity. It is a reaction to lack of experience. Philosopher and wise man, Jason Lotterhand, told the story that when he was first studying tarot in New York City early in the 20th century, discussion turned to The Devil (tarot key 15). The discussion took place in a home where there was a preschooler. The discussion group decided to ask the young child what he thought of key 15. The little boy looked at the card and said, "Oooooo!!! A funny bunny!" Then he laughed, and so did the adults. The child was too young to have been taught much about "good" and "bad." He was also at a young age when exploration is part and parcel of almost every daily activity. In short, the preschooler was in the courageous and confident posture of The Fool (key 0). He "didn't know any better," so he did the appropriate thing: he thought for himself.

Suppose that we've learned from the story of this little boy and have decided to have our first tarot reading. What could we fear from that? We can worry and be fearful of what cards will turn up. Will the cards tell me I'm doing everything wrong? Will they tell me that something dreadful is going to happen? Will they tell me I'll never make a billion dollars or find my soul mate or be famous? As Mary Greer pointed out in one of her tapes, these questions are really all about lack of confidence in ourselves. They are about insecurity. Why do we have this insecurity? Largely because we don't get much praise in life for our explorations and we get quite a bit of comment about our short-comings. This results in a double whammy of diminished self-confidence: diminished self-confidence through lack of experience (as when we isolate ourselves from our daily environments) and lack of self-confidence through lack of social reinforcement for our explorations.

The Justice card in tarot is very interesting in this respect. It can be one of the more off putting cards for many people. It has been observed at The Thursday Night Tarot weekly gatherings that attendance can fall off when the subject is Key 11, Justice. Why? Courts of Justice allot punishments for infringements or crimes against what is agreed upon in a society as optimal behavior. Courts of Justice do not convene for the purpose of awarding prizes and merit badges to people who have helped with anger management in their neighborhoods, or kept the streets clean, or planted trees, or promoted bicycle paths, good public transportation, low cost fresh food, or affordable housing. We tend to overlay one circumstance (daily life, or what we think of as daily life) with another (tarot, in this case). The result is "I don't like the Justice card. It means I won't get what I want, and I'll be punished" – for example.

Among the very good reasons for studying tarot, we come to know attributions, such as Mirth being the function associated with Key 15, The Devil. (No wonder the Devil was an archetypal funny bunny to the little boy who was shown Key 15!) We learn that Justice, Key 11 (or Key 8 in some decks), is a central figure of balance, a powerful aspect of reciprocity in the receptive (feminine) aspect of all our personalities, a supportive assistance, a friend. All archetypal study systems – tarot, mandalas, traditional icons, spirit figures, and others – help us have the courage to explore life. Experience in exploration brings confidence. Confidence, little by little, replaces fear.

New York / San Francisco, July-September 2010

"In some ways, studying the 'old magic' is more a matter of learning to overcome our preconceptions of what we think that magic was, and learning a new way of seeing."

A conversation with REECE HENDLEY, tarot reader

I would like to start this dialogue with the word 'null'.

I actually like the shape of that word, a lot. It sounds and feels all fluffy, like a small ball made from a teddy bear's skin. This word lends a levity to the tongue that makes it very easy, and pleasant, to pronounce. In the tarot world we use that word now and then, when we talk about the 'null hypothesis'. This idea was brought forward by Michael Dummett, about how the tarot trump sequence has no narrative intention, but rather, it is more or less a capricious selection of motifs that where popular at the time of the tarot's creation. What I fail to grasp, and I would like your help here, is how someone can play with unnumbered trumps if they are not organized in a meaningful way. I am well aware that our brains are wired to find meaning, and more precisely, to close any random selection of events into a narrative gestalt in which we tend to assume that the earlier events may have caused the later ones. But still, it is hard to imagine that all those people would have been playing under the spell of a collective cognitive illusion! (Not that this is impossible, mind you. After all, the whole divinatory tarot seems to be a collective cognitive illusion).

In a conversation with Marco Ponzi, he made a very important distinction between a narrative and a hierarchy. A hierarchy is not just a succession of events. A hierarchy adds a sense of priority, by ranking these events in order of importance. The idea of these motifs being popular at the time is very important here. That sense of priority among these motifs has to have been evident. It was that clear sense of value what made possible for a card to trump another one. What are your thoughts on this? Is there a discernible narrative in the tarot trump cycle?

I find your take on "null" fascinating. The word hits me quite differently. I see a man coming home from work to find his apartment empty and his wife and children have left him.

Null,
the hollow hull,
an empty skull.

I recall an image from Hollywood of a human skull getting caught in massive gears and shattering into oblivion. That's like null made even more null, or as my three year old niece says after finishing her supper, "Gone gone…"

I do think there is a discernible narrative woven into the trumps hierarchy. I had seen a clear influence of the *Dance of Death* and Boethius' *Fortuna* on the trumps. Finding Mike Hurst's work, I was introduced to the themes of *De Casibus*, and the *Fall of Princes*, and more paths to explore. I agree with Hurst's general conclusions. They are exactly what one would expect to find in a didactic work of the place and time tarot arose. They are the very same 'highbrow' themes that made their way into popular consciousness via the morality plays and pageants, and would have been familiar even to the illiterate butcher, baker and candlestick maker. The popular theater of the time may have been the biggest influence on both the choice of subjects of individual cards, and the nature of the narrative, and even may have been why this particular game was so popular. We may be looking at the first "movie tie-in" merchandise.

In a conversation with Dan Pelletier I shared with him this quote from Don Quixote:

> Don Quixote was about to reply to Sancho Panza, but he was prevented by a cart crossing the road full of the most diverse and strange personages and figures that could be imagined. He who led the mules and acted as carter was a hideous demon; the cart was open to the sky, without a tilt or cane roof, and the first figure that presented itself to Don Quixote's eyes was that of Death itself with a human face; next to it was an angel with large painted wings, and at one side an emperor, with a crown, to all appearance of gold, on his head. At the feet of Death was the god called Cupid, without his bandage, but with his bow, quiver, and arrows; there was also a knight in full armour, except that he had no morion or helmet, but only a hat decked with plumes of divers colours; and along with these there were others with a variety of costumes and faces.

Your comment brought it back to my mind. The whole episode starts with Don Quixote wanting to fight these personages, and ends with him realizing they are part of a masquerade. Isn't that something? A man famous for taking windmills for giants can actually acknowledge the farcical aspects of theater!

Now, forgive me for asking you to 'psychologize' a whole subculture but, why do you think that linking the tarot with notions such as 'morality' or 'virtue' finds so much antipathy in the tarot community?

I think even beyond the tarot community, notions such as 'morality' or 'virtue' find a lot of antipathy. I think a certain amount of 'leakage' from various social ideologies, particularly from the 1960s has made the ideas of morality and virtue quite unattractive. You know, if it feels good, do it. I recall a quote from the English writer Dorothy Sayers,

> In the world it is called Tolerance, but in hell it is called Despair, the sin that believes in nothing, cares for nothing, seeks to know nothing, interferes with nothing, enjoys nothing, hates nothing, finds purpose in nothing, lives for nothing, and remains alive because there is nothing for which it will die.

I think it illustrates well a great schism between the "old morality" and our modern values of universal tolerance and unconditional equality.

Nietzsche said that the fundamental principle of Justice was to not make equal what is unequal! This goes against our current ideals of equality. Of course Nietzsche loved to throw out shocking statements like this, but actually what he is saying here is pretty close to how Aquinas explained Justice. For Aquinas all just order in the world is based on this: that man give man what is his due. His argument goes into by what right one has to claim his due, how one is or is not owed his due, and that giving someone something that isn't his due, that he hasn't earned, is in fact an act of injustice. Aquinas is clearly not a socialist.

A moral allegory like the tarot trumps could be considered rather un-hip, maybe even politically incorrect. We'd best ignore that part of it.

Now, call me crazy, but I think it is fundamental to acknowledge the moral allegory as the most likely narrative to be present in the tarot's trump cycle, if one wants to reach a sober understanding of the tarot. At a formal level, it accounts for a brilliant design. I guess this is only relevant if one has a sensibility about design. If you do, you cannot help but have your respect for the tarot, as an artifact, strengthened. At a practical level, and here I am venturing into unpopular territory, understanding the moral allegory in the tarot makes the images more useful for us, today. In all these conversations I am having with people within the tarot world, the debate seems to center on fortunetelling versus therapy. More precisely, it seems that, if you take fortunetelling off the equation, we are left with some sort of projective test whose usage is somehow therapeutic. As someone who doesn't feel comfortable in neither band, the idea of the tarot as a visual sermon is very useful. I personally find it deliciously limiting. Here is this hierarchy of these notions we, in the Western world, consider important, so let's choose a few to reflect on them and on how they might apply to your life, here and now. I find that pretty consistent with what I expect from images: to give me strength by eliciting the beauty in me. I guess we could define that as 'inspiration'. What about you? What do you expect from images?

Hmm? That's hard for me to say. I tend to have a somewhat atypical relationship with images, at least tarot images. I don't see them as images really, more as concepts that have been embodied. I tend to look for conceptual relationships between the different cards and don't focus so much on the specifics of how a given allegory was represented. This may be why I find your reading methods so fascinating, Enrique. It is a peek into a very different way of looking at the cards from my own. It is a bit like an odd attraction between a very conservative accountant and a buck-wild super model. I won't go into which of us is the accountant, and which is the super model. No point stirring up rumors!

If we follow the logic of the middle section of the trumps in Dummett's scheme, Love and Fame are on one side of Time and Fortune. Defamation and Death are on the other side. The idea of the ups and downs of Fame/Success/Power is universal and easy to understand. What fascinates me is the way the sequence seems to pair Love and Death as opposites. This suggests, to me anyway, that the designer intended Love to represent something more than simple romantic love. Perhaps we could go so far, if we wanted to try to apply this moral allegory to our own lives, to say Trump VI is our joys in life, particularly the pleasures of our youth, the sort of things we see on the old representations of the Children of Venus, the sort of memories we cherish and pine for again when we are too old to walk with Venus, and Saturn (Death) has come a courtin'.

Details can be useful. A pattern found between the details in two images have us mapping metaphors from these details, to a target domain, while ignoring the rest of the images. Our own mindset is crucial there. What are we looking for? A question from the client certainly helps. A man is about to be expelled from college. If we have The Emperor aside The Hanged Man, we can find a pattern, a symmetry, be-

tween The Emperor's scepter and one of the poles enclosing The Hanged Man. We can say that he has a problem with authority.

Then, you mentioned a notion that interests me a lot: 'embodiment'. In a conversation with Art Rosengarten I contrasted the primary metaphor LIFE IS A PURPOSEFUL JOURNEY with The Fool. A metaphor like that one is so embedded in our thought processes that we cannot help but see The Fool walking, not through the landscape, but through life! We are practically wired to fall into the trap of reading a 'Fool's Journey' in there. Isn't that amazing? We unconsciously map bodily experiences onto abstractions. There is another primary metaphor called ACTIONS ARE SELF-PROPELLED MOTIONS in which the bodily experience of moving our bodies through space is mapped onto the subjective experience of action, that also informs how we perceive The Fool, but also, The Chariot, or The Hermit. It is no wonder that all these images seem to speak about something that goes beyond literal representation. Our own experience automatically links them into the broader realm of our bodily experience, outside their initial allegorical intention.

Take Judgement, for example. There we have a fair and square depiction of the resurrection. Period. Still, there is a primary metaphor we all use daily without even paying attention to the fact that it is called the HAPPY IS UP metaphor. It accounts for the correlation between the subjective, affective state of being happy, and our upright posture. When we are sick, or when we are dead, we lie horizontally. Being upright means we are alive and healthy, so we understand the subjective emotion of 'happiness' as consistent with that posture. We only 'rise' from the dead because for our physical bodies, to stand up is to be alive. That metaphor extends to things like having our thoughts "arising", we are going "up" to Heaven, being "lifted" by joy, feeling "up"… All these are notions we almost automatically map onto the image we see in Judgement.

We see the primary metaphor INTIMACY IS CLOSENESS expressed in The Sun. There is another primary metaphor: AFFECTION IS WARM that we can also see expressed in that image. Notice how all the iconography flies out of the window in a way that feels so natural! We see the primary metaphor UNDERSTANDING IS SEEING expressed in The Hermit. The STATES ARE LOCATIONS primary metaphor can be read into The Tower. I like to play with all these things because it implies tapping into an understanding the client already possesses. It would be interesting to elucidate to what extent these primary metaphors define the way in which we *choose to represent these concepts in an image. But still, I like to think that the scope of what we can expect from these images is defined by their original iconographic intention. I mean: a man may want to know if he is going to get suspended from college or not, but the answer we get is about his attitude, and how his attitude will define his fate.*

If you were to resume the whole message of the tarot to three cards, which cards would you pick? The three moral virtues? The Fool, Death and The World (or The Angel)? None of the above?

With your examples, I think you've already picked the two best ways if we were to sum up the message of the tarot in three cards. The Fool – Death – The World gives us a nice snap-shot of the narrative, an "everyman" whose mortality may be overcome through Christ. It fails to show us how this is done however. That, of course is by way of the virtues. The virtues are the essential message. They penetrate the whole cosmology. Diagrammatically represented[1], Justice descends from Heaven, from "goodness" itself, showing us how to behave when we are fortunate. The Pope and Emperor are ideal examples of that. A good leader is fair. From the movement of the celestial spheres, the Stars, Moon, Sun, arises the movements of Time and Fate. Is it not the constant change, impermanence, and fluctuation of the world that requires us to be strong and have courage? From the Devil and his Hellish house comes Death and Misfortune. Through moderation we curb his dark temptations and lessen our misfortunes and trump Death with Life Everlasting. Below we see those who are intemperate – Fools and Deceivers. Be fair, be brave, and go easy on the creme brûlée. That's the message of the tarot.

Albecht Dürer has an engraving which sums up the middle section of the trumps very well, I think. In his 'Promenade', two lovers stroll through the country side lost in love's intoxicating spell, yet never far behind, Death is lurking. Walter L. Strauss, in a commentary on this piece said: "The figure of Death does not necessarily indicate a warning to lovers, as this was not customary in the fifteenth century. Death was, however, frequently pictured as a reminder that life on earth should not be solely devoted to pleasure and luxury." This statement altered my view of the meaning of the middle trumps somewhat. The message is not, "Hey

---

1   see for instance here: http://i180.photobucket.com/albums/x172/melanchollic_photos/templeoftarot.jpg

Buddy, you're gonna fuck up and die!" It isn't a warning, but a reminder. Enjoy life's pleasures and one's successes, but keep an eye on the big picture.

Around my neighborhood an artist has been posting some signs. Right on my block he posted one that reads: TOTAL NUDITY FROM 2:00 TO 6:00 EXCEPT FOR SOCKS. It lasted a few hours since he placed it right in front of a catholic school. My point is that when people go berserk because of the Christian content of the tarot it is because these story lines transcend Christianity. These are Western values, relevant even from a secular point of view. Now, allow me to get biographical. If I understand correctly, at one time you were living in Mexico, and then you moved to Japan. Did you get a sense of how the people in these two countries approached divination? Did you have any experiences worth mentioning?

That's hilarious! "Except for socks!" Yes. The 'morals' of the tarot do transcend a strictly Christian frame, despite the yummy chocolate having been poured into a Jesus shaped mold! These same virtues were valued by the ancient Greeks, and Fortuna is of course derived from a Roman goddess. We just have to get over the shape and enjoy the chocolate.

In both Mexico and Japan, also Korea and China, I've found people are far more utilitarian in what they ask about. 90% of the questions I get in Japan are about potential romance. "When will I get married?" "Where will I meet my wife?" I've gotten some interesting questions like, "Is the Fairlady Z a good car?" "What breed of dog should I buy?" "Which shop sells the most reasonable hammers?" even a few about deaths, "When will I/my father/my mother die?" It's very much like the sorts of questions you see in old astrology manuals, like William Lilly's, "Where is my stolen fish?" I don't think a lot of modern Tarot readers know how to handle a question like "Which shop sells the most reasonable hammers?"

I've made it a point to try traditional divination methods when I'm overseas. Generalizing somewhat, they tend to be short and sweet. When asked where to get the most reasonable hammers, they say "Mao's Hardware." You pay, they bow. Finished.

I went with a few Westerners to try a traditional Korean fortune teller some years ago. The girl who went first told the man how she felt anxious and couldn't find her bearings, and wanted to reconnect with her sister, and also her step-mother, and was putting on weight, and didn't have much confidence with her new job.

The man immediately replied, "Mao's Hardware!" Just kidding. He did look confused as hell though. He didn't know how to handle a question like that. He seemed to have been trying to find the specific thing she wanted to know. She kept spiraling in fuzzy emotional limbo.

I forgot to mention that our understanding of The Lover card seems to be informed by the LOVE IS A JOURNEY metaphor. That is why the choice between vice and virtue, between women, etc., is understood as we being at a 'crossroad'. If Love has us as travelers, that is, as active actors moving along a path and sorting out all kinds of obstacles, Death, at the polar opposite you suggested, has us as passive objects at the mercy of an external force. Our understanding of Death as an skeleton harvesting the land with a scythe, seems to be informed by the CAUSES ARE PHYSICAL FORCES primary metaphor. When we map the bodily experience of exerting force over an object unto the subjective judgement of achieving a purpose, we see Death as the executor hand of the Grim Reaper, but we also start seeing many other, more contemporary, meanings in the card: 'digging' down into the soil/ unconscious, 'breaking through', 'severing' ties with the past, etc. (Obviously, the LOVE IS A JOURNEY metaphor informs our reading of the lower half of The Lover card. If we were to focus on Cupid, which occupies a big portion of the card's upper half, the CAUSES ARE PHYSICAL FORCES metaphor will also become relevant, since we won't be choosing the object of our love, but Cupid will 'make us' fall in love with someone).

Notice that I am not saying that this is what these cards mean, but that the way we unconsciously make inferences allows for a rather intuitive reading of these cards, especially if we take them out of context.

I once used the tarot to help a woman to re-do her kitchen. We went from "what kind of wood to choose for the floor" to "which contractor would do a better job"? It is fairly simple to define things like that if you have the client picking one card for each option, and then you compare the qualitative feelings of these images. It is not the kind of questions I am usually asked, and I don't really find them interesting, but I took it as a therapeutic session. The woman was under a lot of stress because of her job, she was about to move to a different country, she wanted to leave her apartment in mint condition to rent it for a higher price, and she had no one to talk to about any of this. The reading gave her the answer she was seeking, but more importantly, it allowed her to vent.

Sometimes I suspect that, in the Western world, readings have become a luxury item, while in other cultures they are still a necessity.

Christian Bök, one of my favorite poets, wrote: "For 'pataphysics, any science sufficiently retarded in progress must seem magical". The phrase in itself is a pun on Arthur C. Clarke's, "Any sufficiently advanced technology is indistinguishable from magic". But then, is it not more evocative to suspect the magic in that which is dated, knowing that our amnesic history will always have a few lagoons, than to be blown away by what we don't yet understand but will be unavoidably unveiled to us?

In some ways, studying the "old magic" is more a matter of learning to overcome our preconceptions of what we think that magic was, and learning a new way of seeing. I did a survey some years ago of pre-modern Western astrology and found it fascinating how the supposed system worked. It was like a new language, one completely different than our modern one, even the language of modern astrology, which took something that made perfect logical sense in its given paradigm, and tried to attach it to some basis in "science" and has resulted in the worst sort of nonsense.

I guess I'm a black sheep, as I never saw the TdM Love Card as being a choice between two options, probably because I had studied Greek philosophy before encountering the image. It seemed the man was surrounded by three options – Eros (Cupid), Philia (to the right), and Agape (to the left). I wonder if the word *Lamovrevx* may actually mean "The Loves", as in the three types of classical Love. Obviously, I lean toward literalism (laugh). I later discovered the TdM card is based on Alciato's popular Emblem for Faithfulness.

I want to pick on something you said before, about the practical nature of these questions people from other cultures ask readers about. Why do you think we tend to ask more 'existential' questions? Do you think that this may be the result of one hundred years of psychoanalysis?

Yes, I think much of the worldview of psychology has influenced the way we look at things. I remember Lucy from the *Peanuts* comics back in the 70s, who was always psychoanalyzing the other characters. I also think we have become far more self-centered than our ancestors. We are much less focused on useful tasks like getting a good hammer so we can be of use to our family and neighbors, but instead on why we don't have the happiness we've come to believe we are entitled to.

Also, I would like to know, what made you interested in the tarot in the first place?

What made me interested in the tarot in the first place? Oh, that's easy! It was Jane Seymour!

Do you care to elaborate?

I see you're not a James Bond fan! Jane Seymour was an actress who played one of the "Bond Girls", who was a Tarot card reader, called Solitaire. I was crazy about her when I was 14.

They had a special deck made for the film (*Live and Let Die*), and later, US Games I believe, sold it as the '007 Tarot'. That was my first deck. It had non-illustrated pips, and very little in the way of added esoteric overlays, so it was a pretty good deck in those respects. I had studied a bit of card magic, so I could always pull the death card and predict my friends deaths. We were all into Heavy Metal then, so that was "way cool"!

At Aeclectic Tarot forum you shared a method to read the tarot that you defined as 'the conundrum'. As with anything of real importance, it isn't clear if you are joking or if you are being serious. I any case, your method bears lots of resemblance with some Ericksonian techniques. Erickson would tell a patient: "go to the top of a mountain and wait there until it happens", leaving it to the patient the task of figuring out what, if anything, was supposed to happen. The thing is, most of the times the patients would actually experience some sort of epiphany that was no doubt self-prompted, with Erickson simply creating the space for them to be more receptive, or to pay more attention. I also believe that, given Erickson's authority, and given how easily our respect for authority could evolve into faith, people actually gave more importance to any happenstance occurring during the prescribed time. Variations of this technique would include the prescription of breakthroughs happening on a certain day of the week, or while experiencing a certain color, or sound. I want to know if you are aware of these techniques. If not, how did you came up with 'the conundrum'?

I have only one suggestion. When you say:

There are many ways to read Tarot. This one is one of the most profound, as the cards speak directly to you, and only to you. Only you can understand this message. I can not know what the cards are telling you. This message is for you, and you alone. I am merely translating the images into words for you. This message may not make any sense to you at first, and may require you reflect on what it means. No one has ever failed to come to the realization of the cards' message. It may be immediately obvious, or it may take a day or two of careful reflection to understand. Most people will 'get' the message within a week, usually less. In a few rare instances it has taken as long as three weeks. Call me as soon as you understand the message, or if you haven't understood within a week, call me and we'll work through it together.

I would say:

"There are many ways to read Tarot. This one is one of the most profound, as the cards speak directly to you, and only to you. Only you can understand this message. I can not know what the cards are telling you. This message is for you, and you alone. I am merely translating the images into words for you. I wonder if this message will make any sense to you at first. I wonder when you will be ready to understand this message. I wonder if it will be immediately obvious, or if it will take a day or two of careful reflection to understand it. I wonder if you will 'get' the message within a week, or in less time. Call me as soon as you understand the message, or if you haven't understood it within a week, call me and we'll work through it together."

When you "wonder" about whether something is going to happen, you are implicitly suggesting that it is going to happen. You are suggesting that it is a matter of time, or willingness, but the options become 'now or later'. The option of not getting is is out of the picture. Wondering when the person may be ready to understand the message puts all the pressure on them, but not the blame. It is not your fault they aren't getting it, and it isn't their fault either, they may just not be ready yet. But that is O.K. It is only a matter of time for them to be ready.

Even if you made the whole thing up as a joke, this can be a powerful technique, not as a standard bread-and-butter style of readings, but for certain situations. In a way, it can be as potent as forcing the Death card!

I'm glad you saw that post, I thought you'd enjoy it. No, I wasn't joking. The "conundrum" is real!

Yes, I know a bit about Erickson. This method came about, firstly by just using the trumps as an "instant proverb machine". Three cards are drawn – subject/verb/object. I tried to keep my readings rather literal. For example, Fool – World – Temperance becomes "Moderation Lives Through Folly." I loved the way some of the results were like riddles. They reminded me of Zen Koans. I'd been a serious student of Zen some years ago, even gaining the privilege of being admitted to study at one of the Honzan, or big monastic training centers in Kyoto. Don't worry ladies! I didn't have to take the vow of celibacy (wink). I understood the effect giving one of these 'riddles' could have on someone. I threw a few out there, and got some interesting results. How can you not get interesting results when you tell someone to meditate on "Folly Emboldens Nobility" after they've asked about patching things up with their father (laugh)!? Oddly, Westerners tend to take to the "conundrum effect" a lot better than Japanese. Interesting, eh?

Now, that is interesting. I would guess the Japanese people would be more inclined to apply receiver-oriented communication, in which you are supposed to fill in the gaps, and not be told everything.

What you are proposing interests me a lot. One of the things I struggle the most with is how to incorporate more silence into my readings. Proverbs grow in the untold. It is hard sometimes, when a client has paid for one full hour, to give them silence. But silence is a very important part of any communication. Especially when you know that the most effective things are those things we say in the off-beat moments. You can spend hours telling a woman how great she looks, and all it takes is a vendor saying "let me see, what do we have in Extra-Large!" to demolish her confidence.

Now, subject/verb/object. Brilliant. A little visual sentence, or a visual haiku. In that case, I would rather talk to my client about the haiku than about the cards! I like to think that any random sequence of cards is an anagramming of the original trump series. It is like finding a new word inside of an old one. Like finding 'Cheery Needle' in Reece Hendley. By the way, you only carry with you the vowel E: E E E E like the trail a fox would leave on the snow! I think the literality of a reading is very important, especially because our words are rarely taken literally! When you say "Moderation Lives Through Folly", the person in front of you may be seeing herself doing a head stand and being fed beer through a funnel! That is the beauty of a short sentence like that one. It is an oil stain.

What I would like to know is: what are your expectations when you do a reading like that? How do you think they match your sitter's expectations? Talking of expectations, the other day I was thinking of airplanes, and how, as we sit in them, we are given a set of instructions "for our own safety" which in truth is intended to make the crew's job easier. I thought of crafting my own list, to make my job easier. This is what I got, so far:

To Better Enjoy Your Tarot Experience, Please Remember:

> *– A detour starts with one false step. Don't worry about the future. Focus on where you are standing now.*
>
> *– Behind a worldly question there is a deeper question, and behind that, there is fear. It is that fear that the tarot addresses.*
>
> *– Images remind us of things. The rest is up to us.*

In which context you do this kind of readings?

Well, it might be worth mentioning, I always read for free, and that most of my readings are done in public. I have a set of beer and wine stained Grimaud TdM trumps I carry around in one of those nice leather cases Flornoy sells for his Dodal trumps. (I keep those in the box.) Over half of my readings are at bars, pubs, or coffee shops with several other people sitting there. Obviously those situations have a different atmosphere than a one-on-one reading in your dining room. I keep these readings light, and amusing. They are for "entertainment purposes only". I really only read 'privately' for people I know, or sometimes for people I've read for before outside who want a more intimate reading.

The first few conundrums I tried were "trial balloons", so I tried them with any and all sorts of questions. I tried them at parties, and at home. I tried them with people wanting a reading for laugh, with people who took it very seriously, with friends, and with people who wanted to 'mock the weirdo'.

Generalizing somewhat, the method seems to get best results with the 'true believer', the sort who would pay to have a reading. Generally it seems to be helpful for situations where people have some sort of dilemma and can't make a decision. I think focusing on the 'conundrum' takes some of the pressure off of having to make a hard decision, and the 'epiphany' is their just being able to see what they really want, without having to worry about making the wrong decision.

Obviously this is not the method to use for a question like, "Which shop sells the most reasonable hammers?" Although I did throw a couple out there for questions of that nature. In the interest of science, of course.

The more I think about the subject/verb/object structure the more I think it addresses beautifully a problem of syntax in that, for me, spreads never really solved. I tend to focus too much on the sequences of the cards as words: trumps as vowels, pips as consonants, where the little corners of some letters resemble the little corners of some other letters: the letter M is like two letters I holding hands, the letter X like a letter V drinking from a pond, which is just a way to see in very graphic terms what is going on between all these details in the cards: The Queen of Deniers is holding the Ace of Deniers in her hand, and if she is not careful, Le Bateleur could vanish it, or switch it for a fake one instead. I really like your idea of giving one of the cads the attributes of a verb, which is a way of making that card able to carry the narrative forward in a way that gives the other two cards very specific roles.

You mentioned two things that are interesting to me. One is that you read for free. I suspect that gives the reader lots of freedom to use silence. The other one is that you mainly read with the trumps alone. I know you have a very well thought-out method to read with the pips. I like the pips too, but about three months ago something interesting happened to me. I was at my usual coffee shop, reading for a lady I have seen every Friday for the last four years, when she interrupted the reading to compliment some guy's T-shirt. This guy had a T-shirt that said: "Fuck You Very Much!" and she thought it was hilarious. The guy came over our table and started talking about the T-shirt, then about some other thing, and then about something else, rambling enough as to make evident he wasn't O.K. 'up there'. He saw my tarot, asked if I was giving readings and said he would wait outside for one. The lady and I continued our reading. I could see the guy outside, waiting. When I was done, the coffee shop's owner came to me and told me to be careful about that guy since he was kind of dangerous. Do you know what my reaction was? I put the pips back in their case. Isn't that something? I instinctively decided that I only needed powerful images if I was to deal with a dangerous guy. The guy never came back. But I learned a lot about what I expect from these images, thanks to one simple gesture.

Why do you only use the trumps? Is it a matter of their fitting right into your pocket, or there is something else?

I've come to view the tarot as a work in two distinct parts. The evidence tells us that the regular 52 card deck came to Europe from North Africa, and that the Tarot trumps were a later innovation. Obviously they worked well together as a game, but as a system of esoteric knowledge or as a divination system no one has been able to concoct a really impressive way to combine the two sets. Each set has the feel of a harmonious whole to me, so I tend to use them separately. I always found it odd how some tarot people think that if they can't use "the whole deck" they aren't good tarot readers. If I remember correctly, one early divination method just used the Coin pips. Maybe I'll think of a way to just use courts. I love to play around and build little systems.

The trumps, of course, are what most people think of when they think of tarot, so they're great for when I'm out and about. The yellow spotty circles and criss-crossing thingys just don't have the same visual appeal as a skeleton chopping' heads or an angel making cocktails, do they?

Exactly. You can't grab a madman's attention with a bunch of scimitars that look the same if you look at either Eight or Six of them. My understanding of all these things changes about every 72 hours, but at the moment, I think I understand those designers of new decks. If you want to say what the tarot says, a tarot like the Noblet or the Conver says it perfectly in 22 images. There is no need to improve or change anything. But if you want to say something else, well, you are welcome to scramble the whole thing up as you please. I think I agree with you in that, so far, none of these new propositions seems as impressive as the original one.

Now, back to your subject/verb/object scheme, I was thinking that what any middle card accomplishes, as a verb, in a three-card sequence is what the three Moral Virtues accomplish within the whole trump cycle. By describing attitudes they define actions and move the hierarchy up, don't you think?

Interesting view of the virtues as verbs! I was getting some great insights into the trump's 'moral teachings' the other day by using the bottom rung (referring to the footnoted diagram earlier) as subject, the middle trumps as verbs, and the top rung as object. For example the Fool, Death, and the Devil form a vertical row. Could the message be, "Through Sin the Foolish do Perish"? Or down on the Pope's end, "By Way of Love the Faithful enter the Kingdom of God", and so on… You get the idea. Every row seemed to have a gem of inspiration.

I think what you are sharing turns the tarot into a very viable, and useful, literary tool. I don't mean it in the sense of using the tarot to write books, but using it to generate living poetry.

I would like to end this conversation by asking you: we have all these proverbs, these ideas, these virtues... Then there is all the research that leads to these conclusions, and then, the countless encounters with other people through these images and through these ideas. In which way, if any, has the tarot made you a better person?

One effect the tarot has had on me has been in helping me overcome a lot of prejudices I had about "religion", and even morality itself. I doubt I would have bothered reading Aquinas without a curiosity about what those virtues were doing in "the Devil's Picture Book". After I'd read a bit about it, I thought, "Wow, there's more to this than a bunch of nuts picking up rattlesnakes and screaming 'I Believe'.

An easy way I've found to bring those virtues into focus, for ourselves or others, is to interpret them as 'solutions' when we read the cards. "Here's Temperance. She warns us about the problems we cause ourselves through our excesses. How do you think this could be relevant with your situation here?" No doubt something will come to mind!

I definitely think I've absorbed some of the 'lessons' of the trumps, and I do make an effort to be more fair, courageous, and moderate. Of course, when a beautiful woman has caught my eye, I'm right back to my 'Juggler' ways, playing the 'Fool' (laugh).

New York / Nagoya, Japan, July 2010

"Personally I am interested in the poetic charge of magic and the magical charge of poetry."

A conversation with ERIK DAVIS, culture critic, author

Let me start by asking you: is it poetry 'perfected magic', or is it magic 'perfected poetry'?

If we could hop into that way-back machine I am sure we could cruise back through the centuries to find, fairly rapidly, a point where magic and poetry were one thing. But today I believe they perfect one another partly by remaining in some ways separate – or rather, as overlapping fields that resonate but do not collapse into one another. Poetry has its own claims and dynamics, its own practices and presences. Magic as well. (Of course they both have multiple claims as well). But the relationship between poetic magic and magical poetry is clearly very tight.

Personally I am interested in the poetic charge of magic and the magical charge of poetry, but I am neither a good poet nor a dedicated magician. The orders of poetry and the orders of magic, as the California poet Robert Duncan would say, are not the same, but they correspond. Correspondence is the key, the shared spell of metaphor, of linking this and that, this image to that concept, this gesture to that ancient persona. In *The H.D. Book*, Duncan compares Poetry and Hermetic alchemy: "The rhymes of this poetry are correspondences, workings of figures and patterns of figures in which we apprehend the whole we do not see." That's part of the key: both systems remain open. The presences they call are in the field but not identified with the things we make that conjure the field.

In my personal process the tarot became a gateway to the alphabet. I mean, I called on the alphabet to understand the tarot, only to end up rejoicing in the alphabet. There is a quote from Vito Acconci I like: "Poetry is an attempt to get through language and arrive at a state of pre-language – it's a cry, a gasp, a screech", to what I would say, why not a gesture? The tarot is full of gestures, and when one studies the Marseille tradition, one finds that these gestures contain many words, the words we use to describe them, words that are homonyms to other words, which are also metaphors for many other words. All these words blue-print thought pat-

terns, but I like the virtuality of their relationships. I sympathize with what you said about not being a good poet, because I can't bring myself to believe in one definitive arrangement of words long enough to call it a 'poem'. I need to keep shuffling.

I was very taken by some of Jack Spicer's thoughts on the tarot. I like his notion of letting a certain voice take over us, like that fungus that is inhaled by the Stick Ant and grows inside its brain until it ends up controlling the ant. I might disagree in the need for the 'outerness', since I suspect that one of Western art accomplishments has been to make creation a secular process. Perhaps we are our own fungus. But in any case, he talks about letting that voice take you 'beyond' yourself. Right there, I can't help but see many parallels between the dictation of poetry and the reading of tarots. I confess I never think too much in differences.

Speaking of similarities and differences, to me, one of the most useful books to 'get' the tarot was Scott McClouds's Understanding Comics. Perhaps that's one of the reasons why I found your comparison of the tarot to a comic strip so exciting. You probably know this, but Italo Calvino's initial idea when he wrote his Castle of Crossed Destinies was to add a third part to the Castle and the Tavern: a Motel of Crossed Destinies, for which he would use comic strips instead of tarot cards. Calvino was somehow hinting at that connection you made in your article. Then we have Alejandro Jodorowsky, of course, a comic author who is also a tarot author. Now, I would say that, even today, comics are some sort of fringe art. The tarot is also some sort of fringe phenomenon. But the fact that both are fringe manifestations doesn't means they necessarily mix well. I know lots of tarot enthusiasts who would be offended, or even put down, by your comparison. It brings to mind last Saturday. I took my kids to a vampire-fangs workshop. They cast their own fangs in a professional FX workshop. They were the only two kids among a group of adults, and I could tell they kind of ruined the experience for some of the other guys. I mean, to be 40 years old and to want to be a vampire is a very fragile dream. If you bring kids into that dream you are somehow underlining the childish side of it, and if this makes you blink for too long, the whole dream collapses. Do you think that comparing the RWS tarot to Little Nemo in Slumberland can also threaten some people's occultist dream?

Possibly, but only if they weren't thinking very hard about either comic books or the tradition. Especially about comic books. Today comic books, aka graphic novels, are taken pretty seriously, more like cinema than the pulp kid's stuff that people think about generically. Part of the reason they have that fringe rep is that, even though they are a modern form (barely a century old) the attempt to tell stories with dense highly coded pictures is of course very old. Mayan codexes, medieval stained glass, and, yes, the tarot are within a broad stream of visual practices that reach back into myth and the deep imaginal life of human beings. Rather than "dragging down" Tarot into the realm of pulp children's lit, I think the comparison rather "raises up" comic art into a potential vehicle for esoteric lore and experience. Witness all the comic book writers and artists, from the Golden Age through the Alan Moores and Grant Morrisons of today, who are deeply immersed in esoteric lore and express it to varying degrees in their work—parts of *Promethea* are functionally identical to Tarot symbolism and experience, even if the images come already established in a linear form.

But I would also have the opposite response to those whose occultist dreams are threatened: your magic will be weak if it does not draw from the fringe, the marginal, the childish, the mad. Where else would the powers and presences flee to when rationalism and science unfurl their engines of disenchantment across the world? I love your story, because it makes me see the pathos of the 40 year old vampire wannabe. But I can also imagine another 40 year old "vampire" who exults in the fact that there is still something you can do as a 40 year old that is imaginative and frowned upon by adult society. There is still a margin to occupy! The presence of the child – or the trace of the comic book in the Tarot deck (which is quite obvious in many contemporary decks – is also a reason to celebrate.

I guess part of the low reputation comics still have may precisely come from the idea that a 'pauper's bible', any pictorial book, is intended for the intellectually impaired. This goes against the complexity and richness of contemporary graphic novels, or course. But still, don't you think we look down at pictorial forms of communication, like comics, codices or the tarot, due to some sort of 'alphabetic hubris'?

Sure some people still do that, a lot of them actually. But a lot of the ones that do are also addicted – and I do mean addicted – to television shows and popular cinema, whose motion does put them in a different category from pictorial literature but whose content is rarely more sophisticated. But yes: there is an alphabetic prejudice that we inherit from the Gutenberg galaxy. But really, in America anyway that galaxy is rapidly being eclipsed or at least supplemented with streams of images that often draw from the great ramshackle storehouse of the imagination – ie, the nation of images.

There is something else you mentioned that I think is important: the margin. Perhaps the most important element in comic strips is the only one that is invisible: the white frames between images. I would say that the amount of inferences one automatically makes when reading a comic book, going from one frame to the next one, makes these white frames the busiest space on the page. Here, a door opens. In the next frame, we see a corpse. Still, we understand what happened. A whole crime is being told in the white strip between these two images. One can see the same thing happening among tarot cards. Here we have The Lovers. The next card is The Devil. A whole story happens in the untold, the non-illustrated, in the crack between images. So, I wonder, do you think that finding these cracks, or watching them is part of the magician's job description?

Great question. Yes, absolutely. Magic is liminal: it takes place in between, in the leap, the breach. On the one hand this is the leap between things that are related in the poetic act of metaphoric correspondence and analogy: this thing (or gesture or scent or word) is *like* that thing (or emotion or image or presence). That *like* is the magician's bridge, the hermetic crossroads. But is there anything *in* it? There is so much *stuff* in magic – lists of correspondences, jars of herbs, packs of cards, images that fill up everything to their borders with content – but there is also a nothingness in magic, a pregnant void, a Buddhist "emptiness" that allows the truly surprising and lively connections to emerge. That's why most cards (maybe all the good decks) have borders around the images in addition to the natural borders created by the physical card edge: it is crucial for the poetic imagination to go wild but inside a border, a border which can delimit both the extent of the imagination *and* leave room for silence, for the white that is all colors.

As you pointed out, we consume images like no other culture in the history of humankind has done before, yet most of the time we have a rather passive attitude towards images. I see it happening with the tarot just as it happens with TV, the image comes to meet our eyes but we don't go 'out' to meet the image. There is something I have asked almost everyone I have had a conversation with, because I think it is key to understand our relationship with the tarot: what, if anything, do you expect from images in general?

Here I think the Jungian discussion of the image in active imagination, especially as it is elaborated by James Hillman, is really key. Not the whole archetypal kit and kaboodle, but the very practical relationship to the image that combines passivity and activity. Whether with dreams or the potent images we encounter in revery or poems or Tarot or things out of the corner of the eye, we must create a space, a clearing, of encounter, a place where our ego is not directing the show. But this is different than the passivity of watching TV, because it is a highly attentive (ie "active") passivity that calls out to something in the image, that lets the image bloom into a presence (if it wants to be). This is where magic (especially pathworking/scrying), the Tarot, poetry, and Jungian practices meet: they are united in the question: what does the image want? They learn to follow the image. This is why sometimes having a supernatural belief – that the cards are always right, that they are a message from the true heart of the world – is helpful, even if some of us (myself for example) can't spend much time there. Not because it is true, but because it encourages that polytheistic allowance of the image to do its own thing. But it can be done without such beliefs as well, and may be more wonderful for it.

Yesterday I was waiting to cross a street when I saw a woman coming my way that I felt immediately impelled to salute. As soon as I was about to say "hello" I froze. I realized then that I 'knew' that woman from a TV show. You mentioned that we have become addicted to TV and I would add that we possess now a whole storage of memories that aren't ours. They happened to Chevy Chase or Harrison Ford. I guess that at some point these memories could be useful (especially coming from Chevy Chase!), just as by picking tarot cards we can borrow a dream we can enact if our own dreams don't come to us. I could say I knew that woman on the street, from a 'dream'. Watching her on TV is like dreaming her. If we were to bring a Siberian shaman to our cities, and have him walking on our streets, he might end up thinking the Western world is the most spiritually developed place in the world. We broadcast our dreams, and we have more of a hundred channels to the underworld we can access through a remote. AT&T, Sprint and Verizon offer us several plans so we can talk to spirits all the time, we send our thoughts across the globe to people who we have never seen but know what we're thinking, Prada and Chanel provide us with talismans and potions to succeed in love and business, and we access the akashic records of Google whenever we need a piece of knowledge we don't possess. I know I am playing on Arthur C. Clarke's quote: "Any sufficiently advanced technology is indistinguishable from magic." But IF technology can be said to be, for us at least, a form of prosthetic magic, what is it that 'real' magic has that makes us feel we aren't getting it through our current gadgets and gimmicks? In other words, what promises are in magic that technology cannot fulfill?

For me it is precisely the open-ended, ambiguous "poetic" function that we have been talking about. This kind of meaning is not as programmed as consumer culture, and when it results in the invocation of active presences – when the images take command – there is an organic living quality to it that the rounds of technological simulacra very rarely have. (They can have them to, as in an excellent high-tech party where all the media go into creating a ritualistic ecstasy with cognitive punch.) When the computer or the robots on the corporate help lines "talk back" to me I know that they are algorithms; when the image in last night's dream returns during meditation and speaks to me, I know that it is not. Perhaps that distinction will erode eventually.

What is your earliest memory of tarot cards?

My first exposure, I believe, was an episode of the television show Kung Fu.

Finally, I would like to know, in your view, what do you think it is reasonable to expect from tarot cards that comic books can't give us?

The fact that the Tarot sequence is always new and unexpected gives it a multiplicity of possibilities that allows you to keep coming back to the "same" images over and over and finding new stories and new implications. For that reason, they can weave themselves into your actual life more readily. Because of the synchronistic framing of the performance of the cards – their "randomness – the analogy between them and comics utterly breaks down. The montage or correspondence between the panels is not directed by the artist or writer, but by your own heart and mind and subconscious. We become the bridge.

New York / currently exiled in Houston Texas (but Californian by birth),
September 2010

"I think reading Tarot is very much like singing: everyone can sing and most people are pretty awful. Some few people have a natural gift, others can work hard to develop a better-than-average talent into something transformational and thrilling."

A conversation with VALENTINA BURTON, magician, tarot reader

Why the tarot? Do you remember the first time you saw some tarot cards?

I have NO memory of the first time I saw Tarot cards; reading the Tarot grew out of my childhood fascination with reading playing cards. I have a very old IJJ deck that was probably given to me then. I sort of don't remember them not being in my world. I still love playing cards! They are so in-your-face direct. There is no wimpy bullshitting with playing cards! Tarot is great because you have more cards, more images (than a playing-card deck). I almost always read with card combining, so there is just more space for more-specific answers with Tarot.

I love playing cards too! As a matter of fact, and even when I love the looks of antique cards, I truly believe that a brand new pack of Bicycle playing cards is one of the most perfect design objects in the Western world! Now, it is precisely because you are "in the trenches" that I think that talking to you would be fascinating. If I understand correctly you do readings in a public setting four times a week. That on top of your private appointments. Are those two completely different kind of clients? Is there any difference, in your view, between the way a person who decides to get a reading in the spur of the moment and a person who makes an appointment in advance, and how each relates to you and to what you have to say?

Yes, I adore every kind of playing cards! I read fortunes with cards before I ever did any magic effects with them, and made the choice to be a professional magician because it seemed less strange than being a professional card reader... how's that for some goofy thinking? I was a magic/circus/comedy/variety performer for twenty-five years. I wore myself out, and have NO regrets about leaving that field.

I read at a luxury hotel in Dallas called Hotel Zaza, and the clientele there initially related to me completely differently than my private clients. I've been at the Hotel for five years, and I stay there because it keeps me humble. (And because I've become something of a Tourist Attraction... out-of-towners go see Where Kennedy Was Shot and then go see That Fortune Lady at Zaza)

Just last week, I had a woman plop down in the chair and loudly say "Well, this had better be really GOOD, for thirty dollars!" It was all I could do not to reply "My regular clients think I am underpriced at one hundred dollars. Go Away!"

It's a pretty masochistic thing, but getting feedback like that reminds me of what the Great Unwashed Masses think of what we do. They have no real frame of reference for what a solid reading can do for them, and why should they? By the time that woman left my table, she was ready to build me a Temple. Being able to do that requires I have solid chops as a Reader and not get lazy!

Since I've been at the Hotel for such a long time, I do have many insanely loyal Hotel clients, and they are constantly bringing new folks to see me; but the same dynamic plays out... the newbie will be polite and get a reading because their friend/business associate pushes them to, but they think it's all hogwash and bullshit. They sit in front of me like a stone, minimally mix my cards, and give off body language that tells anyone passing by that they think this is silly and not important, or they flirt with me. (How pathetic do you have to be to hit on the middle-aged card reader?) I read for them and when I'm done, they say "Wow. That's pretty amazing! How do you do that?" and then fill me in on their divorce/company reorganization/custody battle/crazy family member/new film/house remodel/sick doggy/drug lord boyfriend/book tour.

In the space of just fifteen minutes, the whole dynamic shifts. I'm probably just arrogant (what magician isn't?), but it's fun to do that, it feels powerful; and it keeps me really sharp. In my office, things are very different.

First, it's not easy to get an appointment with me, I limit the number of clients I will see in a day, and won't read on days I have a big party or late night at the Hotel; so clients feel lucky to get in... they don't tend to be stinky and irritating because of that. My office is a very specific atmosphere (it feels like New Orleans in about 1936), and that makes it my turf, they are special guests in my world, if they don't behave they can't come back. My Hoodoo certificate from LuckyMojo hangs on my wall, and nobody in their right mind would cross a Hoodoo Gal, right? So they behave. My biggest issue at the office is scheduling and making clients understand that I will not see them more often than every six months.

So, to be more succinct: After all is said and done, there is no difference between how both types of clients relate to me or what I say. The only difference is time. Office clients are ready to get a real reading, and Hotel clients have a bunch of crappy ideas in the way of a real reading. Once the crappy ideas are blown away, the final effect is the same. Hotel clients just waste more time getting there.

Do clients react differently to playing cards than to the tarot? How would you characterize that difference?

Currently, I only will use playing cards if they are somehow more appropriate for divination. Usually, that will mean something like an event with a Western theme (where I would costume with a Miss Kitty outfit, something like that. No tarot cards in the Old West!) Clients usually don't like playing cards as much as I do. They almost always view them as too mundane, not magical enough. Tarot gives them a thrill, it's exciting for them. (So Spooky!)

Most modern folks are actually surprised to see someone telling fortunes with playing cards. It used to be very common (reading with playing cards). Now, if I pull out a playing-card deck, guests will assume I'm getting ready to play Texas Hold Em (and they never think I'm about to do a magic trick.)

Another reason to use playing cards or Lenormand cards with a client IS that fear factor; goosey clients (again, this client is frequently the Host of a trade show or other event, worried What People Will Think) prefer non-Tarot divination. Tarot has had such a run of creepy-movie-type publicity that it really has a Public Relations problem right now!

People (again, I am referring to the General Public, just in my experience) think a reading with playing cards or Lenormand cards is cute and charming; they are more shaky about Tarot, it seems more SERIOUS to them (There is that DEATH card…!)

Do you think the fact your readings are so matter of fact or down to earth could somehow reflect the fact that you read with the Lenormand deck? Sometimes it is hard to get real when one is looking at 'Judgement' or 'Temperance', but a house, a sailboat and a hand extending an envelope are pretty straightforward. I have always marveled at how close to storytelling all these fortunetelling decks are (Petit Lenormand, Kipperkarten, Sibillas, etc).

I primarily read with the RWS deck (the Original, love the colors, love Pixie's artwork). I think my readings are very down-to-earth because I read in combinations (triplets), and they just speak to me in a very practical way, they are very clear. I look at them, and the story the cards are trying to tell will just seem so obvious. It goes beyond the "meanings" (and beyond the picture), although I consider myself a more old-fashioned Reader, not at all modern or "intuitive" in my card interpretations. I like RWS because clients like them. They are very pretty.

I think it is very possible to "get real" with those hugely-full-of-meaning Majors like "Temperance", "Judgement", or "Hierophant". It just depends on how you read. I will occasionally use Lenormand cards, I love them too! The reading you get with a Lenormand deck is similar to a Playing Card reading. Again, old-fashioned and to-the-point, no fluffy stuff, no New Age thinking.

Do you use any kind of system to read with these decks, or do you go by the image?

Are you asking if I use a layout? I will sometimes use that very old square layout, where you begin with the Questioner's card, and then look at what is close by, then farther away, etc. It always works, but sometimes I think it takes too long to do. For about a year, I began every session looking at the Querent's Natal Chart and then that particular layout of Lenormand, before breaking into Tarot to answer the client's particular questions. For the last couple of years that has just seemed too laborious and time-consuming. My clients want to get in, get what they need, and get on with their lives.

Many times for a party or corporate event I will use Lenormand or some other oracle deck, because they are so interesting and unusual (and non-threatening and pretty). The alleged historical connection of the Lenormand is fun to talk about with guests, too. I will typically use a small layout plan of triplets, and vary it depending on the number of guests. I almost always need to read fast and accurately, and I base the layout on that (how much time I have per guest).

I don't think I have answered your question about "system vs. image"! I guess for me, the system IS the image, along with the old meanings for that card, mixed with the other cards that share its placement. I both know and read with the classical meanings, and use them as a jumping-off place for something more. I just re-read that, and it sounds ridiculous!

I think trying to explain how I do something as personal as divination is like an artist explaining how they are inspired to create a piece. Maybe explanation is not possible.

How do people react to these images? Do you explain what they are?

How do people react to a Lenormand reading? The same way they do to a Tarot reading. Normal people (meaning, not-into-tarot) will either start chattering away about how amazing it is that those little cards just presented exactly what is going on in their life (and these are the folks that are difficult to get out of the chair, and will not shut up...), OR they will silently look shocked for a moment (sometimes blushing or coughing), and then stumble away from my table muttering something like "Well, Little Lady, I don't believe in any of this stuff, but you hit the nail right on the head" (Remember, I am in Texas...)

I think you are tapping into something very important: people fear the tarot. Is there anything that can be done about it? What do you think?

I feel that the only thing any of us can do (meaning, Tarot Readers), is to be the very best Readers we can possibly be, especially those of us who read in a public setting. We don't control anything else! I *do* believe that more public readers, reading for folks who don't usually seek out Tarot readings, helps... but this work is so *hard*! Why would any sane card Reader take this up?

We need to give our clients the amazing experience the cards can deliver, without any ego from us (I know, that's hilariously funny coming from ME! I can't help it, I have Leo rising.) What I mean is that quality of stepping aside and letting the reading come through.

When folks have an amazing, powerful, transformational experience with a Reader, they will tell others. Eventually, (hopefully) the general public opinion will see the cards as an adventure, not a threat. To add just a bit to that, if I may... I really don't want Tarot to become ordinary, commonplace, so I really don't think it's advantageous to have Tarot *everywhere*. I like very much that it is special, and not everyone can read cards well.

I think reading Tarot is very much like singing: everyone can sing and most people are pretty awful (just watch American Idol auditions!) Some few people have a natural gift, others can work hard to develop a better-than-average talent into something transformational and thrilling.

I would like to ask you one last question: what do you think it is that makes your readings memorable?

This is just my opinion, and I can only answer this question based on feedback I get from my clients: I think my readings and the way I read are memorable because I am pretty earthy and direct (My business partner David would probably say TOO earthy and direct.)

I think the way I read is very old-fashioned. I am very to-the-point, and I do many things that make more New-Age-Ish Readers flinch. (I will PREDICT! I will use the cards to see how another person thinks and feels! I will mix Tarot with Lenormand cards and Astrology! I am a *very bad girl!*)

I think the way you know a reading was *memorable* is if the client returns, and if they recommend you to others. David and I both have a very high rate of repeat and referral clients. Those clients refer/repeat because we give them stuff they can really use in REAL LIFE. I have a long-time client who actually tapes all readings and then has his secretary transcribe them. He delights in showing me "This is what you said, *exactly*; and this is what happened!" He thinks I don't believe I'm as good as he thinks I am; so to him the *memorable* is all about accuracy.

For most of our clients, it seems that *memorable* is about useful.

So, I guess my point is that memorable is relative, just like everything else!

New York / Dallas, Texas, August-September 2010

"Tarot is a logical system of divination that can be immediately apprehended and does not require, in my view, any special esoteric training or even reading of books, many of which, I think, are bogus, as are the reformulated occultist decks."

A conversation with STEPHEN SCHWARTZ, journalist, columnist, author

I would like to know, to satisfy my own curiosity, what do you remember from Allen Ginsberg?

I remember that every time Allen met me, from the time I was 17 to the time I was, literally, 36, he made passes at me. Every time I laughed and brushed him off. He and Gary Snyder taught me to read the *Heart Sutra* in Japanese on top of Mount Tamalpais above San Francisco in 1966 or 1967. I remember a great deal more. I was not a great fan of Allen's writing – I preferred Kerouac. I knew almost every one of the Beats personally except Kerouac, whom my mother knew and disliked because of his drunkenness.

It would be a long story. Is this for any project in particular?

My question to you was more of a personal nature, since I am interested in Ginsberg's work and personality. I am interested in poetry. I am interested in a traditional poetry form called tarocchi appropriati. *This consisted of using the tarot trumps (the 22 famous cards) to improvise poems with. The poet will give one or more cards to a person, and then he will say, in poetic form, why he chose that particular card for that person. There were several variations of the game but that is the gist of it. We are talking about something that started right when the tarot was created, around 1440, and continued up the 16th Century.*

I like *Howl*, but not all the rest of Ginsberg's work. Then there was that posthumous book of poems. I liked it, but I don't think I can be objective, knowing that those where the poems of somebody who knew he was dying. There was a playful, careless, quality in them that I found refreshing.

I was for about 18 or so years a devotee of the Marseille tarot, which I read intuitively and based on gematria or Kabbalistic numerology. I also used the 22 major arcana to compose poetry, but rather by casting cards and then basing a sequence of events or sentiments on them. Not simplistic. Sometimes I would invent the sequence of events and then cast the cards and match them up by simply paralleling the event and the arcanum without attempting to draw or elucidate an esoteric meaning, so see if some new meaning would emerge

I became a Muslim and am now a Sufi. We disapprove of tarot but are not hostile about it.

I never liked much modern American poetry. Snyder, McClure, and Lamantia were exceptions but even they lost their lustre for me. I still greatly admire some of Patchen and some of Rexroth. I became a fan of Spanish, French, Catalan, Russian, Croatian, and Albanian poetry, in that order and in the original languages, as well as Sufi poets like Haxhi Bektashi Veli.

McClure had a set of special cards made called *DreamTable* that used words to create new combinations. He also created a luscious set of psychedelic cards with the artist Bruce Conner.

Jerome Rothenberg has explored the poetic 'wisdom' of gematria like no one. How did you use gematria to work with the Marseille tarot?

I did gematria with the major arcana by correlating them to the Hebrew alphabet and its numerical values. But this was a very, very long time ago – 40 years.

I only work with the Marseille tarot and never had any interest in any of the decks that came later on. But I don't use Kabbala or any other external system. As a matter of fact I have been trying to piece back what can be defined as the 'Marseille tarot's optical language' which emerges from the visual symmetries we find in these images. We can see it as playing with the visual homophonies we find in a card sequence, and ascribing experiential meaning to them. There are a few authors in the 20th Century who have written about this: Paul Marteau, Tchalai Unger, Alejandro Jodorowsky, Philippe Camoin, Jean-Claude Flornoy. All of them are either French or based in France. In fact, the Marseille tarot's optical language seems to resonate with what in France they call La langue des oiseaux, *the language of the birds, which is also a form of word-play based on the consonance of shape, or verbal* homophony. *Incidentally, some people suggest that* La langue des oiseaux *has some connection with The Conference of the Birds, that beautiful poem by Farud'din Attar; but there doesn't seem to be any practical connection there. A couple of contemporary French authors have dealt with* La langue des oiseaux. *One is Yves Monin, the other one is Luc Bigé. There is lots of enchantment about the French language on what they explore and, I suspect, a bit of made up stuff. As you might see, it is all rather removed from the occult!*

You seem to have witnessed an interesting moment in American poetry, and I would be interested in your memories of how the emergence of what we now call the New Age informed or was informed by these poets.

The language of the birds is a concept securely present in Sufism and Kabbalah. It is said that King Solomon understood the language of the birds, in both Judaism and Islam. There are two notable medieval authors who wrote long poems with similar titles – the *Parliment of Birds* of Chaucer and the *Conference of Birds* by Farud'din Attar, the very great Persian Sufi, and many enthusiastic types assume similarities without reading the books, but having examined them I can say that the only item in common is the title, though Chaucer traveled in Muslim Spain.

The surrealist poet André Breton championed an eccentric author named Jean-Pierre Brisset who wrote a book claiming to decipher the language of birds. I had it 10 years ago but have not looked at it in years. I believe there is an excerpt in Breton's *Anthology of Black Humor*. Rexroth, Duncan, and Lamantia founded the post-1945 new age in America based on the influence of Buddhism.

How did you became in contact with the tarot?

Through interest in esotericism, occultism, and Surrealism.

Did Lamantia, Rexroth or Duncan ever talk to you about the tarot?

Rexroth never mentioned the tarot to me. When I knew him he was coming out of Buddhism, had turned first to Anglo-Catholicism, and finally to Greek Orthodoxy, in which faith he died, although his funeral service was Russian Orthodox. I never got a straight answer as to why that happened but at the time I was not so interested. I believe it is credible that the Greeks would not accept him – they are very particular – but that the Russians were short on congregants in San

Francisco then. I did attend the funeral reception, which is called a *panikhida*. Rexroth did say to me that his basic attraction to Orthodox Christianity had to do with the Gospels having been originally written in Greek. He also had an interest in Renaissance esoterism. At the specific moment he told me that about the Gospels I was more interested in Roman Catholicism and he knew quite a bit about that, too.

Duncan's crowd was quite entranced with the tarot at some point – I was not as close to them as I now wish I had been. I always considered Duncan a better poet than Lamantia. One of the great regrets of my life is that their circle was considered close to anyone not gay – I would have liked to have studied more with them. My parents knew them very well. The science fiction writer Philip K. Dick was part of their circle but was kind of driven away because he was not gay.

Because of Lamantia's rather peculiar and even questionable association with the French Surrealists, about which I am now convinced he lied, Lamantia would allude to the tarot from time to time and I believe there are references to it in his poetry. I have a recollection that he had one of the occultist decks, like the Waite, and that he had a *taroccho* set from Italy. I think he said his father or other relatives played *taroccho*, a card game using some but not all of the tarot cards. I also have a vague recollection of purchasing a *Marseille* deck for him as a gift.

In the early 70s I think the only one in the circle of which Lamantia, myself, and Paul Nagy were members in San Francisco who actively did tarot readings was me, but seldom publicly. Maybe once at a party at my house and a few times in a cafe. And I don't recall doing it for money but may have once or twice.

I have not touched a tarot deck for use in divination since 1984, except for one time in 2005 or so when Paul Nagy and I were at a party in DC.

Tarot is a logical system of divination that can be immediately apprehended and does not require, in my view, any special esoteric training or even reading of books, many of which, I think, are bogus, as are the reformulated occultist decks. It is what it is and what it is is extremely obvious; a map of the strengths and weaknesses of general personality types plus the immediate fortunes of four social classes: aristocrats, financiers, people of religion, and land workers. Aristocrats and land workers are male, financiers and people of religion are female. These were the four social classes of ancient Sumeria, in which monetary tribute and religion were administered by temple prostitutes. The major arcana come from the Hebrew alphabet but one does not need to know the Hebrew alphabet or anything about Judaism to comprehend them, since they are illustrated. How the two systems were combined is anyone's guess, but that they were once separate is demonstrated, as far as I am concerned, by the survival of the regular playing card deck. The major arcana might have come via the Aramaic rather than Hebrew alphabet.

Lamantia claimed a considerable knowledge of emblematics, a medieval esoteric system similar to tarot, and of alchemy. But in the 1960s he became intoxicated with the purported Egyptian sacred mathematics of Rene Schwaller, who called himself Schwaller de Lubicz. He died faithful to that creed. In about 1971, when we were very close, seeing each other almost daily, he confessed to me that the Schwaller movement had a Nazi background, and I realized from reading a later memoir by Andre Vandenbroek, another Schwallerite who married Lamantia's ex-wife Gogo Nesbit, but who was Jewish (i.e. Vandenbroek), that the entire fixation on Egypt by Schwaller was anti-Jewish. Schwaller loved Pharaoh, not Moses. Lamantia's references to this greatly shocked me because my father was Jewish, and I was a leftist, although I was not brought up in the Jewish faith and was more drawn to and knew more then about the Christianity of my mother, who was Protestant, and of the Catholics, one of whom I married.

My father had given Gogo Nesbit a job in a store where he was an executive, as I recall, when she and Philip came back from Mexico in 1956 or so, and Gogo gave my mother a couple of turtle neck sweaters which were too small for my mother but which I wore as a teenager.

Lamantia's admission about the Nazi background of the Schwaller movement was the beginning of my alienation from him, which was rather loudly consummated in 1974 (the police were called) and which was never truly restored. It was said by another San Francisco writer, more recent, named Jack Foley, that Philip always needed to try to prove he was smarter than anyone he met. But a very great deal of his knowledge was superficial. And, as noted, I believe he lied about André Breton and I know he lied about other things. For example, he bore a particular hatred for the physicist Bernard Harden Porter, a poet and very gifted scientist who published Philip's first and misleadingly titled volume, *Erotic Poems* under the colophon of Bern Porter Editions. In about 1998 when Philip could speak civilly to one another for about five minutes, I mentioned to him that Bern Porter had been a key figure in the development of the atomic bomb and had been investigated by the federal government while he worked on the Manhattan project, as it is usually miscalled – the correct term was "the Manhattan Engineering District." Porter had published the only paper in the world at the time on the separation of isotopes from uranium and was put in charge of the whole operation at Oak Ridge, Tenn. That enriched uranium, Porter had even published, without security clearance, was a surrealist text about the atom bomb before it was dropped on Hiroshima, which text seems to have gotten past the feds. He was only investigated because of his associations with leftists in the Manhattan staff.

Porter was not above embroidery of the past – he claimed the FBI questioned him about Rexroth and Lamantia, which was absurd – the FBI did not hear about Rexroth until 1951. When I mentioned this very interesting fact about Porter's scientific work to Philip he said it was all bullshit about Oak Ridge and the bomb and any involvement with Porter, to which I replied that the investigation of Porter was an official public document anyone could read. That riled him up again and we did not speak much after that. I did say, as I recall, that it was a matter for irony that Porter was working on the atomic bomb while publishing an anarchist poet, as Philip described himself at the time.

Lamantia's was a tragic case, and in my final view he was not the great poet he was made out to be. In a strange loop of surrealist coincidence my ex-wife's family had associations with his family of which Philip was unaware, and my main girlfriend's family had similar links with his family – all Sicilian connections. Through the girlfriend I was able to check some statements of Philip's about his life in the early 1940s in SF.

I think the most interesting aspect of all this is that many Beat and other intellectuals of the time knew Christianity, Judaism, and Buddhism as well as various pagan traditions but almost none knew anything serious about Islam. I had begun reading in Islam quite early, in the late 60s, and introduced some things to Lamantia. About five years before his death Lamantia told me he was reading Corbin, the "traditionalist" apologist for Shia Sufism – a good person in his own way – and he seemed quite swept away by Corbin, as he had been by others before. But by then I was reading Gimbutas on Indo-European paganism! I now like

Corbin quite a bit except for his "traditionalism" – which I first encountered at 19 and immediately recognized as neofascist. In the end I saw the same dread trends in Gimbutas's triune social model of Indo-European pagan society – aristocrats, priests, peasants – no financiers – i.e. no Jews.

Most of the Beats were more interested, like the hippies, in I Ching and astrology than in tarot, most were indifferent to alchemy, and I don't think any of them except Lamantia knew about emblematics, which I surmise he had picked up from the Surrealists. Philip had read Qur'an – this is the subject of an allusion by Ginsberg in HOWL – and he knew about the Muslim kingdom of Sicily, because he was Sicilian himself and had read seriously in that topic, at least.

Do you remember what kind of text they created by using the tarot, or in which way they used the tarot as a writing tool?

No – it was just a passing mention.

Do you have any idea of what kind of "humiliation" the poet Jack Spicer received from the poet Charles Olson*?

I was about a tiny child when it happened and heard a lot about Olson from my father – who did not know, I think, that Olson served as a Soviet spy, amazingly enough, but nothing about Spicer until I was a teenager. But you can search (Kevin) Killian's book on Spicer and find it all – Marseille vs. occultist decks plays a role.

In our conversation Paul Nagy told he he remembers Lamantia telling him that the only true tarot was the Marseille tarot. That is what Breton seems to have thought. Did Lamantia ever said that to you? Why do you think Breton was so important to Lamantia, or perhaps, let me ask this in a broader sense: where is, in your view, the pull, the attraction, Surrealism had in those American poets?

I learned about Breton and the Marseille tarot before developing my adult relationship with Lamantia. My recollection of it is that I reminded him about it.

The Duncan-Spicer "axis" was quite interested in tarot and used it to develop literary texts – I was reminded of this by a new article on Spicer.

During the second world war most of the main European Surrealists lived as refugees in the U.S. and Surrealism had great currency as an avant-garde movement in America, although there were few American Surrealists. It especially appealed to ex-Communists like Rexroth or ex-Trotskyists like Duncan. Its influence was also crucial in the emergence of the abstract expressionist movement in painting.

As a Muslim now I eschew divination although I accept the wearing of amulets, to which most of the Muslims I know object, except for certain Sufis.

New York / California, July 2010

---

* In their book Poet be Like God. Jack Spicer and the San Francisco Renaissance, *Lewis Ellingham and Kevin Killian recount a scene in which Jack Spicer visited Charles Olson, and to ingratiate with him, he started laying tarot cards on the carpet. The deck he had brought was the one designed by Pamela Colman-Smith, the deck now we assume is the 'default' tarot. As the story goes, instead of impressing Olson, Spicer brought some embarrassment on himself, since Olson was partial to the Marseilles tarot. There are a couple of words used to define the Rider-Waite deck: 'phony' and 'corrupt in every term'.*

"'Artificial dreams describe the Tarot cards so nicely."

A conversation with JAMES RICKLEF, Tarot reader, lecturer, writer

What are the differences, and similarities, between a tarot spread and a haiku?

First, I would say that the general definition and rules about Haiku are what's analogous to a Tarot spread. A specific Haiku poem may be considered analogous to the specific use of a spread for a reading, and one's interpretation of a Haiku poem would be comparable to one's interpretation of a Tarot reading.

Based on that, I can see a few similarities between spreads and Haiku.

There is a structure for both, although that structure is flexible. Haiku novices often rely on their grade school instruction that a Haiku must be three lines with the syllable counts being 5, 7, 5. However, serious Haiku poets of the last few decades (at least those writing in English) no longer slavishly adhere to that rule. This is similar to the use of a spread. I do lay out the cards for a reading based exactly on the spread I have in mind (assuming I am using a structured spread), but as I do the reading, if tangential questions or issues come up, I'll deal another card or two as seems appropriate. Also, in her wonderful book, *Tarot for Your Self* Mary K. Greer talks about how you can move the cards around after you've read them as they were laid out.

Haiku and spreads are also similar in that there is the possibility of gaining great depth of meaning from very little input for both – just a few words for the Haiku and just a few cards for the spread. And both a Haiku poem and a specific spread of cards suggest a story without specifically spelling one out.

Finally, you can create an infinite number of Haiku poems based on the Haiku structure, and you can do an infinite number of specific readings based on a Tarot spread.

The major difference that I see is that there is no right or wrong interpretation of a Haiku poem. That may be true as well if you are doing a reading for self-reflection, but if you're doing a reading for someone's specific question, that is not true.

Maybe you know this, but John Cage was very enthusiastic about the I Ching. I found this quote from him that I think summarizes his views on it:

> I use the I Ching when it is useful, just as I turn on the water faucet when I want a drink. I find the I Ching useful to answer questions, and when I have questions, I use it. Then the answers, instead of coming from my likes and dislikes, come from chance operations, and that has the effect of opening me to possibilities that I hadn't considered. Chance-determined answers will open my mind to the world around.

I love the simile between the I Ching and the water faucet, and I wonder: when do you think it is useful to look at the tarot?

For my own use, I find the Tarot to be a wonderful road to insight. It helps me understand myself and my world better. I also like to pull a "card of the day" to give me something to consider about my life in general or about my specific actions or circumstances for that day.

It is also useful to turn to the Tarot for guidance in making a decision. However, it's important to make the distinction here that I don't use it to actually make those decisions. When I do a reading of this type, I prefer to ask questions like, "What to I need to know about this situation to help me make the best decision possible?" I find it unfortunate when people want to use the Tarot to make their decisions for them, which I feel reflects an abdication of their responsibility for their life.

What is 'chance' to you? Is that a notion you find useful? Do you have a better name for it?

"Chance" (i.e., a random, accidental, or unpredictable occurrence) stimulates creative thought. It takes us out of our rational thinking and moves us to use our intuitive mind instead.

Many years ago, I came across a study in which business people were given random images to consider as they made decisions and worked on problem solutions, while other participants in the study were not given any images. The people who were given the random images did a better job of making decisions and solving problems (I wish I could give you a reference to that study, but it was so long ago.) So, even if we merely consider a Tarot reading as a way to deliver random images, it could still be useful. However, I don't think it is merely that. I think there is more to it, which is due to what Jung called "Synchronicity."

I think of "chance," as it relates to working with the Tarot, in terms of that word. Working with the Tarot is the vehicle through which Synchronicity operates, through which the Divine communicates with us. As another way to put it, consider this quote from an article on Wikipedia:

In the 1984 film Repo Man, ... [t]he Miller character states that while many people see life as a series of unconnected incidents, he believes that there is a "lattice o[f] coincidence that lies on top o[f] everything" that is "part of a cosmic unconsciousness."

Call that overlying "lattice of coincidence" what you will – God, Spirit, the Universe, the Divine. Perhaps we can call it "Informed Chance." Whatever you call it, though, I think it's what brings the right cards to a Tarot reading.

It would be great to know more about that study! Now, changing tracks a little bit, yesterday I had a client who wanted to know why her dog didn't like its vet. She laughed and admitted it was an unreasonable question, but she wanted to know anyway. How would you handle a question like that one?

I wouldn't.

What would be your line of action then?

I might start by pointing out that most pets hate to go to the vet. That's not a real mystery. Beyond that, I would suggest that maybe we could do a reading about what she needs to know about working with her dog. I find the best uses of the Tarot include things like finding out how we can deal with life, not what other people (or dogs) are thinking or doing. Of course, if the Universe wants her to know what's going on in her dog's head, if It truly thinks that's what she needs to know, then the cards will tell us. But I find that's not usually the case. Typically, what's important is our own self-exploration, our discoveries about ourselves.

I guess any question reveals something about the person who asks it. For any question we are asked, there is another question we could ask our clients in turn. As you say, in this case the important thing is to understand the dynamic of the relationship between the person and her dog.

There is something else I would like to say about that situation too. In such circumstances, where a client insists on a reading of this sort, I might wonder if this indicates that she is coming to depend too much on the Tarot to deal with problems or decisions that she should be able to deal with on her own. In that case, could doing that reading for her be considered "enabling" her self-disempowerment? This is something that we, as Tarot readers, should keep in mind.

Now, there are two main metaphors used to explain what the tarot does: the fortuneteller metaphor and the 'poorman's shrink' metaphor. The first metaphor promotes the idea of telling someone her future, while the second one promotes the use of the tarot to 'understand' the cause of a person's problems. How do you feel about these two metaphors? Do they work for you at any level?

Metaphors are helpful in discussing things since they serve as a simple model, but as such they are also limiting. I don't want to try to shoehorn myself into either of those models, but I guess they are useful for the purpose of discussion here.

To let you know my take on the first one, let me give you my professional "tag line" – I tell people that I am "a Fortune Helper, not a Fortune Teller." I don't think the future is etched in stone, so I feel that using the "fortuneteller" metaphor is somewhat disempowering because it implies that the client has no ability to change his/her future. Whenever I talk about the future during a reading, I call it "the probable outcome" and I generally explain to the client that I feel we always have the power to change our lives, at least to some extent, if we choose to do so. By the way, I think that's the message of the Justice card, when you think of it as an indication of karma, or "cause and effect."

As for using the Tarot to understand the cause of a person's problems, that's much closer to what I do. But I also use the cards to help people explore options for their lives and consider possible solutions for their problems. And I use the cards to help people create a better future for themselves. For example, I have posted a series of short Tarot readings my blog, and at the end of each one, I give the seeker a few Tarot Affirmations that they can use to help manifest the changes they want.[1]

---

[1] http://jamesricklef.wordpress.com/category/readings/ask-knighthawk-readings/

Personally, what attracts me the most to tarot readings is the absurdity of it. There is something counter-intuitive, and subversive, in the act of turning to printed images every time we have a problem. This is of course no different from praying to a saint's image, and no different from the act of looking at a drawing or a painting and feel lifted by it. Man is the only animal who can craft artificial dreams. The result of such a poetic act is to enrich reality by derailing it, in those moments in which our usual, 'reasonable' strategies have us going in circles, without leading us forward. We enrich the perimeter of our thoughts by exposing ourselves to random input. But we also enrich the perimeter of our possibilities by testing imaginary solutions instead of simply repeating the few strategies we already know. Obviously, it is the seemingly unreasonable nature of a tarot reading what is objected by those who scorn them. But this is also why some clients confuse doing something seemingly unreasonable with expecting something unreasonable.

I think it is easy to understand why a person who maps herself onto the tarot, finding all kinds of pertinent analogies between the cards and her life, may think the process also works the other way around, and the situations seen in the cards will find their way back into reality: "if I can see myself as The Fool, and the Fool is walking towards the Ten of Coins, then I should be walking into a pile of gold in no time". What is farfetched is to promote such line of thought. The tarot provides an opportunity to imagine possibilities. The rest is mainly up to us.

Now, given what you describe in terms of your tarot practice, I would like to know: what can you offer that a therapist can't?

First just let me say that I like that quote: "Man is the only animal who can craft artificial dreams." "Artificial dreams" describes the Tarot cards so nicely.

As for your question of what can I offer that a therapist can't … It's interesting that you ask that. More than once, after doing a reading a client has said something like "My therapist has been trying to tell me that for years!" So apparently one thing I offer is a drastic cost savings over that of a therapist. (I say that with a grin, but I'm not being totally facetious here.)

Now, I'm not sure what a therapist has to offer, but I would say that another difference is that I offer practical help in addressing a person's problems. Like I said previously, I don't think the "poor man's shrink" metaphor accurately applies to my Tarot work since I also use the cards to help people explore possible solutions for their problems and I give them helpful tools like affirmations.

I also offer intuitive insights that come to me during a reading, which might be something that a therapist (or at least, a traditional one) wouldn't feel comfortable sharing. And from time to time, I get a flash of insight that I can only explain as being psychic. I don't bill myself as a psychic, but it does happen, and people coming to a Tarot reader are going to be open to that, while those going to a therapist would look askance at any such pronouncements.

Surrealist poet André Breton used to say that poetry should give us "practical solution to the problem of our life". I think that fits perfectly to the tarot. I have a small concern about professional therapists: madness is a profoundly creative state. One rarely finds a therapist who can match it. Picking on what you said, about giving practical advise. I wonder, where do you draw the line between giving advise to your clients and taking responsibility for their problems?

To answer that succinctly, on my Tarot Ethics page[2], I state: "My goal as a Tarot reader is to allow my clients to take responsibility for their own decisions and actions."

I think that solutions and answers that people arrive at themselves have more power than those handed to them by someone else, so I do not make choices for my clients. For example, if someone is faced with a choice between Option A and Option B, I won't tell them, "It sure looks like you should choose Option A." Instead, I'll help them examine the pros and cons of each option and maybe we'll look at some other deciding factors as well. For those "Should I do this or that?" questions I generally use a "choice" spread that is designed to show the client what they need to know about their situation to help them make the best decision. In my book *Tarot Tells the Tale* I describe and do sample readings with a powerful and flexible set of 3-card choice spreads that does this. A very basic version is this type of spread is this:

> Card 1: What you need to know about Choice A?
>
> Card 2: Other information that can help you make this decision.
>
> Card 3: What you need to know about Choice B?

---

2 http://www.jamesricklef.com/Ethics.html

To facilitate a deeper examination of a client's choices, my other book *Tarot: Get the Whole Story* presents an eight-card spread ("The Expanded Choice Spread") that adds positions for things like alternative choices and probable outcomes. And if that's not enough, that book even introduces a twelve-card choice spread.

I have a final question. What would you like to see happening in the tarot world in the next five years?

Wow, that's a really big question. Okay, let me give you a few thoughts about that.

First, I would love to see more networking and cooperation within the Tarot community. For example, I have begun a series of blog posts that I am calling a "Deck creator forum" with the intention of helping get the word out about people who have created interesting Tarot decks, especially, but not limited to self-published decks. And your own series of Tarot interviews, Enrique, is another example of supportive cooperation.

Things like Facebook, online discussion groups, and blogs are really helping to bring people together from all over the world, but unfortunately they sometimes have facilitated some contention too. Internet communication (vs. face-to-face) can be tricky, partly because we don't have non-verbal clues with it and partly because the relative anonymity seems to dull some people's sense of social etiquette. Also, if you insult or berate someone in a blog post, for example, (whether intentionally or inadvertently) the whole world can see that, so you have to be very careful about such communication. Of course I realize that we're only human, so most of us trip up now and then. It's a new set of skills for humanity, which evolved relying on face-to-face communication (and we're far from proficient at that either, I guess).

Anyway, I think this issue of positive and supportive communication is important for the Tarot world. We are still a nascent group and a niche minority, so cooperation is imperative at this point. Naturally, we're not always going to agree with one another, but I would hope that for our common good we can all try to disagree without the rancor that I've encountered sometimes.

Connecting over the Internet is great, but another thing I would like to see is more real-life Tarot events. At this point, we only have a few (relatively) big Tarot events in the US. A few months ago I went to the Annual Readers Studio in New York, and it was so wonderful to get a chance to meet in person so many people involved with the Tarot. There are a couple other similar events here (MATS in Minneapolis and BATS in San Francisco), but it would be great to have a few more scattered around the country for people who aren't able to travel so far. I'm sure that's the case for most other countries too.

I would also love to see more intermediate to advanced Tarot books. Do we really need more Tarot beginner's books? That still seems to be a huge focus of the publishers. I've wanted to write more advanced books, but I found it hard to interest publishers in that, which is part of the reason why I self-published my book, *Tarot Affirmations*. And perhaps that's what will help – this new ability to self-publish Print-On-Demand books may help fill that need. For example, Bob Place recently did that with his beautiful book, *The Fool's Journey: The History, Art, & Symbolism of the Tarot*, and I may again go that route with my work-in-progress book provisionally titled, *Tarot and Your Spiritual Path*.

Finally, I'm really hoping that the Tarot community can help the lay population gain a better understanding of the Tarot. There is still too much misinformation, too many misconceptions out there. I mean, come on. The Tarot is not the work of the Devil, it is not just the tool of gypsy fortunetellers, and a Tarot reading is not spooky and scary. (Well, not usually). These ideas are slowly giving way to reality, but slow seems to be the operative word. I still frequently encounter people who don't want to get a Tarot reading because they're scared of it.

There is something I hope can help – more, and better, media portrayal of the Tarot. (Mary Greer's Tarot blog has a great article about Tarot in TV and movies.) It would also be nice to see a good crossover book on the subject, something to explain to the lay public what it's all about. Maybe it could be called "Everything You Always Wanted to Know About the Tarot: But Were Afraid to Ask."

Thank you for giving me the chance to participate in your series of interviews, Enrique. These have been very interesting questions and I've enjoyed talking to you.

New York / Los Angeles, October-November, 2010

"I certainly believe that readings are, in part, an illusion. But then I think that pretty much all the components of our lives are illusions: constructions that are the consequence of our own individual interpretations of reality."

A conversation with DOUG DYMENT, scientist, mentalist

All these conversations are focused on the tarot and on the dynamics of readings. Since you have put together the most comprehensive list of resources on cold reading, I think it could be interesting to talk about that specific craft.

OK. Let me caution you that I have never done tarot readings; I've always felt that it's difficult to distinguish oneself with this particular oracle, as so many use it. At various times, I have used palmistry, PsyCards, and regular playing cards, but now I mostly give readings using Zener cards. (In fact, I plan to publish a book on Zener card reading early in 2011, as I feel that nothing particularly credible has ever been written on this topic.)

I would like to know why. What interests you about cold reading?

I come to readings in much the fashion of most mentalists. I learned how readings "work" by studying the literature, and then used cold reading casually in the course of mentalism performances, to give more depth to my presentations. As anyone who has ever done this will tell you, it fosters requests for more detailed readings, usually in private. I responded, found that I enjoyed that kind of work, and felt that I was able to at least entertain, and often help, people by using that skill, so I continued with it.

As I become retired from regular platform performance, I find that I do more of this personal work, and less of what we normally think of as "mentalism", though I still engage in both activities.

I didn't know you do readings! I personally find that the most challeging aspect of my work as a reader consists of dealing with people's expectations about the kind of 'beliefs' a reader allegedly has. People immediately assume I believe in all kind of things that have no interest to me. I believe in readings because I believe in the usefulness of random, unexpected, input. I suspect that reasonable thoughts tend to return to themselves, and many times, whatever we can reasonably think about a topic, reasonable thoughts have us going in circles. But an unreasonable thought usually leaps forward, taking us into unknown territory. I cannot stress enough how the absurdity of a reading is useful in itself, for it implies to break our thought-patterns to include new patterns, and test other imaginary solutions. But my bottom line is simple: I do readings because I can create beauty by doing them.

We obviously have a lot in common in this regard: I could easily have written that entire paragraph myself. I don't disagree with a single thought expressed therein. I love your comment on "creating beauty".

How is your own relationship with beliefs? Do you adhere to any particular belief?

I'm a scientist/engineer by training (Ph.D., Computer Science, former Professor) and by inclination. Which makes me a skeptic on everything. But a true skeptic, not one of those debunker/disbelievers who are just as invested in their own beliefs as those they attack are in theirs. I think that things have natural (as opposed to paranormal) explanations, though I have no trouble with those who hold otherwise, and feel no compulsion to try to change their minds. Actually, I assume that "paranormal beliefs" exist as they always have, as a placeholder for things we don't yet understand. And I'm perfectly happy to admit that "I don't know" when I don't. As I have written on the back covers of all of my books, "I am too skeptical to believe in the impossibility of anything."

And of course I didn't know you were interested in Zener cards.

Actually, three of my books (*Mindsights*, *Stimulacra*, and *Tricyclic*) contain Zener card material, albeit for traditional mentalism purposes, not readings. For that matter, two of them have tarot items, one of which ("Major Arcanum", from my first book) is used, I know, by a number of readers as the only piece of mentalism they ever do: the one 'convincer' demonstration used prior to delivering a reading!

I don't want you to give too much away but, what kind of readings can you do with Zener cards? Are those more personality-oriented readings?

They're appropriate for both types of readings ("personality/lifestyle" and "situational", in my terminology). I give examples of layouts and procedures for both in the upcoming book.

I tend to hope for beliefs to be like bridges that will somehow take you somewhere, instead of beliefs being like ponds where you sink down. One of my pet peeves with mentalists turned into readers is that many of them tend to think that, as soon as they pick a deck of tarots, they are supposed to also pick up all sort of clichés and superstitions, "because the client expects it". How do you approach this? Do you feel that approaching readings from the perspective of a scientist/skeptic detracts from your listener's experience?

I don't think so. Again, I'm an actual skeptic, which means something completely different from the opinions and attitudes of most self-proclaimed "skeptics" (who are not skeptical at all, but have beliefs that are every bit as strong as, but contradictory to, their "opponents"). I don't present myself as a scientist/skeptic, but merely as a reader who has studied the art of interpreting the symbol patterns. In fact, I find it more helpful to approach readings as someone who *seeks* the answers, rather than someone who *knows* them. That way, the reading becomes more of a joint exploration than a prescriptive exercise. Of course, I need to be authoritative in the role of the person who has mastered the oracle, but I also need to be open to the perspectives of the clients.

On a related note, many people in the tarot world tend to align cold reading with deception, or with those who do readings for unscrupulous purposes. I tend to suspect that cold reading, either if we are talking about picking up clues in a person to make educated guesses about her situation, or if we deliver stock phrases to a person, are as valid a reading method as the tarot, or palmistry. (Then of course, we often read a person 'cold' by using any known oracle). Would you consider cold reading to be an illusion, and if so, to what extent could the concealment of that illusion be defined as 'deception'?

Wow, a complicated issue/question! To begin, I think that discussions of this topic are almost always subverted, rather than assisted, by use of the term "cold reading". As for myself, I define it literally, a reading (of any type) done "cold" (i.e., with no foreknowledge of the subject). Actors do cold readings, and nobody suspects *them* of nefarious intents (it used to be that if you did a Google search, the top results would all be theatrically related, but lately the conjuring version has taken precedence, including its erroneous Wikipedia definition). Experience has taught me, however, that most non-theatrical people do not employ the term in such a neutral fashion, but rather give it a personal interpretation, one equated with behaviours that are not present in the definition. They often use it to mean "stock readings", or "personality analysis", or (frequently) anything involving deception. They assume that it's some sort of magicians' "technique", or a scam. So I think that serious discussions of these matters can only benefit by avoiding the term entirely.

I certainly believe that readings are, in part, an illusion. But then I think that pretty much all the components of our lives are illusions: constructions that are the consequence of our own individual interpretations of reality. Sometimes we are aware of their illusory nature, and accept them for the convenience they provide. More often, we are not. Were we all blessed with an accurate (and complete) perception of reality, there would be little need of readers (or armies, for that matter).

Does the intentional concealment of the nature of a particular illusion constitute "deception"? Sure, any concealment is a form of deception, but this is pretty much a tautology with the previous topic: deception is omnipresent in our lives. The real question, I suggest, is to what extent any purposeful deception (assuming that it exists) is harmful. It's easy to slip into a false dichotomy here, as the consequences of deception (1) lie on a scale from good to bad, and (2) are difficult to evaluate. (If you tell a person that death is not imminent, when you know that it is, are you causing harm or benefit? There are broadly differing opinions on this, and they often depend on the makeup of the person being deceived.) Most people consider medicine an honourable profession, yet it is rife with deception: placebos, Rorscharch tests, "bedside manner", etc. And then there are the many religious businesses. I think that the practice of giving readings is neither more nor less ethical than any of these. All of this assumes, of course, that harm is not *intended*: unscrupulous practitioners can be found in every endeavour.

I think you are touching on an important point there: a reader has to have the appropriate mix of authority and openness. I like to see a tarot reading as a dialogue through images. In that dialogue, one cannot dismiss the way people react to the cards. This is very important to me, as I have come to see a tarot pack as a set of images that carry, from a completely visual standpoint, either positive or negative suggestions. My work consists on building up on these suggestions, so, when a person is faced with a positive image, I will give her suggestions to enact these positive actions, feelings or emotions, when the time comes; if we are faced with a negative card, my work consists of giving the person suggestions so she can have the strength to endure, and to face, these negative processes when the time comes. More than 'predicting the future', my aim is to suggest a way of dealing with any possible future. At one level that implies that I have to know what these images are; but at another level, it also implies I have to work with the way the person reacts to the images, to the point of forgetting whatever I know, if it contradicts the person's experience of a specific card.

This is the great strength of tarot (and Psycards), though simultaneously a drawback, as you note. The client is presented with images that are immediately identifiable, and with sufficient complexity to invite interpretation (even of the uninformed variety). This is good, in that it encourages the participative approach I lauded earlier, but it can also be challenging when the client forms unsettling/discouraging/inappropriate interpretations.

I guess my 'complicated question' was directed to know your thoughts on the use of any kind of information that doesn't comes from the tool at hand. Some people seem to find that notion conflictive. I tend to suspect that we, human beings, are better at reading signs that we think, and we all, consciously or unconsciously, automatically seize any person we are introduced to. We make educated guesses based on the person's gender, age, or appearance. I think that initial impression informs the readings we give. There is nothing deceptive about it, and there is nothing paranormal about it. It is just the putting into practice of our human experience. What do you think?

I think that to a considerable degree this will happen naturally, unless you are doing readings from a hermetically sealed room! But that said, I think it is also perfectly appropriate to draw upon information that does not emanate from the oracle. One's purpose as a reader is (obviously) to provide a reading of the oracle. But a reading does not (or should not) exist in a vacuum. Any reading must be interpreted in a particular context, and that context is as much a part of the reading as the tool being used. A given card will have a different significance for a fifteen-year-old boy than it will for an 85-year-old woman.

A reader can be considered a person building a bridge between a specific oracular construction and a particular moment of person/place/time. It is extremely difficult to fabricate a bridge if you only know what the connection looks like at one end. Anything discoverable about the client can only be supportive of the goal of a more accurate (and pertinent) reading, and is consequently both useful and valid, in my view.

Marcel Duchamp used to explain that the reason why he chose a urinal for his ready-made was because he felt aesthetically indifferent to it. He didn't especially like the urinal as an object, he didn't especially dislike it. I was thinking of what you were saying about the impossibility of looking at an image without interpreting it, either in a positive or a negative way. Sometimes it is very easy to build a reading on top of a person's empathy with a given image; but it is a little bit harder when you have to work 'against the image', by defusing whatever negative reaction a person may have to it. Obviously, working 'against the image' would be a mistake. I usually remember Milton Erickson's approach whenever one of his kids took a fall: he would acknowledge the pain, suggest it would get worse, and then suggest that just as the pain would get worse, it would recede. Following the same logic, one has to acknowledge the negative aspect of an image, one has to accept that such challenges could truly become overwhelming, and then one can define these feelings as a cue for the person to elicit a positive response. Erickson would say that when a kid hurts himself, and the grown up says "don't worry, it is nothing", the kid's reaction is to think "this guy doesn't know what he is talking about!" That is very much the same reaction one sees in people, when a reader tells them about how great it is to get The Devil, because "it is a release of creative energy", and nonsense like that.

My initial thought reading your response was "no image is devoid of suggestions". Then I thought of Zener cards. Are they different? I mean, when we see The Tower, we see a collapse, we see people falling down, we see fire. When we look at Death, we see a skeleton swiping limbs with a scythe. We can rationalize these images to 'explain them away', but the fact of the matter is that, from a visual point of view, those are scary images. On the other hand, a circle, some wavy lines, a square, a cross, or a star, as presented in Zener cards, seem way more open. They don't seem to be especially positive, nor especially negative. I wonder if those images are like Duchamp's urinal. Now, would you say this is an advantage? I wonder about it because the emotional connection between a person and the cards she got, no matter if they are positive or negative cards, can be so strong as to become magical. Can that be achieved with Zener cards?

The Zener shapes certainly don't bring the richness of detail present in the tarot and Psycards, but what they do offer are universal symbols, omnipresent in art and human experience back through recorded history. Anthropologist Angeles Arrien calls them "Signs of Life" (in her book of the same name). And as such, they do carry specific meanings. But beyond their purely symbolic interpretations, they act as archetypes for the classic wood/fire/earth/metal/water elementals of the Chinese Wu Xing (which boasts a literature that dwarfs almost any other subject!). And classical Chinese beliefs on these matters are more interested in transitions than static states, another aspect that is well suited to divinatory needs.

So yes, the Zener symbols don't give you the "instant emotion" that can come from oracles such as tarot; they require more interpretation by the reader. But, on the other hand, they offer more of a blank slate, and are less likely to invoke a prejudicial response from clients (as you are undoubtedly aware, many people exhibit a *prima facie* fear of tarot; there are areas of the United States where producing a tarot pack – or even a pack of playing cards – can lead to trouble)!

One last question: Can a broken spider be fixed with crazy glue?

Hmm-m-m... well, *people* with disconnected anatomical pieces have been fixed with crazy glue, so it ain't impossible.

How do you approach life? Where does the engineer end and the mystery performer start?

I take life as it comes, with no grand plan. My background and temperament incline me toward the (truly) skeptical, but I'm disinclined to ridicule the beliefs held by others. I'm endlessly curious about how (and why) things work. I strive to preserve the "anal" in "analytic". I try to do good by doing well.

New York / San Francisco, December, 2010

"I think our contemporary world needs what we offer now more than ever."

A conversation with DEAN MONTALBANO, tarot reader, hypnotist

Do you remember the day you decided to become a reader? What lead you to it?

Well, Yes and No. I am 5th generation, as far as doing readings goes, though I am the first to ever do so professionally. I started reading Tarot before I even went to kindergarten, in fact I was surprised to find out EVERYONE didn't do this thing. I went through a phase where I didn't do it, and picked it back up (oddly enough) when I pretty much gave up magic and went to work for a large mouse.

I saw a sign for a psychic fair and decided to ask the organizer if I could read there. She said she would call me back. She did an hour later and said she would LOVE to have me there. During that hour, that lady – now a very good friend – would later tell me that she called 3 people to see if anyone had heard of me. All three said they knew me and I was wonderful. None of them knew me and no one in this area could have ever had a reading from me. So, I guess it was supposed to be.

A few successful psychic fairs later, I decided I should look for a regular spot. Someone called me, again rather out of the blue, and without being asked or provocation said "Hey restaurant such and such is looking for a new reader" and I called them up and was the head psychic there for over 16 years until having just recently stepped away.

I am so jealous! I have never experienced that sense of flow. Whatever I do, I have to push it hard, and if I stop pushing, it stops moving forward. I became a tarot reader because there was nothing else I wanted to be, and I have to say, it was somehow what this city was willing to accept from me. Even so, one has to flirt a lot with this city for the city to flirt back! Only recently did I discover that my great-grandmother used to read cards. It happened about three years ago. I was sitting at my usual coffee shop, the place where I used to do my readings, and a very elegant black man came to me and asked me "who is the old lady?" I didn't know what he was talking about, but he kept asking "who is the old lady, the one who passed on the gift to you?" We never got past that point in the dialogue, as he kept insisting there was an old lady, and I kept telling him there was none. Then, two years ago, when my brother died, I went to see my parents, and at some point I mentioned the story to them. "That was my grandmother", my father said. She was an spiritualist, and she read cards. She promised to 'pass' that down to my father, but my father never really got into it. So, I guess I got it. Although, of course, that is not the way I experienced my process of becoming a reader. But it is a nice story anyway. Can a nice story be useful without being true? What do you think?

As a hypnotist, I have learned that there really seems to be no "Truth" that is for all, but only truth (Little "t"), meaning, as we see it, or as it affects and effects us. In other words, all truth is subjective.

So, can a story, nice or otherwise, be useful without being True? OF COURSE! Even if it is not True, it is true. I am fond of telling people that ALL my stories are true. Even if they never really happened in this reality, they certainly did somewhere else, and they are all true to my vision of telling them.

When I became an Ericksonian Hypnotist, I was already doing about 3 thousand readings a year and it was really interesting to me to see how Hypnosis and Reading overlapped. Every story we tell invokes the power of our "Once Upon A Time" trance from childhood and there we learned many things from the safety of our parent's knee or the knee of whatever teller of tales had our attention.

We, as a society, have forgotten MUCH of this power and do not recognize many of those who would use their stories to access that magical other than conscious learning part. The News, Advertisers, Fear mongers and such…

Related to Tarot, can one think of a more powerful story than one that is written for you, by your higher self, and channeled through a series of archetypal symbols to be delivered right to you when you most need it? Ah, what fun!

I agree with you about the little 't' in 'truth', although I also see how, for the average person, a story that isn't real is perceived as less relevant. I am talking specifically about the context of a reading. The client expects for the story to be 'true' and measures the reading in terms of 'accuracy'. I rather see the content of any reading as an imaginary solution. 'Imaginary' is a word that has mostly negative synonyms: invented, made up, concocted, fancied, illusory… Which is funny given that every single thing humankind has achieved started out as imaginary. To me, the future is an imaginary carrot on a stick. You know? I tend to have a problem with the notion of 'living in the moment'. I think that there are times when it is important to focus all of our attention on whatever we are experiencing. But sometimes, the moment 'sucks'. Here is where we, human beings, have a powerful evolutionary advantage no other animal seems to possess: we are the only animals who can choose not to live in the moment. As far as we can tell a duck has no other choice but to live in the moment. A duck is always sitting in the moment. We are no sitting ducks. We can always project ourselves into an hypothetical situation, to give ourselves relief, or hope, or to test imaginary scenarios and come up with solutions that aren't present 'in the moment'.

All this takes me to the topic of readings and hypnosis. This is something that interests me a lot, as I think that a reading works through hypnotic patterns. You mentioned Erickson, whose work is of great interest to me. Now, Erickson had a very peculiar way of dealing with his patient's problems, and there are hundreds of anecdotes about his practice; but I suspect Erickson's goal in all of these diverse cases was the same: to help the person recover functionality. Not to understand, not to intellectualize, but to get the person back on the saddle. Life moves through more or less defined patterns, and the very notion of illness supposes an inability to follow these patterns. Somehow, I see my work with the tarot like that: the body has a memory of what being healthy and functional means. Sometimes, pain can distract the body from this knowledge. After all, pain is a rather interesting phenomena. But in the vast majority of cases the memory of being functional runs deeper than the memory of being wounded, one only has to find the means to remember these memories. I think that, to some extent, that is what the tarot does. The tarot is a group of images that lost their memory, hoping they can find a place in our memory.

Now, when you brought up "the memory of our father's knee" I wonder if you meant that a reading elicits in the person the spirit of a child, in terms of openness, capacity for wonder, even hope. I was also reminded of something I was discussing with Scott Grossberg. He pointed out that a person who comes for a reading needs to "suspend her disbelief". Would you agree with that?

I am not sure that the person coming for a reading needs to suspend disbelief – maybe because I think of that as a magic phrase. I find the people coming to me for readings DO believe (as do I for that matter) that this is a "real" thing and has value in it. I do think that some of my clients might need to more suspend BELIEF, in other words, not looking for someone to give them parental type answers (do this don't do that, if you make that face it will freeze that way) but rather create a little disbelief in the message and the message giver (Reader) and instead take the message and allow it to become a poem, to flow and morph, within their own minds and extract the metaphors and messages that are within the reading and can only be understood by their lower self (using the Huna terms here.)

This, of course, depends entirely on the style of the reader though. Some readers give messages like : "If you want that job you need to write a new resumé and bring it in by hand." There is not much metaphor there. If the message is: "Be a scribe and be your own messenger." That might mean the same thing as above in the end. But it is far more metaphoric.

I do think that the Child part, the Once Upon A Time Part, is indeed elicited in a reading, but I think that we really are all always children. We get bigger and get jobs so that we can continue to feed the child and keep him or her safe, but that is only because our biological parents can't take care of us forever. But who we really are IS that child.

Recently I read a quote from Lacan, saying something like "the purpose of therapy is to explore human nature". At one level, I will be happy to run with it, but at another level, I find it pretty unrealistic. A person goes to therapy because she has a problem, just as a person goes to a reading because she has a concern. It would be great to think we can all spend time and money on spiritual musings, but the truth is, we tend to be more practical than that. What can you provide through a reading? What is that people get? And also, is it what readers offer something that has any stand in our contemporary world?

Yeah, I would have to say I can't agree with that quote too much. To me the purpose of therapy is to become more functional, have more choices, become more congruent and so on. OK, maybe we need to go meta and ask Purpose for WHO? Maybe that IS the purpose for the therapist. Most therapists are attracted to the field because they hope to figure themselves and their immediate families out, so maybe for THEM that is the purpose (Or the positive intent). But I still think for the client it is to function with less pain.

Through a reading I hope to provide: Perspective, Confirmation, Alternatives, Choices, Peace of Mind, Comfort, Remove Confusion, or simply entertain. Now, weather people GET that or not is at least 50% up to them. I can point to a path, but they have to be willing to see it, examine it, think about it and then follow it or not.

I think our contemporary world needs what we offer now more than ever. But I think the word reader could be replaced with Minister, Counselor, Guide, Elder, Teacher, Parent and have virtually the same meaning. People are less and less in touch with their child, and less and less in touch with spirit, less and less in touch with the Elders – in the USA at least.

TANGENT ALERT – I often think, perhaps I was born a hundred years too late, for I look at society, even when I was younger, and see one in the US that has really scary, messed up values. "We" value Now, Money, Things, Experience, Diversion over what has been, Knowledge, Learning, and People. It really kind of scares me sometimes, saddens me other times, amuses the dickens out of me other times. BUT don't mind me, I am pretty nuts.

I am with you: any counseling is aimed at helping the person in need to regain functioning. That is something I especially like about the tarot: it "preaches by example" by showing physical postures and attitudes one could mirror. Let me get back to metaphors vs. literal statements. How do you establish which one works better for a specific listener?

Typically, I start by listening to the client a bit, if THEY tend to speak with abstracts and have an abstract question. I start there but lead to more concrete direction. And Vice Versa.

I have many Wiccan and new age clients. These are the folks who come in and ask when they are going to find a new job. You ask when they last applied for anything and they say "Well, I lit a candle and did this spell... But I STILL don't have a job." They are the ones who need to be told to fill out an application. LOL... If that makes sense.

More often than not, I have them ask questions AFTER I do my reading. I start with them not saying or asking ANYTHING aside from the question "Have you ever HAD a reading before?" Then, I explain, "Well, the cards are just used as a tool. I do a general overview of now and the next few months, and at the end you can ask a specific question. It just has to be specific and it has to be about you."

So, the first half tends to be metaphors leading to specifics, followed by a specific question and whatever impressions I get about that.

I find very hard to guarantee the value that the content of a reading will have in a person. I would be as bold as saying that we cannot guarantee the reading will have any value at all for a client. So, what are we really charging for? The value of the information? Its accuracy? Its relevance? Are we simply assigning a value to our time?

Well, I charge for my time/energy. But as I say, everyone is entitled to one free reading (that is to not pay me if they feel there was no value) and I am entitled to never read for that person again.

A doctor doesn't guarantee you will heal, nor a lawyer that you will win your case. You pay for their time, and expertise. And how many doctors or lawyers will say "if you're not satisfied with what I have done, don't pay me." For years I did readings in an environment where people paid after the reading whatever they felt it was worth. I never got stiffed.

In an entertainment environment, readings at parties and conventions, I charge for my time.

One more thing: when was the last time you got a reading?

Hmmmm. Last time I got a reading was about two weeks ago at a tea leaf class I taught from a student who had never given a reading but "obviously" had been giving them for centuries.

New York / Orlando, Florida, December 2010

"Tarot is like breath."

A conversation with DONNALEIGH DE LAROSE, tarot reader, radio host and podcaster

What made you think that talking about the tarot on the radio was a worthwhile occupation?

Funny question, because occupations tend to bring money in, and I'm putting money *out* on this one (grin). My goals for *Beyond Worlds* include making tarot accessible, modern, intelligent, and giving it dignity while pulling away the curtain on some of its mystery. Tarot cannot be completely demystified, however, as it has such a curious and mystical way of "knowing" and has such a sense of profound wisdom that can't be explained even by people who have used it a lifetime. But being able to connect with the mystical in such a tangible and poetic way is a profoundly personal and spiritual experience. There are a myriad of ways to use tarot, and we hope to share with the world that it is more than a gypsy lady under a neon sign (not that there's anything wrong with that) nor just a beach-side trinket-shop novelty experience (not that there's anything wrong with that, either). It's a tool for self-insight, psychology-digging, divination, meditation, intention, creative writing, personal growth, dream-interpreting and for finding answers and clarity, just for starters.

So while our tarot broadcast is not bringing me income, it is wildly rewarding in that I get to learn – along with tarot lovers worldwide – how to connect with those 78 cards and gain some serious self-insight while improving personal reading skills. The payback has been in the touching letters and emails sent to us almost daily from people worldwide sharing how the show has impacted their lives, how they feel more capable of connecting to tarot and providing better readings, and how finding a like-minded community has released them from a sense of isolation or "being different." Some have kindly written that we've made a larger difference in their lives related to tarot than any other source, and that just bowled us off our feet and inspired us to continue.

When we started the show, we never dreamed it would draw the attention it did. There were literally hundreds of shows featuring metaphysical topics, readers, psychics and interviews, and we figured we'd be lucky to get a small audience of interested listeners. We were blessed to have somehow been noticed in the crowd and embedded as a part of the larger Tarot Community. We eventually learned how to become different, developed a stronger format, and I became connected with three of the world's best and most vivacious tarot readers, each bringing decades of life experience with tarot in different ways. So what started as a tool for quiet self-learning has since evolved into a shared community of people worldwide who also love using tarot. We've really honed in on serious tarot education, making our show a one-of-a-kind weekly free service that has featured the world's best tarot thinkers, doers and creators. And while *Beyond Worlds* has become my second full-time job in terms of the time used to prepare for it, the income received is solely in satisfaction that we're able to provide something that benefits both modern tarot and its users worldwide.

I have recently been thinking of the notion of 'profit' and my conclusion so far seems to coincide with your thoughts: there are several ways of making profit other than money. Yesterday I was looking at a book on Rudolph Steiner's influence in the arts in the the 20th century. Most notably, for me, was an interview with Joseph Beuys. I knew Beuys was a follower of Steiner, but not an anthroposophist, and I also know that even those who followed Beuys never shared Beuys' passion for Steiner. Now, in this interview, Beuys was asked if he considered himself an 'occultist', to which he replied that such a word is somehow "fatal". Beuys was one of the very few artists I know of who managed successfully to bring magic and myth into the contemporary scene. Even so, he rejected the 'occult' label. How do you feel about that word: 'occultist'? Is there space for it in an "accessible, modern, intelligent, and dignity" view of the tarot?

What a great question. The word "occult" has so many connotations, depending on who is the interpreter. Taken point-blank as a definition from the dictionary, it is simply:

1. of or pertaining to magic, astrology, or any system claiming use or knowledge of secret or supernatural powers or agencies.
2. beyond the range of ordinary knowledge or understanding; mysterious.
3. secret; disclosed or communicated only to the initiated.

    (www.Dictionary.com)

Interestingly, my childhood roots in Christianity or any world religion would also be considered "occult" under that definition. So I guess we should first realize: any religion could be defined as an occult science. If the system has a God (or god/desses) or miracles, it is supernatural. Only those Baptized or initiated know the inner secrets. And if their members were asked if their system was intelligent or modern or dignified, I'd be willing to guess we'd get a resounding and respectful "Yes!"

Is there space for an "accessible, modern, intelligent, and dignity" view of the tarot? I'd say, "Absolutely, yes!" The secrets of tarot can be accessible, although there always seems to be a bit of the secret remaining, such as when we still continue to ask "how does Tarot work?" long after we've learned to interpret the cards fluently. To many, tarot is a spiritual system with profound wisdom and dignity. I personally have deep respect for the wisdom it gives to me, and I perceive it as coming from the Spiritual. Others may see it coming from our own Inner Wisdom. While tarot's roots are not in what many would consider "modern," it is certainly a system we can apply to our modern questions and concerns, much in the same way any ancient sacred text of the world's great religions can be used to give modern folk ethical guidance to today's wildest topics. While the tarot is not a religion, it definitely holds the spiritual and can be used by anyone of any spiritual persuasion and can be used as a powerful bridge to the seemingly untouchable.

A former (and recovering) Catholic myself, I am no longer bound to any organized religion but finding myself a healthy hybrid of many of the world's spiritual wisdoms. The world "occult" in my childhood held very different meanings to me than it does now. From the way it was said with a whisper or with caution in my youth, it seemed to be defined more as, "forbidden," "dark," "sinful," "sinister," or even "demonic." I realize now that that is most definitely not what the word "occult" means (nor what the word "tarot" means) and being able to say the word "occult" without feeling it is a dark word was a journey I'd taken as I released my old religious roots. I've since opened to something I think man can't define by rules or boundaries: the Spiritual. And the Spiritual is highly intelligent, wise, dignified, and timeless.

Occult methods can be highly intelligent, being practiced by our world's best scholars. Having a Master's Degree myself and having experienced challenging, high level college courses, I can easily say that something like Qabalah, Astrology, and systems of divination like tarot have really given me a stretch of my intelligence. I doubt I'll ever be able to grasp astrology the way I wish I could, a highly systematic and intelligent occult system in itself. I've found tarot to be a wonderful mix of intelligence and emotion, putting the two parts of a person together into one system, logic and intuition melded as one story. The symbols become a story in our psyche and challenge us to see things outside of the scope of our ego. And if that is "occult," it is a gloriously bright thing.

Saying the word "occult" to my Catholic or Baptist friends would likely be "fatal," in that it would be the end of that debate or understanding. They'd hear another word/definition in place of the one I was using. So in that manner, Beuys may have been onto something. When we use vocabulary, we're often both using the same word but with different reference points or definitions. To those friends of mine who have a negative connotation of the word "occult," I'd likely remove the actual word and explain techniques friendly to them so they can hear the message first. When they hear a "spell" is analogous to a "prayer," it often opens eyes. I've witnessed people argue over things when they *think* they have opposing views, where if you actually break down the conversation, they are agreeing on everything but how a word is defined.

As for me, I rarely use the actual word "occult" because I fear it will be misconstrued depending on who the listener may be, but I can't deny that what we do is "beyond the range of ordinary knowledge or understanding, and mysterious." And that is the definition of "occult", or any Spiritual system. So if someone were to say of my love of tarot, "you're honoring the occult," I'd have to respond, "Well, so are you, my friend, when you honor your God/dess, whomever that may be." And that can be a good thing.

How did you come in contact with the tarot? How did the people around you reacted when you started to delve into it?

I was awaiting a biopsy for a lump that was removed from the back of my skull. With two vacation days falling within that week, receiving the biopsy results was dragged out and I was feeling a lot of tension and worry while waiting. I drove past my local psychic's shop and turned around, deciding to stop in and ask her what she saw if for no other reason than to keep myself busy. While I had other (powerful) readings from her in the past, it was the first time I really looked at the cards instead of at her. She also does readings with rocks, a fascinating experience, and in the middle of reading them she stopped the reading, looked up at me and said, "You can do this, you know." I had no idea what she meant, but she somehow felt I was "a reader." Huh? I'm an audiologist.

She showed me how to read rocks that day, and I practiced on one of her clients in a free reading experience that blew me away. I bought my first deck that day and wanted "exactly the same one" she had. I came home with the Universal Waite box in slick shrink wrap, and had no idea whatsoever what to do with it. The cards looked like random, meaningless coloring book pictures to me. The deck was shelved for a year while I practiced doing hundreds of crystal/rock readings, trying to prove to myself that their accuracy was just a coincidence. It was not. I experienced a huge spiritual shift that year.

A year later, I learned how to read tarot, starting through literature and audio classes, slowly building a comfort with the cards, listening to MP3 classes while on my commute. What I learned through tarot is that the cards can answer extremely precise questions that the crystals cannot. The scope of what the cards could do awed me and when I denied that they were accurate and apologized for what they said, it turns out there was no need for apology: it was I who would have been wrong. The cards saw beyond my human scope and perspective. There was almost nothing I could not ask. I felt like the Universe had suddenly opened to me and I felt inspired and excited at the potential for learning.

Now I use the crystals for people who might be fearful of tarot (who fears rocks in their hand?), and I have found that the rocks are great for defining someone's life if they have no specific question. It organizes the good parts of their lives, the hairy parts, and the prickly people and situations. When they have further questions and want to know specific answers about those prickly people, that's when I say, "let's consult with the cards...."

My family was distraught at what I was doing when they found out. I had kept it secret for a few years, but eventually I did share with them. My mother went into a severe, clinical depression, convinced that I was consulting with the Devil (which I no longer believed was real, other than our own egos which I believe cause the world's problems). She consulted with her pastor, convinced that I was a lost soul, and it put a strain on my relationship with her, a very difficult process for me as she was my best friend as a child. I realized, though, that I was not choosing between tarot and her, but instead was choosing between my authentic self and becoming what she thought I should be or was supposed to become, something that no longer fit. It was one of the most difficult experiences of my life, and one from which there are still bruises.

In the midst of this evolutionary process, I was studying in psychic circles and a psychic medium connected quite surprisingly with my late grandfather (he was the closest I've had to a soul mate). My grandfather said through her that "you are seen as your family right now as being down here" and she motioned near the floor with her hand. "Soon you will see, it will change, and you will be seen up here," and her hand lifted just above her head. It was a toiling process, but she was right. This past year, I've given readings to several of my family members who privately asked me if I might use the cards for them, each who were amazed by the detail and wonder of the cards. Often family will call to ask just to get together for a reading. My mother heard that her sister had a reading and asked if she might have a turn. It was unnerving for me to think about reading for my mother, but it happened. And it was a joyful experience for both of us. She even ended up doing most of the reading herself as she became very excited about the symbolism she saw before her that related to her life. That reading was just this past summer, and we used the gentle Gaian Tarot, which is rich in imagery.

There are people I cannot share my passion with, although most of the people I'm close with in my day job know I love tarot and they will often ask for a brief reading when something serious happens to them or if they are unsure about a situation. There are friends I used to have that I no longer connect with because our spiritual system was our connector and mine shifted, but those shifts were more by my own choice than by theirs. I ended up meeting new people, respecting the old, but bringing in those with shared interests. My medical job makes it taboo to discuss anything of a spiritual or esoteric nature, which is fine. There is a clear line between work and spiritual system discussions for most people anyway.

This year I bought my 14 year-old son his first deck, which he will be getting around the holidays. He loves anything with dragons, so I bought him Lisa Hunt's Celtic Dragon deck. He may never read from it, but tarot is such an inherent part of me that I can't imagine not handing down a piece of the legacy to him. He may pass it on to his own children someday as something "Grandma used to love." And I hope by then that tarot is seen as less "woo woo" or weird, and seen more as intelligent and dignified by the general population. (We're working at it).

Your experience is characterized by something most people I know has trouble with: the whole compendium of the esoteric experience (all these things that stand behind the word 'occult'). Do you think it would be possible to separate the tarot from all the other beliefs and practices you have mentioned? I mean, most people I know, who oppose these metaphysical beliefs, still get benefits from the experience of the tarot. But many people would dismiss the tarot along with all these beliefs. They don't get to experience the tarot, assuming the tarot is about all these other beliefs. Have you had that problem?

I'm not sure I know what you mean. Do you mean is it possible to separate Tarot from any spiritual system? Or that we can use tarot and still adhere to other spiritual systems, perhaps?

I think I meant option one. But now I am intrigued by something else you just shared. Last week I did a reading for a woman who was sitting on the passenger seat of a car. Suddenly, out of nowhere, her window exploded. No one was injured, nothing happened, but since then, she started thinking about death, and more important, about what it means to be alive. Do you think you would have ended up reading tarots if you didn't have that lump?

I do not think I'd be reading tarot (or reading anything for that matter) had it not been for that lump. Truly out of our darkest moments come some of our brightest gifts. Turns out it was just a benign gland, but boy, did it turn my life around and for the better. Looking back on many dark or painful moments of my life, that very same form of expansion and change was happening and it ended up for the better when I emerged from the other side.

When you ask if it is possible to separate tarot from any spiritual system, I guess that is like asking me if I can separate breath from spirituality. They are different, and yet they are intertwined. Breath doesn't contain all that is spiritual, as spirituality is so much wider than that. But breath contains our chi, our life force, the very DNA of its source, and we are of the Divine. And we all breathe the oxygen shared with others as our world contains a finite amount of oxygen that we recycle, so we are all intertwined. We all breathe each others' chi, experience each others' true essence and spirituality right to the core of our lungs and blood streams.

Likewise, tarot is like breath. It doesn't contain all that could possibly be spiritual, as spirituality is so much wider than tarot or anything physical that exists. But tarot represents our life force, our spiritual natures, our physical realm, and our thoughts and emotions and passions. It represents the very DNA of which we are made. Yet it can intertwine with all that is. It can blend beautifully with any spiritual system that allows it in. Tarot represents anything we ask of it and more, and yet there are no rules or boundaries other than we as humans make. And how can the spiritual be defined by borders? That is where we fall as humans. The spiritual cannot be fully understood, bound, or defined other than what we create as boundaries in our own minds. Spirituality is fully understood by no one, though sought by many. And tarot is just one bridge to witness some of the wisps of spirituality that we might possibly grasp. Can it be separated from spiritual systems? I don't think so because tarot is all that is. It is not bound to any laws of dogma though others may bind it to such things. It belongs to no specific spiritual system, and yet it is a part of all. I often say that people may be prejudiced against tarot, but tarot holds no prejudice against anyone. It is completely free of ego.

Tarot often forces us to look at a painful part of ourselves when we realize what we are doing is uncomfortable because it is our ego screaming to us. It sees from outside us, very objectively, and becomes a great teacher. There are times I know it is telling me to do the right thing, and it may not feel satisfying because my ego wants otherwise. But if I listen to tarot, it will take me to a better place in the end, even though I want to resist it at times because my humanity gets in the way.

I do think that, sooner or later, most of us get a shattered window. Hopefully, it should make us better, or at least, more interesting. I am not sure the ego is the problem. Perhaps too much ego may be a problem. The ego is the tonsils of our soul. For years, doctor's policy was "take the tonsils out first, ask questions later". Now it seems these tonsils actually had a purpose! I am not sure that a completely egoless person would be able to bring beauty to the world.

Now, there were you, doing readings, exploring the tarot. How is it that such a 'shattered window' put you in front of a microphone?

I think you are right. The world without egos would be very bland and "vanilla." And we wouldn't learn very much. We like our movies exciting, I wonder what our lives would be like without the involvement of egos? I think a balance of it can be a rather precarious line to walk (I hope I can find it).

My shattered window was threefold:

1) The lump on my head exposed me to an important tarot reading that initiated the journey.

2) The physical loss of my grandfather from this life (the most difficult event in my lifetime) released me from worrying about being judged for what I was doing, as he was the one person who I truly cared about not disappointing. When he was with me in spirit, he actually encouraged me and pushed me forward.

3) The struggle with my mother as I learned to release becoming what others thought I should be and embracing who my soul was yearning to express and become was a journey of inner growth that was profoundly necessary and honest.

When the shards of the smashed window finished falling, I went on a journey of tapping into the Spiritual world and for the first time receiving back, rather than just pushing energy out toward it with prayers or requests. Even though I became more open about sharing it, it was still a very solitary and lonely journey. There were profoundly miraculous moments with no one to share them.

My friend, Dawn Simpson, was going through a similar process at the time, and we reconnected through our having found these spiritual systems: hers through angel cards and angel communication, and mine through tarot. Shortly after, she'd been asked by someone who found her on the internet to do a radio show about her angel communication, and she was incredibly excited, but as it turns out, it was just a marketing ploy, as being on the show would have cost her several thousand dollars every couple of months. She was disappointed not to be able to do it. But I'm not one to watch things go undone.

I had learned about *Blogtalk Radio* by hearing the *Tarot Talk Podcast* with Georgianna Boehnke and Raven Mardirosian, and so I told Dawn I could make it happen for free. And *Tarot Talk* was winding down with their final episodes having been announced a few months before. So Dawn and I nervously started a show (with embarrassing starts as we learned to find our on-air voices). But I have a lot of fire, and I was the one with the technical experience, so with all my planning behind the scenes and interviewing, and my personality being bolder than Dawn's, the show became more tarot-centered than angel-focused, and Dawn naturally had a much quieter presence than I did. It seemed my voice somehow overshadowed hers and I began to feel guilty. I wasn't able to maintain the interest in angels as they didn't seem to have as many layers of learning or systems that tarot did (in my own little head, I'm sure they actually do). I no longer felt I was honoring Dawn's vision.

We went through a shifting process where *Beyond Worlds* (a name I originally chose so it could encompass anything metaphysical, which I now regret) became heavily tarot-focused. Dawn started an angel-only show with my encouragement, and it allowed her to find her own voice, her own leadership and on-air confidence and presence, and from there she was able to focus solely on her passion: angelic energy. I was able to focus solely on my passion: tarot. I added an addendum name to Beyond Worlds that I originally wished I'd called the show: "Tarot Tribe," and purchased the URL for that (www.TarotTribe.com). I then went down a road that was completely self-fulfilling and educational, fast-moving and wild (very "8 of Wands"), pulling in all the facets of tarot that I wanted to learn, while finding that others were very interested in the same topics. The real magic to the show began for me, however, when I pulled in like-minded people who I admired deeply in the field, and who had shown strong support to the show.

First, Storm Cestavani was asked. He'd been incredibly supportive of the show and a constant presence in the chat room. I'd wanted to ask for his partnership on the show for many, many months, but he is the type who would not say no due to a sense of obligation, and I didn't want him to feel pressured to have to say yes to something he felt required to do but didn't have the time to do. As it turns out, it was a magical mix of chemistry, and his merging onto the show was instantly seamless and with a few comments he made on one particular show, we actually pulled in who was to be a future co-host as well as several new listeners who liked the new, gutsy approach.

Next, Georgianna Boehnke joined us, a natural radio talent from *Tarot Talk*. Georgie is known for her sensual voice, her bright, positive spirit, and her incredible tarot insights. She was a natural blend to the show, but as perfect a match as it was, I knew there was yet one missing link.

Theresa Reed, *The Tarot Lady*, hosts a once-a-month Blogtalk show that is a wonderful showcase for her incredible talent with tarot. Calm, grounded, clear and concise, she makes tarot instantly accessible to anyone who felt it seemed difficult to understand or "out there." Her interpretations of the cards were also a great learning tool for readers who were looking to expand their tarot vocabulary. When Theresa agreed to join *Beyond Worlds*, the show felt instantly karmically complete, and a force had been created that I wasn't quite prepared to recon with. The learning amplified, the discussions became deeper, the camaraderie of the show and the community amped up, and suddenly I felt we were able to create college-level learning about tarot for the community with a friendly twist and some deep discussion. We each read tarot so differently that I hope the show gives many facets of tarot to those who listen, and make people aware that tarot is not a "one size fits all" system. It is what you make it and it becomes a very personal journey and method.

The journey is no longer solitary for me, and the magical bonus is that others also have found a sense of connection through the show. I get several kind letters from people around the world every week thanking us for taking them out of their solitude or feelings of being alone, and that they were able to learn and grow and find other like-minded people through the community of our "Tribe."

So the shattered window released some things for me that would have held me back. It can be a jarring surprise, a Tower moment when things suddenly crash, but eventually comes the Star in the wake of the dust and we begin to find what we were looking for. Our goal now, with the new vision of the Fool beginning again for us again, is to bring more youth to tarot, so that young people can become aware of tarot's depth at an earlier age. All it takes is one deck of cards, so the expense can be minimal, and the rewards profoundly enriching.

At the beginning of our dialogue you mentioned you work with three of the best tarot readers in the world. What in your opinion makes a tarot reader great? What makes readers great?

Experience (lots of it), clear and consistent understanding of the cards using whatever method they use, clarity of readings, being able to connect cards clearly to situations consistently, having an ongoing interest in deepening one's understanding of the cards, confidence, respect for the client, genuine honesty, gentleness, professionalism and respect, and not going back on what is seen in the cards – being forthright. But ongoing life study of the cards, consistent searching for more, passion and experience really make someone stand out. I love working with people who are in love with the system, and who have felt that way a lifetime. I also appreciate people who are respectful of others' reading styles, that there are many ways to read, and that we can all learn from each other.

New York / Woodstock, Connecticut, January 2011

> "The Tarot gives us the means to unlock that information, which on the deepest levels is looking at the patterns that lie beneath daily life."

A conversation with EMILY CARDING, deck creator, author

Why the tarot? Why did you choose to get involved with these images and all what they represent?

Why the Tarot? My fascination with Tarot began at a very early age. Before I was born, my mother had been interested in Tarot and the occult, not in a serious way, but enough to have a Rider Waite deck and a couple of interesting books. Although she stopped when she married my father, the books remained on the shelves with their fascinating titles, amongst them, *The Devil's Picturebook* by Paul Huson. Of course the fact that as a child I was not allowed to look at them made them all the more fascinating! I used to sneak peeks at these forbidden words and images. When I was older, late teens, she gave me her old Rider Waite Smith, along with stories of an adventure with a Ouija Board and awful things happening at her school to the people involved! Indeed, the deck was rather malefic in its portents, and despite many cleansing attempts I didn't use it for readings, though I kept it for many years.

After having interests in spirituality and magick from an early age, I found myself free to pursue this when I left home to go to university, and right from the beginning I was doing readings for my fellow drama students with my first deck, the Hallowquest. Here was a deck so unlike the RWS, (which it took me a long time to learn to appreciate), and one in which the artwork seemed to speak to me personally. From my knowledge of Arthurian Mythos but also a strongly developed visual imagination, I found I could interpret the images on an intuitive level. Other early decks that spoke to me in this way were the *Sacred Rose* and the *Ancestral Path*.

Through the years, Tarot has been a part of a larger magical and spiritual path, and very natural for me to be drawn to, as it combined my love of things mystical with an appreciation of art and symbolism. I had always painted since childhood, for pleasure, so when I became a mother and a career in theatre was no longer an option, I decided to make a career from my art. Combined with more time and opportunity to train and explore within my magickal and spiritual path, creating my own Tarot was a natural step towards this. Then I just got in everyone's face with it until I started to be noticed! The fascination with the Tarot and the energies behind it is a journey which gets deeper and deeper and more fascinating with time. Looking for new ways to portray those energies and symbols is an addictive compulsion!

Interestingly, returning to the old RWS of my mother's, I decided to finally destroy the deck and burnt it in a ritual, one card at a time. Not only was it shortly after that that I started to recieve inspiration to create my own deck, but at the same time my mother revived her interest in the Tarot. I now believe that it was her blocking her natural magical leanings for all those years that caused the negative energy around the cards, and that burning them with respect in a sacred fire caused a release of energy and inspiration! (Don't try this at home though, kids)

Burning the deck, wasnt that a little bit harsh? Which card did you burn first?

True. But it was pretty. The coloured ink made lovely green flames, and it was all done very respectfully! Gosh, which card first? I wish I could remember. As Granny Weatherwax would say, we've all passed a lot of water since then.

There are two things I wonder about, regarding the creation of your own deck. First, what was missing in the pre-existing decks that made you feel the need to create your own? Second, I would like to know more about the dialogue between what you brought to the table and what was there before. In other words: how much can one add to what the tarot is, and how much should one keep from what the tarot was, in order to innovate without loosing the tarot's identity?

Well, let's not forget that the first deck I painted was actually *The Tarot of the Sidhe*, not the *Transparent*. I think because the *Transparent* was my first widely-released deck, that's what is seen to have come first, whereas the complete *Sidhe* is only just now being released. So really when I was first creating a deck, it wasn't a huge innovation, at least not as obviously as the *Transparent* was. And in fact none of my decks have been created as the result of finding anything lacking in existing Tarot, far from it! *Tarot of the Sidhe* was created out of the urge to explore the symbolism of Tarot from the inside-out, in a way an educational process for me as creator. Up to that point I had been largely an intuitive reader, and the traditional meanings had never truly clicked in my brain. It was also more importantly an act of spiritual service, to create or strengthen the bridge between this realm and the otherworld. So the creative process was that I would meditate on each card's meaning, studying both Rider Waite and Thoth-based decks, (not really the Marseille tradition), and the Sidhe would send me an image which I would do my best to interpret. The aim was to create a deck which others would be able to read the way I first learnt to read, with symbols that spoke directly to their subconscious. Now I'm not saying that other decks don't do that, but I have the need to act upon inspiration when it comes.

And really that's how the *Transparent Tarot* came about. It was literally a bolt of inspiration from the blue, which woke me up in the middle of the night and made me sat bolt upright! I had wanted to create something that hadn't been done, it's true… again, not for anything lacking in what already existed, but just to try and find some uncharted territory. Perhaps I'm a Tarot explorer? (Aren't we all?) I had NO idea that an idea would come to me that was as radically different from anything that had been attempted before! Then after the idea, of course, comes the technical process of making it work. A part of that was certainly considering what needed to be kept to make it recognisable as Tarot. For me that is the structure and the energies behind the cards. Although I have played with non-traditional symbolism in all my decks, I have stuck to the 78 card structure and my own interpretations of recognisable meanings within that. Also I find the elemental association within the suits very important and always try to emphasize that more than the symbol which represents it – except perhaps in the *Transparent*, where in the minors I had to be SO minimalist to make it work. The stylised figures are in the corresponding colour of their element, (apart from swords which are purple, as yellow would have been practically invisible!), but the traditional suit symbols and much Rider-Waite based symbolism remains in their poses. I didn't want to alienate people, I wanted them to have something that was still familiar and safe. With the Tarot I have painted, (*Tarot of the Sidhe*, *Tarot of the Black Mountain* and the current WIP the *Neverland Tarot*), I generally emphasize the nature of the element and the story of the card over the traditional symbols.

As to what my decks have brought to the table that wasn't there before, well the *Transparent* has brought a way of reading that wasn't physically possible before, only in the imagination. Now instead of the standard 78 images there are billions of possible combinations that you might get as images to interpret. It has given people a tool to encourage using their intuition, but in a playful way. Anyone who has sat with the deck in front of them knows how playful it is – you just have to fiddle with those cards! And that gets through boundaries, it gets people thinking outside the box.

Would you say that reading the tarot is a way of making the unconscious conscious? If so, whose unconscious? Your unconscious or your listener's?

Well that's a really interesting question and one which there can't be a definitive answer to, not even on a personal level. How the Tarot works is a mystery, a wonderful mystery into which we can delve as deep as we choose to and there's always questions and more to explore. When reading for another person, I think a strong energy connection is created, provided the sitter is actually open and not sitting there cross-armed and challenging. You could go into some sort of rational process of analyzing the reading, looking at who is shuffling, who is selecting cards etc., but a good reading is the child of a meeting of energies between both reader and sitter.

I do have my pet 'scientific' explanation for how tarot works, which does not negate the spiritual or take the 'divine' out of the divination, but rather shows that there is more to it than woo-haha in the eyes of a sceptic. That is that we are all exposed to more information than our conscious mind processes on a day to day basis, and that, as you say in your question, the Tarot gives us the means to unlock that information, which on the deepest levels is looking at the patterns that lie beneath daily life. If you believe everything is connected, as modern science is starting to prove, then it follows that even seemingly random events that we witness may be giving our subconscious clues as to apparently unrelated events elsewhere, even the other side of the world. Butterfly wings causing tornadoes and all that jazz. So leaving the spiritual out of the equation, you get pretty much the same answer. Yes, the Tarot helps to translate the language of the subconscious – it's like the babel fish of the deeper levels of the mind – and that includes your subconscious perceptions of the person you're reading for. Of course for those of us of a spiritual or magical persuasion, there's a lot more going on, but the same basic principle applies. The tarot is a babel fish, whether it is translating the language of your mind or the messages from spirits or Gods.

I would like to go back to the Transparent Tarot *now. Any opaque tarot gives us a limited set of elements we can permute by shifting their position in a two-dimensional plane. Any tarot image can be said to be 'in dialogue' with other images to the left, or the right, above or below them. The idea of transparency brings a third dimension into the picture, as now an image can also be in dialogue with images on top, or behind, itself. I have two questions about that: do you imagine that what such transparent logic gives us is a better depiction of our own thought process? And then, have you considered the possibility of exploring other media different from painting to make this formal departure even more radical?*

Other media, like computer applications or film for example? A number of people have suggested a Transparent Tarot app for the iphone or ipad or similar, but I'm not that technically literate! I'd love to see someone else do something like that with it, but there are issues there with the publishers and so on. So really what I would like to see is other people who have strengths in other media taking the idea and running with it in new directions. I would be really interested to see that. Also different people's minds and perceptions work in different ways. I do think that the Transparent decks offer more fluidity and that does reflect the wondrous dimensions of the mind as well as the spirit realms. I'm also aware that not everyone can get their head around it!

I think that, at some point, you might want to look into the Marseille tarot, which is said to be 'transparent', as cathedrals are, so the details in an image can be overimposed on the details of another image.

What I wonder is, what does transparence means? I remember, for example, how the notion of overlapping two elements was foreign to printing processes until relatively recently. As long as printing was achieved by pressing blocks on paper, overimposing two elements was technically impossible. As a matter of fact, it was only when the computer became widely accessible that one could stop thinking of design as 'arranging blocks on a field', and a third dimension, albeit illusory, was achieved. There were people like Neville Brody doing that before computers, but it was only thanks to computers that these visual resources became available for everybody. Every media brings its own ideas. Computers made possible for typography and image to fuse. Before that, pictures were treated as squares one had to compose with, treating the image as one would treat a letter. Is your transparent tarot a response to what has become our predominant visual landscape, or do you see transparency having specific advantages when it comes to creating meaning in a reading?

Yes, I should perhaps at some point look into creating a Marseille. If I ever do another *Transparent* deck it will either be a *Marseille* or a *Lenormand*, or perhaps eventually both. But the process is so fiddly and exhausting, just working out how everything will fit together, that it's not something I'm planning just yet. I have a lot of other projects lined up. I do love cathedrals though, and often dream of impossibly large ones...

As to the nature of transparency, well, when I first had the idea, that is, it burst into my head, and I had no idea if it had been done or then if it COULD be done. I presumed that if it could be done, then someone else must have thought of it already, and I was thrilled and amazed when I realised that not only was this idea completely original, but that I could find a way to make it work. Some have called it a step in the evolution of Tarot. Well, that would be nice, but unless someone picks up the baton and develops the idea, then the Transparent decks are more like a genetic freak, the X-Men mutants of the Tarot world! As the idea was not a result of a conscious process but rather a startling eureka moment which I then had to explore whether it was possible, I can't claim it as a response to modern media or the 21st Century environment, merely a direct inspiration. So you'll have to ask my muse. As you hinted at in an earlier question, the idea of layering reflects the nature of the human mind and psyche, and transparency has always been present in nature if not in Art, from when we first looked into a pool and saw both the surface and the depths at once. In fact I recommend everyone tries taking the *Transparent Tarot* in the bath with them!

The advantages I have found as far as using the Transparent for readings goes, it gives extraordinary details, tiny details which can open up such deep insights in completely unexpected ways, just by how the cards interact. Noticeable details, such as whether figures are facing towards or away from each other, or something as subtle as sword blades seeming to break on blades of grass. It's very chaotic, in the best possible way, and often the combinations still astound me. A year or so ago my Grandmother passed away, and I found myself unable to attend her funeral due to a cancelled train. I happened to have my Transparent Tarot with me, so sat in a cafe eating breakfast, I pulled three cards to see if I could get some sort of message from her. The image that was formed astounded me, beause the three cards came together in such a way as to not only give a message of love and forgiveness, but formed a very clear image of Christ on the cross. My grandmother was a firm Catholic, and it seemed to me she was saying that she had returned to her God. A powerful moment. That is the kind of fluidity and flexibility offered by the Transparent decks.

I have a final question: what makes life worth living?

What makes life worth living? My goodness, Life itself! Every breath, every drop of rain, every ray of sunlight, every dog fart, every moment of awe. In fact every moment of everything. Life is a great adventure, life is a tragedy, a sit-com, a romance, the world is full of all kinds of magic and beauty and I love it all. I feel things very intensely and I wouldn't have it any other way. Oh, and chocolate, of course!

New York / Cornwall, (South West UK), January 2011

"We revolutionize the person, the person will then revolutionize humanity."

A conversation with ANGELO NASIOS, tarot reader

I enjoyed very much reading your article on the "Myth of the Fortuneteller". I found it very lucid. The way I see it, the New Age market has made a true huge, orchestrated effort at sanitizing the tarot and making it apt for contemporary audience's consumption. I really admire the whole enterprise. Something I find especially intriguing is the fact that, besides making the images more bland, the main strategy sees to actually be based on defusing certain words, like 'fortunetelling', as you aptly pointed out. So, in the New Age world 'death' is not death, but 'transformation', and there are not bad cards. Nothing is bad, but 'challenging', and we are all looking to feel 'empowered'. I can see how the effort was aptly applied and these ideas permeated the writings of most relevant tarot authors, from the 70s onwards. I am very interested in this as I myself strive to find my own words to talk about the tarot. In fact, I think that the tarot's main function is to heal language. But your article also gives enough ammunition to those like me, who think that, at this point, it is obvious that the New Age's strategy has failed. The New Age market has grown, but it is a ghetto.

Society at large still sees tarot readers with suspicion, no matter what they call themselves. I suspect this has to do with the fact that the tarot and the main assumptions it represents are at odds with the way our culture at large sees itself. I am well aware that the average tarot reader would face that reality with a patronizing "it is up to the world to wake up and realize what they are missing". But to be honest, I wonder if we have given the world any reason to "wake up" at all. When was the last time the spiritual world produced a world-changing idea? Perhaps the last remarkable one was Blavatsky's theosophy, in that she opened a whole market niche for alternative spiritualities. I am not sure. It seems that society at large gets its answers from science and technology because those are the fields that are changing the way we think about the world. Within that context, tarot seems a dated tool for gaining insight, no matter what we call what we do. What are your thoughts on this? Do you think it is time to revise the 'sanitizing' strategy? Do we, tarot readers, really have something to add to the discourse of our times?

You pose some wonderful questions, I like the way you think! When you say the New Age market is "sanitizing" the tarot I assume you mean it is devaluing or rebuking the traditional uses for tarot such as fortunetelling. I feel it is not the market (publishers for example) but the community as a whole that does it to itself. We, as readers, have been trending over the last 15-20 years in making tarot more of a tool for therapy. This is because we want to be less "woo-woo" or the corner crack pot fortuneteller with the neon sign. People have prejudices to most things in life, when people hear that you read tarot they assume you are a psychic, you are telepathic, you are this and that. This is due to depictions of readers in the media via movies and TV shows. We always hear about the frauds stealing thousands of dollars from people. This places a huge stigma on all readers.

The way to combat that stigma is by dissociation from the either the word (fortuneteller) or the practice (fortunetelling). So now we are not fortunetellers, we are "spiritual counselors" or "advisors". It's just a mask we hide behind to appear less on the fringe. I fell victim to this trend myself. When I first started to read tarot I read it for one reason, to make predictions. I wanted to be the fortuneteller, the psychic, the one who could know the future. That's how I approached tarot, as a means to see the future, which is what tarot was made for. Tarot was not originally made for therapy.

When I joined a free reading website in 2006, the same year I went professional, I was told that tarot is not for fortunetelling, that we should not make predictions with tarot. I believed that and said that I was not a fortuneteller. I started using alternative titles. However, on this site we still had "outcome" cards, which in essence is a prediction card. We still did divination, we were still fortunetelling. The only thing that was different was that we denied doing fortunetelling and hid behind the mask of the alternative title. What does this say? It says that we still want to make predictions but lose the baggage of the fortuneteller stigma.

The neutralization of the meanings (Death = transformation) of the cards is expected. We live in a world that is very politically correct. This is no different with tarot. We soften the cards so we don't cause fear in our clients. Again, it goes back to the media. Has there ever been a time when the Death card was not used as a tool for fear and in the prediction of the untimely death of the client? In the movies the readers don't say, "Oh, you got the Death card, I see transformation". They say, "You will die!" As readers in the real world, again, we need to distance ourselves from the assumptions of the client. Yes, the Death card does not mean doom and gloom. But we should not ignore its name and soften it with sugar. The Death card means endings, something is dying, metaphorically, of course. As you say there are no "bad" cards, but "challenging" cards, this belief has to do with being politically correct, but there is more to it. Nothing in life is black or white. Nothing is good or bad, everything is subjective. The tarot is highly subjective to the reader and to the client. So 'bad' and 'good' have blurry lines. We should not even use words like 'good' or 'bad' because it implies morality in the cards. 'Positive' and 'negative' are better words, they do not imply morality. The cards have positive and negative meanings in them, and depending on the cards near them, the meanings change, enforcing or suppressing any given meaning. We think the Tower is a bad card, but next to the Sun and the Ace of Pentacles it is a great card. The positiveness in the tower is enforced by the surrounding cards. The Tower next to The Devil and 3 of Swords expresses more negative qualities.

What can we offer the world to "wake up"? I feel that people, deep inside, desire to be awakened to something higher than themselves. It may start at an early age or later on in life. I myself knew at the age of about 7 that people died and that I would die one day. It has been a constant source of personal anxiety, and I am thanatophobic. So I went into a spiritual direction early in life. I started reading tarot at 13. I have been studying theology and philosophy for some time as well. Others ignore the spiritual dimension and live only in the material world, and come to spirituality later in life, if they do it at all. What have we given to "wake them up"? I can only speak from my own experience. Tarot has offered me a way to connect to the divine and understand who I am. People want science to explain the world and make sense of the world because we live in a scientific world. We want facts, proof, evidence and experts. Nothing is wrong with that but science has limitations. Science cannot tell me about my psyche or who I am. Science cannot offer self understanding, science can't interpret my dreams, science can't connect me to divinity. So when people want to understand the things science can't help them with, they will turn to things like tarot and spirituality in general. We offer them what science can't, answers to the unknown. I also don't think tarot readers have to offer anything that will revolutionize humanity, because we are already doing it in each person who reads tarot or gets a reading. We revolutionize the person, the person will then revolutionize humanity.

Joseph Kosuth, one of the most relevant conceptual artists "in the books" suggests that when a culture that believes in technology needs that "something else" science can't provide, it turns to Art. He even calls our time the "Art Era", in which art stopps being just decoration and has become a tool for epistemological pursuits. Woody Allen also said that "art is the religion of the intellectuals". My feeling is that, no matter how big the New Age world can be, in numbers, the world at large is not buying what we have to sell. Now, let me be perfectly clear: it is O.K. The market is big enough for all of us to make a living, even if we have no bearing in the big picture. But still, what is it we are offering? You mentioned something essential: tarot readers have been playing the "poor man's shrink" for about 20 years in order to legitimize what they do under the guise of 'therapy'. Curiously, though, it seems that psychology only has something of relevance to offer when it gets out of the therapist's couch and goes scientific by means of academic research done through tested, falsifiable, procedures. There is a whole body of research now on what is called the psychology of happiness, that seems to be providing useful insights and which didn't emerge from a black chaise longue. Therapy seems, in itself, a form of artless shamanism in which a rather uncreative person, the therapist, attempts to face a creative phenomena, mental illness, with a few stiff diagnosing tools. So, if we aren't there to do that, and if we don't believe in predicting the future, what are we doing? What is what a person can get from us that ten years of therapy aren't giving her, if this is not a bunch of lottery numbers?

If we live in an Age of Art and art is the religion of the intellectuals then tarot readers must be the most intellectual people in the world. Simply because tarot is art. Each card is a small piece of art and some decks are masterpieces in their own rights. I like it that you brought up the topic of art and intelligence. It was in the the late 1800s that Sir Francis Galton (cousin of Charles Darwin) believed that intelligence was inherited. One test he used to prove this was to show great works of art to people in the aristocrat class and then to common poor people. The aristocrat people who were educated in looking at art and described art, interpreted the art, and talked of it as a metaphor for some idea or concept. They spoke about what the art meant to them and what it represented. The poor people would look at the art and say "it's pretty" or "nice". Galton believed that the people in the aristocratic class where more intelligent because they could look beyond the superficial and see the whole picture. They had more perception, and Galton thus believed that they were more intelligent. This, however, was founded to be untrue, of course, because anyone who becomes educated can do the same, so intelligence is a skill learned not inherited.

Art does appeal to the 'intelligent' people. When someone who is 'intelligent' learns facts, dates, formulas and objective information they may become bored and require a challenge. Art provides a challenge to people who are 'intelligent' because without that challenge they would not be able to truly understand what a certain piece of art means. So when they require that 'something else' as you stated, they go to art. Art also is a reflection of us, art represents us as people, as a society and as a species. Normally people turn to religion or spirituality to understand who they are and to understand life. The intellectual will turn to art because it can serve the same role as religion. Art teaches us about who we are, where we came from, and it shows our unconscious and our nature.

So back to the main issue, what are we offering? Since tarot is art we really can appeal to the spiritual and to the intellectual. We like to think that tarot is this magical thing and that it is somehow supernatural. However, as I explain it in my forthcoming book, tarot can either be supernatural or natural. We might be connecting to God, our guides, and the cosmic unconscious. We might also be just reading images that are random in nature, but our minds put what is random into meaningful patterns. I honestly don't care which one it is, I only know tarot works. What do we offer? No matter the person, be it the spiritual seeker or the intellectual, they are both seeking meaning to life in one form or another. I believe that, esentially, tarot offers a way to bring meaning and understanding to our lives. The rest of the world might not be buying into it because of all the "woo-woo" in it. When we have a reader who goes on a popular daytime TV show to do a reading for a show host and explains that tarot is mysterious and the origins of tarot are linked to Atlantis we are going to have people who will be turned either on or off in respect to tarot. Tarot needs to be presented in both fashions, as a spiritual tool for those who seek spiritual enlightenment and as an intellectual tool for personal psychoanalysis.

With regards to psychology, it does appear to be artless shamanism at times. Psychology is somewhat in a gray area in science. Psychology is both science and philosophy. Most of what psychology is based on is theory and little fact. The theory seems to be about the art of psychology. However, the trends now in psychology is to go the scientific route via neurology, for example. That is when you lose the art in psychology.

Psychology, and psychoanalysis specifically, has a lot to offer, and tarot has a lot to offer. Reading tarot for yourself or another, we can think of it in terms of doing psychoanalysis. Psychoanalysis, also known as the "talking cure", focuses on the client talking about what is troubling him. Talking the problem out of its skull and coming to a solution. Tarot provides the same. Clients talk things out and come to solutions. The only difference is that with tarot you have visual triggers that prompt reactions, memories, feelings and thoughts that might speed the process up and not take 10 years like the case may be with a therapist. If you are trained in psychoanalysis and if you can use tarot, I think you have a combination for great results when it comes to understanding what is going on in people's minds. I do think tarot is here for this kind of approach and tarot is here for predicting future, minus the lotto numbers. You can get profound revelations via tarot in a three card spread and it only takes minutes to read, so the results are faster than in an hour long therapy session. In the end, however, we are not therapists and should not pretend to be therapists. Tarot readers will forever be in a separate group to everything else, and I say, let's just stay that way. We are doing just fine the way it is. There will always be people who want what tarot can offer, which is understanding, meaning, and, of course, predictions.

I rejoice in the fact that the word 'portrait' has the word 'tarot' hiding inside. Perhaps reading tarot could be a form of portraiture, in which we are telling someone this line: "look! This is you! You are here!" And then again, I believe it was Ingres who said that, for the painter of portraits the client is the worst critic as we all tend to envision ourselves less wrinkled than we are! How do you perceive the distance between telling someone what he needs to hear and telling someone what he wants to hear? Is there a difference?

Yes, there is a big difference between telling people what they want to hear and telling them what they need to hear. Telling them what they want to hear is not beneficial at all, it can actually be damaging. When you tell people what they want you pose no challenges to them, you do not make them think, and they don't reflect on what you are saying, so they won't learn and thus grow spiritually. They will stay where they are. When a client calls 20 psychics and asks if she will get into a relationship with someone who she could never be with and all 20 psychics say YES, she clings to that notion. However, when one psychic says NO, and here is why and here is what you should be doing, that will cause change for the client. When you tell people what they need to hear you provoke challenges in them. I think that when the client gets a reading you should challenge him or her somehow. Make them think about the issue at hand and about things they have not considered. That is how you get to progress and change in a person, by making them think. I think most people don't think enough or think superficially, without any attempt at critical thinking.

They say it takes two to tango, well, I'd say it takes two to tarot. The client needs to be active in the reading and not just sit and listen to me. My job is to read the cards, and the client's job is to think about what I am saying. Telling them what they need to hear can be hard, and sometimes what they need to hear can be hurtful. If you have a client who is self-destructive in her relationships and comes to get readings on why her partners leave her, and to know what is wrong with them and not her, the real problem needs to be addressed. She has a problem, or is the problem, not everyone else, and she may need to fix herself, not everyone else. Showing her how to fix her habits can be the difference between having other five failed relationships or a few good ones and finally the one she always wants.

At what point do you lose hope in a client?

I believe in the good in people, and I try not to lose hope in them. I want them to realize their potential, I want them to come to a personal revelation about who they are. There are, however, people who do not want to change or feel they can't change. There is one situation when I lose hope, when a client keeps repeating their mistakes while expecting a different outcome. I have a friend whom I would read for about her relationship. She knew that she should not have gone in a relationship with her ex, but she did and now wants to leave again but can't separate herself from him. All the readings I do for her tell her to leave, and she tries or does leave but somehow she always ends up back with him. No matter what I say, nothing changes, and her habits don't change. It is in situations like these that I start to lose hope, but I never lose hope completely, because there is always that possibility that she will leave for good. That she could change one day is what keeps my hope alive. I believe that just about everyone can change.

Just last week I had a woman like that: crying aloud for a man she met 22 years ago and never ever had a relationship with her. It is not the same case, of course. This woman was a lot more radical in her obsession for an idealized love, and different from your friend, as her relationship never happened. Sadly, I have to say that these cases of women who are stuck in relationships that died out decades ago are extremely frequent. In these cases, I tend to ask myself: what purpose does her strategy serve? She has to be getting something from it. She is not getting the love she hopes to get, but here, there has to be something else that is being accomplished by this behavior. But that's where I draw the line and I remember that I am not a therapist. I agree with you in that looking at a few images could make visible some invisible things that the 'talking cure' would take years to unveil. But I really wonder to what extent should we really aim at changing someone. Artist Lawrence Weiner always says: "I don't want to screw your morning with something I posted on a wall. I want to fuck your entire life with it". I think that's a powerful, charming, statement; but I often wonder if our purpose as readers isn't more like the purpose served by road signs. A road sign can tell you: "Dead End" and it is up to you to acknowledge the sign and realize that if you keep driving you will end up crashing or landing in a pit. The road sign doesn't make you ponder if you should keep driving. It doesn't tell you the meaning of anything. A road sign delivers information in such a direct way that it leaves you no alternative but to acknowledge that if you choose to ignore it, you will have to accept some consequences. I am not talking about 'fate' or about a sense of predestination. I am simply suggesting that the future is the punch line of the present, and sometimes the tarot can be very sobering, since there are no mysteries about the outcome of unreasonable strategies. What are your thoughts on that matter?

I agree with you that tarot is akin to road signs, which are very clear. I do feel that many times the cards are very blunt and clear in what they are trying to express. If I feel the cards are relaying such a direct message I tell the client that these cards are very clear and direct. However the cards are not always so direct, they sometimes leave room for pondering. This may be because the question asked requires more internal (unconscious) work to be done by the client. Direct answers come more often when the answer is external or in the conscious.

With regards to the client who never had a relationship with this man 22 years ago but is still obsessed, what being obssessed serves her? In my view, she is living in a fantasy which she feels is better than her reality. She'd rather dream of a perfect world in which she is with this particular person than face a reality without him. Ideally, we want the client to come to a revelation about their behavior and make changes. However, some people don't change or do not want to change. They want the fantasy and will only try to find anything or anyone who will reinforce that fantasy. The extent to which we should aim to change someone is the same extent to which the client is willing to go to in order to change. We can only aim to what the client is willing to work on. When we have clients that don't accept what we say and continue to repeat old behaviors, we can consider not reading for them anymore. This person is beyond the help of the tarot reader, and perhaps a psychologist is needed because there might be a mental health issue going on with her.

How do you improve? What other disciplines are there for you to enrich your tarot work with? Are there any formal pursuits you keep working on? How does a tarot reader keep improving, besides practicing?

There are many ways to improve my reading abilities, how I understand tarot and use it. I want to become more knowledgeable in Astrology. I know enough to understand the planets and how they relate to the cards. However, I want to know more detailed things regarding astrology and incorporate that into tarot or use it separately as an additional tool. Astrology is in my view the most important system to be used when incorporated into Tarot. I do believe it is important to have a well balanced education of metaphysical and traditional knowledge. In college I have taken courses in philosophy, psychology, and biblical literature which all somehow can relate back to the tarot. Psychology is an important tool and I do wish to continue studying it. The greatest way to learn outside of practicing tarot is to interact with other readers. I am a firm believer and advocate of social media as a means to interact with others, share ideas, teach and learn. I promote *Beyond Worlds* and *Psychic Friends Live* any time I can, because I truly believe that they are a perfect example of the excellent product you get when you combine tarot with social media. Interaction is key to becoming a better reader. Facebook is a great way to connect with the tarot community and keep up with what is going on. Do not limit yourself or close yourself off into your own world of learning via books alone. Go online, read tarot blogs, watch youtube videos on tarot, and listen to radio shows and tarot forums.

Do you envision yourself being a tarot reader for the rest of your life? What other things fill your time?

Yes, I do see myself being involved with tarot my whole life. Growing up with the idea of having a 9 to 5 job in an office, and wearing professional clothing was a nightmare. Currently I am doing just that, my day job is my literal childhood nightmare. I knew I wanted a career in something non-traditional, I wanted to do something different. I also knew I had to be my own boss. My family owns our own business, so, growing up I knew my parents as the ones always in charge and never having to be subject to anyone else. My mother told me when I was a kid that I would need to be my own boss if I wanted to be happy. I think she was making a statement about my character rather than a general rule, because I personally don't like to be told what to do and she knew that. Tarot seems to be the path I have always dreamed of. It is non-traditional, very unique, and I can be my own boss with it. Tarot is also something that never gets old. Every reading is a new adventure in a way. Tarot is my true passion and I do see myself in the future developing more and doing more in our community. I am currently writing a book and I hope that it won't be my last. I hope to write more and contribute whatever it is that I can. One day I hope to be considered a respected figure in the tarot community. What else fills my time? I work a full time job which takes up much of my time. I am also in college part time. However, the funny thing is that no matter where I am, I am thinking tarot. I will be at work and thinking about my book, or what to write about, coming up with ideas. At school I try to take what I am learning and apply it to tarot. Tarot seems to fill up all my time, but I am not complaining.

New York / New York, January 2011

"Self-delusion is a beast that lives inside each one of us, and like meaning and love, it is man-made."

A conversation with RICK MAUE, magician, mentalist

I remember talking to Todd Robbins, who told me he was drawn to side show stunts as a reaction to have grown in the deceptive decor of suburbia. Do you recall the first time when you experience a sense of wonder and you realized it was all an illusion?

Two incidents come to mind. One is directly related to my background in magic and mentalism, and one is related to life in general. I will briefly try to tell you about both.

I remember seeing a magician on TV when I was about 5 years of age, and he did a large stage illusion, and after that he took out a deck of cards and did a simple sleight-of-hand trick with just the four aces. And I remember thinking that the stage illusion looked cool, but even at age 5, I was immediately suspicious of the big box that he used. Basically, I thought it had to be a trick, and the box made it work. But the demonstration with the four aces seemed completely magical to me. At that moment, I honestly thought that it could be real magic. After all, the playing cards were not suspicious because I had seen playing cards in the real world and they couldn't make the trick work (remember, I was 5). But after a little more thought, I decided that the demonstration with the cards was probably an illusion as well. It just didn't make sense that the stage illusion was a trick, and then the card piece was a demonstration of real magical power. And it was at that moment that I realized that things in life could be deceptive, on purpose. However, I figured that such deceptions would always be presented as entertainment, and that was how society kept itself from confusing reality and illusion. (Once again, remember that I was 5.)

This story brings us to incident number two. We fast-forward to the early 1970s, and there is a buzz in the air about a psychic that can bend metal with his mind. He can read the thoughts of others. He can start broken watches. And he was saying that we all have the power to do the same things. He was all over the news, so I figured that it had to be true. (Okay, I was no longer 5, but I was still a kid.)

With my enthusiasm building, I searched for everything that I could get about the guy. I also started reading books like *Chariots of the Gods* by Erich von Daniken. After all, this stuff was not being presented as entertainment, it was on the news, so it had to be real. Well, a few months passed, and as I continued to devour everything that I could get my hands on, I began to have doubts. Some of the ideas just seemed too far-fetched, and they just seemed to be what people wanted to believe to be true but without being willing to examine the "evidence" too closely.

It was around that time that I began to realize that beliefs seemed to exist in a special "hands-off" part of our society. If someone believed in something, it was more than a bit taboo to criticize it. Even asking for any type of rational discourse seemed out of the question. In short, none of us like to have our beliefs challenged, and so it seemed that the standard societal defense mechanism was to not challenge the beliefs of others, no matter how preposterous they may be. So I guess it's accurate to say that those are the things that laid my foundation for the connection between a sense of wonder and starting to understand illusion. You could also say that's when I became disillusioned with self-delusion.

I have to confess that I am always looking for the man behind the curtain. The most immediate downside of this is that I can't watch a parade without wanting to rain on it. At some point, finding the man behind the curtain stops being an accidental happenstance, and becomes a way of looking at the world. The thing is, once you spot the man behind the curtain, there is no way back. I guess that would be my own definition of being a 'skeptic'. One wonders how things really work, and one stops taking symbols for concepts. But I guess that the "standard societal defense mechanism" you pointed out has trained me to think that 'maturity' consists, precisely, of refraining myself from raining on other people's parade, and so let them be, as long as they don't force me to march along with them.

Now, within that context, I have spent the last two years thinking a whole lot about death. This was a direct consequence of my brother's death. There is nothing original in that: death seems to be an invisible membrane surrounding us and which we don't see unless it pops. My brother was 38 and died as a consequence of a car crash, leaving us with a sense of rupture in our natural narrative: parents aren't supposed to bury their sons, grandmothers aren't supposed to mourn grandsons, and older brothers aren't supposed to see their little brothers die. (As you might see, one doesn't have to be five to be naive!) I remember that, as I was packing my bag to go to see my parents, I was also mentally packing the stories I needed to cope with my brother's death, and also, the stories I needed to help my parents cope with my brother's death. I was intrigued about the fact that such 'packing of stories' was a spontaneous reaction of mine. I tend to think that neither life nor death have an inherent meaning. Perhaps 'meaning' is in fact that boundary between these two. Death is, after all, the mother of god and the mother of art. In any case, my stories weren't religious stories. I was actually amazed at how ineffective the pseudo-spiritual explanations other people offered to us were. As I became aware of the emptiness of all these "heavens", "paradises", "releases of positive energy into the void", I also became more and more comforted by the actual lack of meaning in my brother's death: it was a random event, and crying was all we could do about it. Even so, I couldn't help to think: isn't that self-delusion too? I bet there is a man behind the curtain of any rationalization we make of the world.

I am telling you all this because I am trying to get at that "disillusion with self-delusion" you pointed out. Do you think that would be a form of 'magician's curse'? I guess another way of asking the same question would be: is there such thing as someone too intelligent to experience a miracle?

Wow, the notion of whether or not a person can be too intelligent to experience a miracle sends my mind going in a number of different directions. It's probably best for me to start by clarifying a few things before we go too far. Now, some of this will probably be unrelated to what you asked, but as Hunter said, "You bought the ticket, take the ride."

First things first, I assume that when you say "a miracle" you are referring to something that is beyond the point of having no known cause, instead, the occurrence actually defies the laws of nature, as we understand them. After all, intelligent people constantly experience things that cannot be explained, but those things are not automatically labeled as being miraculous, their causes are merely unknown. So let's really start there with a simple hypothetical example of a typical paranormal claim.

Let's say that a person experiences noises in their attic, and so they believe that they have a ghost inhabiting their home. Now, although I don't happen to believe in ghosts, I am not going to smugly tell that person that ghosts don't exist.

After all, that would be the stereotypical "skeptic" reaction, and doing so would merely spotlight our two diverse opinions and create two irritated individuals. Worse yet, the "unexplained" noises would still be coming from their attic. All of that is counterproductive, and it actually steers us away from the truth.

Instead, I would talk with the other person, and I would try to understand what they were feeling and saying. Then, I would agree that they do indeed have a source of unexplained noises in their home, and if they really want to discover the cause, then we have to consider all possibilities, including their notion of a ghost. (Please note, by agreeing that they have a source of unexplained noises in their home, we begin the entire process on common ground, and that is what opens the door for us to honestly work together to find a real solution. However, most people who believe in unproven claims don't really want to learn the truth. They simply want the delusion to remain because it makes sense to them. In short, astrology and religion are one in the same.)

So, we would then make a detailed, and honest, list of what could be the possible sources of the noise in the attic, for example, the house may simply be settling; there may be plumbing problems; or heating/cooling problems; or wildlife in the upper crawlspaces; or a ghost; etc., etc. The point is, we would eliminate possible labels one-by-one as we address each possible source, but more importantly, we would agree to not apply any specific label to the cause until we were certain that it was indeed correct. And we would eventually find the cause, or we wouldn't. Either result would be a success because the truth was never compromised with the application of any unsubstantiated labels. However, even in those times that we would be unable to discover a cause, but we honestly eliminated some of the erroneous causes, we would still be closer to the truth because we would have cleared away some of the static, which is an important step toward seeing a clearer picture.

In simple terms, any other type of unexamined phenomena that is merely labeled "a miracle" (or paranormal) is simply a result of self-delusion, wishful thinking, and outright laziness. Truth requires hard work. And that's pretty much how I live my life. I either know something to be proven, or I except the fact that it is not understood. I honestly try to avoid unproven labels, and the need to justify them to myself, or others.

So, can a person be too intelligent to experience a miracle? I don't know, but it's possible for even the most intelligent person to be lazy enough to experience one

But now, to change gears just a bit, I wanted to comment on a couple of points that you brought up in the story of the times surrounding the death of your brother. (More importantly, my deepest sympathies, my friend.) I agree with you when you said that you "tend to think that neither life nor death have an inherent meaning." To me, life and death simply happen. We don't know the exact science behind all of it, so it is all a mystery. There is certainly a cause behind our existence, but that does not imply that there is a meaning. And, there is no evidence that any meaning exists. Things simply happen because they do, and everything has a cause. In other words, there is no such thing as an accident. All things happen due to causes. One car hits another because the two paths intersect. That is the cause. But there is no meaning behind it.

Humans exist, and there must be something in nature that caused that to happen, but there is no meaning behind our existence. Meaning doesn't exist in nature. The concept of meaning is man-made, just like the concept of love. Love doesn't exist in nature. Love is man-made. It is deeply-rooted in needs, wants, comfort, survival, etc. Now, don't assume that I am saying love doesn't exist. It certainly does. Or, at least the concept of it exists on a human level. Love is merely the "label" that humans put on the package of certain wants and needs. But love is simply a label that allows humans to communicate in regard to certain topics. And the same goes for meaning. Meaning certainly exists on a human level. Poetry can have meaning. Paintings can have meaning. Songs can have meaning. As with love, meaning is merely a way for one human being to communicate with another human being, and it is a tool that we use to enhance our own experience. But there is no evidence that the concept of meaning exists outside of human existence. Many things in life have meaning. Everything in the Cosmos has a cause. However, meaning and cause are certainly not the same. Causes are tangible, while meaning only exists in the human imagination.

And finally, I want to address your comment, "I bet there is a man behind the curtain of any rationalization we make of the world." Sure there is. Like I said, everything has a cause. It's when we start looking for meaning (or applying those unsubstantiated labels that we talked about) that the self-delusion sets in. But don't get me wrong, self-delusion is a part of every person's life. Whether we want to accept that fact or not, it is true. It is a defense mechanism. It is a security blanket. It is an often-needed ego boost. It is a way of coping with difficult times. It is a friend that doesn't question us. It is a friend that doesn't judge us.

Self-delusion makes us think that life is important, and that delusion can make us believe that human life has meaning, when, in truth, we're just here because we are. When we're gone, something else will be here. We take it personally, but it's all just cause and effect, but our own self-delusion makes us think differently In short, self-delusion is a beast that lives inside each one of us, and like meaning and love, it is man-made. Self-delusion doesn't exist in nature. Human beings are pattern-seeking animals. That is how we survive. Imperfect as it may be, self-delusion allows us to complete certain pictures, and so it is simply another tool that helps us to survive. All of these things – self-delusion, meaning, love – are merely tools that we use for survival. However, to me, the key is to ask yourself a question that should be asked about every tool that we use in life: Do you use the tool, or does the tool use you?

You mentioned something that is very important to me: we must own our own fictions, but we shouldn't let our fictions own us. Now, you are a lover of poetry. Poetry is weird to me in that I cannot call it 'fiction' and I cannot call it 'non-fiction'. Poetry is language happening. The other day I was looking at someone performing a magic trick and I realized I react to magic the same way I react to poetry. There are poems that I enjoy and poems that blow me away. The difference, I think, is that a poem I just enjoy is a poem I read while knowing, at some level, how it is done. But when I read a poem and I have no idea of how that person came up with that precise form, or those words, when I have no clue as to how that person made that happen, then I am totally blown away by it. Those are my favorite poems. I would say you are a designer of illusions. I don't know if you would agree with that! But I would like to know if what I just described happens to you too.

For the most part, I agree that poetry is neither fiction nor non-fiction, at least in regard to the poetry that I am drawn to. One way to describe the pieces that I write would be what my greatest hero and mentor, Harry Chapin, used to say about songwriting. He stated that even if his "story songs" weren't literally true, they were emotionally true. The same goes for my poetry. However, with that said, you (or anyone else) may read my work and say that it is not fiction, nor is it non-fiction (which I agree with from the viewpoint of any person reading the piece), but as the poet, it is often much more than "language happening". It actually is 100% non-fiction because it is everything that is my life put on paper. And I would think that a number of artists would feel the same way. So I think the perspective is very different from the other side of the creative fence, which I suppose, is rather obvious.

In regard to your notion of knowing or not knowing "how" it is done, this is very interesting. Even though I have compared the art of theatrical deception to poetry many times before, I never looked at poetry through the eyes of "how" before, which, as I said, is very interesting. However, if the truth is told, I rarely look at any strong piece of theatrical deception through the eyes of "how" either, unless I happen to be in "work" mode. But trying to stay with the idea of "how" for just a bit, the experience that you describe of not knowing how a person came up with the precise form or words doesn't happen when I read the work of others. However, it happens every so often when I read something of my own. I get that feeling of "where did that come from?" on those rare and wonderful occasions. As a creator, it is exciting, and humbling, to not know where one of your own creations came from, and it can be unsettling to not know how to harness the muse again. That is the poetry, and the magic, of creation.

Getting back to the work of others, like I said, I don't get the feeling of "how" when I read another person's poetry. Sure, I am often blown away, but I guess I just accept – naively, I suppose – that the person is just so much more creative than I am. Now certainly, I realize that great poetry or prose often causes the writer to sweat blood, but in the end, some people are just incredible writers, and I assume that incredible art comes from them, whether they want it to or not. And when they do choose to ignore it, their genius is simply lost to the wind because they don't bother to capture the moment by writing it down.

And one final point. You described me as a designer of illusion, but you were not sure if I would agree with that assessment or not. In truth, I honestly believe that the human experience, and the human interpretation of existence, is nothing but an illusion. I mean, just like in the previous questions, we create things like love and meaning to reinforce the illusion of the human experience. I just happen to be one of those unusual people who has had the good fortune to be able to point out that fact for a living.

Ah! I didn't know you wrote poetry! What lead you to it? What is in poetry that one cannot find in stage illusions?

Well, I started writing poetry back in the early 1970s, and I became submerged in it rather quickly. But then again, most of the things that I do, I do them to extremes, which is probably why it's really good that I never had an interest in drugs or alcohol. But I was introduced to Poe, and then Blake. Soon I was reading the Beats, and Rimbaud, and I was hooked. The more I read, the more I wrote. But like most people, the stuff was only for me, none of my poetry was intended for the eyes of others. Although that all changed a little more than a year ago, but that's another story.

But poetry originally filled a void that magic simply couldn't back then. You see, the one thing about magic and mentalism that has always driven me crazy is that the vast majority of it never expresses a viewpoint. Much of it doesn't have anything to say. Sadly, that's how it was when I was young, and the same holds true today. Sure, some of it is funny. Sure, some of it is entertaining. Sure, some of it may even be a bit thought provoking. But very little of it expresses a viewpoint or really has anything to say. And even though I have never been one of those magicians/mentalists who debates whether or not what we do is art (because I really don't care), I do have a personal philosophy of what art is. To me, art expresses a viewpoint, or, at the very least, it has something to say. That doesn't mean that every person will get the exact interpretation as everyone else, but that's fine. The key is that the creator/performer knows what he/she is projecting.

But, like I said, when it comes to magic/mentalism, most of it has absolutely nothing at all to say. In that way, to me, both magic and mentalism are more accurately defined as craft. However, I must make the point that I am not speaking for anyone but myself. I don't say these things to start any major debates on the Internet forums. Others may define what they do on their own terms and it doesn't affect me in the least, just like my views are not intended to affect others. I merely define these things so that I can work inside my own creative framework. So, many years ago, poetry became the way for me to express my views, and magic and mentalism allowed me to pursue craft and performance. However, I slowly started to understand that I could incorporate my views and my beliefs into my magic and mentalism, and I began to experiment with that combination. Today, my show has quite a few of my personal thoughts expressed, and it is fun to work in certain places and voice my feelings on topics like religion and politics. For me, the key to success has been to avoid any type of preaching, and merely allow my views to become a bit of additional seasoning that helps to bring out the flavor of my performance character. By doing so, what I do is not threatening, nor is it adversarial. And that's why it works. But yes, regardless of adding that element to my performances, to this day, I still write poetry. In truth, a day doesn't go by that I don't get something down on paper. That's why there is always a small Moleskine reporter's notebook in my back pocket.

What you are saying about (theatrical) magic having nothing to say is very intriguing. I think you are onto something here. I guess a magic trick says nothing more than the trick itself. The problem is, indeed, one of intention. Just as you perceive a lack of meaning in magic, I tend to perceive a lack of aesthetic intention in magic. This is something that, for me, is also lacking in the tarot world, as many readers assume that the aesthetic aspects of tarot end right where the card borders end. It is as if the artfulness of the tarot were reduced only to the artwork on the cards. I wonder to what extent 'aesthetics' and 'content' could be the same thing, or not. In any case, both share that notion of 'intention', as when we inform whatever we do with pursuits that go beyond the thing in itself. When it comes to magic, do you have any aesthetic pursuits? In which way does your poetry inform your work?

I guess that if I have any real aesthetic pursuits in my performances, they would lean toward an organic approach. No flashy props. No music. Very minimalist. It's just me, conversing, and sharing with the audience. I even tell them that what I do is a partnership, and the only way that I can be successful is if I help to make each and every one of them successful as well. And one way of accomplishing that is to help those who assist to relax, and the familiar items that I use play a role in that relaxation process.

I want my show to look professional, of course, but I also want everything that is used to look like it came from an office supply store. And, by the way, everything in my show does come from an office supply store, which is great because I can basically piece together my entire act in a matter of minutes. However, the ease of putting the show together was never my intention. It just happened that way. My goal was to make every item used very recognizable and above suspicion.

After all, each audience member has the exact same items in their own home. Once again, being familiar with the objects helps the audience assistants to relax.

As for the ways that my poetry informs my magic/mentalism, I guess the easiest way to say it is that I have the same passions in life whether I am writing poetry, creating/performing my act, or anything else. The key is to figure out the best vehicle for saying what I want to say. In some strange way, it's a bit like when Warren Zevon used to talk about how certain songs worked better on the guitar, while others just made more sense on the piano. So, some of the feelings that I want to express come out better as poetry, and others as performance pieces of magic or mentalism. And yet, each form informs the other. But one thing that I will say is that all of my creations are more likely to be inspired by music or poetry than by any magic or mentalism. I mean, a high percentage of my performance pieces have come from a lyric or a stanza, but hardly any of them ever come from other pieces of magic.

Your comment about minimalism and having an organic approach reminded me of Tom Wait's glitter. I was watching several clips of him, paying attention to the performance side of it, and I was mesmerized by the way he would reach into his pocket, grab a handful of golden glitter, and throw it over his own head. It doesn't get more low-tech than that! The audience cheers-up every time he does that. As a performer, Waits reminds me a lot of Joseph Beuys. There is that other gimmick he has: stomping on the stage to rise dust, or smoke. It does resembles Beuys' dance on top of an iron plank, with iron-sole shoes.

The thing about Tom Wait's glitter is that there is no deception involved, no trickery, no 'apparatus'. He simply grabs it from his pocket and throws it on his head. Carrying one's pockets full of glitter is poetry in itself! But there is no artifice, and even so, that glitter raises big cheers. I like a lot that lack of artifice. Somehow I feel people are willing to by-pass (not even suspend) their disbelief, to enjoy seeing this rainmaker making rain. One can enjoy the effect, but one can also enjoy the bold lack of artifice. I have to confess that I share the same aim in my work with the tarot. It was the tarot what brought poetry into my life in the first place, as I see the act of looking at tarot as an act of poiesis: a making of meaning by noticing the rhythms and patterns elicited by the coming into contact of two or more images. I hope people can bypass their disbelief, get sucked into the seemingly uncanny relevance of the images, and then snap back, without ever losing sight of all being an illusion, a set of imaginary scenarios, neither fiction nor non-fiction, like a poem. Now, not everybody is able, or willing, to make those leaps. As we discussed before, we are probably high wired to reject such leaps. I wonder what your views are in terms of how far we should go with helping people 'snap-back' into the reality of illusions. How little is 'too little'? How much is 'too much'?

Well, there is quite a bit to chew on in your question, but I want to begin by digging around inside your comments about Tom Waits. Basically, I want to touch on the idea of making assumptions as an artist. In truth, it is a discussion that I have had many times with certain friends. (Please understand that my following comments are not criticism, they are merely discussion.) Yes, as you said, it doesn't get more "low-tech" than Waits tossing a handful of glitter over his own head. And yes, the crowd reacts strongly each time. However, I am not willing to concede that the reaction is based on the idea that the "people are willing to by-pass (not even suspend) their disbelief, to enjoy seeing this rainmaker making rain." To me, that notion is certainly poetic, but I think there is a helluva lot more to it than that. I would argue that the audience reaction to the glitter is fueled by a number of factors. First and foremost is the celebrity status of Tom Waits, or more generically, a famous person performing before his adoring public. That point alone would be enough to generate a strong reaction to just about anything that the performer does. After all, it is very rare for any celebrity to ever be judged objectively, or effectively, by his/her dedicated fans. A typical case of Pavlov's Fans.

But let's try something, let's take Tom Waits out of the equation completely and see how the exact same glitter-tossing action would be met by audiences when watching a complete unknown. For the best test, let's have a street performer use the same technique somewhere in Brooklyn, deep inside the bowels of the NYC Subway System, and we will see what happens. My suspicion is that the reaction would be, at best, one of mild surprise. At worst, the action would be completely ignored. (Much like the street player in the brilliant, and haunting, Joni Mitchell song, "Real Good For Free"). And with each additional toss of the glitter, the subway audience may possibly get into the spirit of the piece, or they may quickly grow weary of the seemingly mundane action. But I would be willing to bet that the reaction would certainly not be the same as when Tom Waits tosses the glitter. And that would leave me to believe that if we could erase the image of Waits from our memory, and we could experience the glitter-tossing action for the very first time beneath the cracked Brooklyn streets, we would not have the impression that the "people are willing to by-pass (not even suspend) their disbelief, to enjoy seeing this rainmaker making rain."

What I am saying is that the reaction at the concert is possibly (and I would even be so bold as to say probably) not due to the action itself, but instead to the overall context. But that's merely looking at the reaction itself. It is something else to assume what the reaction means. So let's take another step and refocus on the original Tom Waits crowd. Is it also possible that the reaction is partially due to the intentional lack of production value, and that the overly-simplistic act of tossing the glitter is actually mocking more elaborate theatrical displays? Simply put, perhaps the reaction is overwhelmingly based in parody. Could that also be a reason for the strong reaction? It could be, but who knows? The reaction could mean so many different things. My point is that I cannot bring myself, as an artist, to ever assume what an audience is thinking or feeling. I can certainly have an emotional direction in mind that I want them to travel, but I can never really be sure if any, or all, will take the same path. For example, I have watched Teller perform his signature piece, *Shadows,* well over fifty times, and I have watched the audience react in different ways over the years. Some crowds are deadly silent. Some react with a nervous giggle, you know, the kind you tried to suppress in school. Others have laughed out loud. There are even times that the reaction of one person drives the rest of the crowd.

In short, I would not be confident enough to assume exactly what each audience was thinking or feeling, or what a specific reaction means. More importantly, I would never be able to assume what every member of the audience was thinking or feeling. After all, each member of an audience sees a completely different show than everyone else in the theater. However, one thing that I do know is that all aspects of art are directly influenced by the artist's level of fame, and reactions are certainly affected by the celebrity/fan relationship.

And now, changing gears just a bit, and yet trying to tie all of this together, I would like to look at your vision of tarot in the same way. I certainly respect your view of people being able to "bypass their disbelief, get sucked into the seemingly uncanny relevance of the images, and then snap back, without ever losing sight of all being an illusion, a set of imaginary scenarios, neither fiction nor non-fiction, like a poem."

In fact, I go far beyond respecting that notion, I actually like it quite a bit. But just like Tom Waits, tarot has an established level of celebrity, and often the masses will only see what they want to see with their celebrities. Which means that the real-world hope that most people will not lose sight of tarot being an illusion, and seeing it as a poem, is a bit too Utopian for me. Although I am trying to avoid cynicism, I must keep my feet planted in realism and know that most people that have an interest in tarot are looking for answers and directions for their life, and I don't mean that in a poetic way. They often want to know what is going to happen, and what they need to do. (You probably knew that my "dedicated skeptic" persona would emerge at some point during these sessions, and you may even be surprised that it took this long. Oh well, I guess we can't really fight who we really are, he said with a grin.)

I only make all of these points so that I can make the following basic points. As artists, we cannot assume how our art affects others. All we can do is put into it what we can, and then it is out of our hands. Once our art goes out into the world, it is no longer ours, and what others get from it, or do with it, is out of our control. We can never assume to know exactly how we touch people.

Now, I know that I have yet to answer your actual question, but I felt that in order to address it properly, I needed to start by putting my response on a bit of solid ground. So how far do we go to help people "snap back" into the reality of illusion? How little is too little, and how much is too much? To be honest, I don't know. Now, I figure that that's not really the answer you were hoping for, especially after the long rant that preceded my simple six-word reply, but I am just being honest. However, instead of answering your question with a specific answer, let me explain why I don't know.

Simply put, the question, like many questions about creativity and art, is looking for a response that could indicate some type of rule. And rules are to art what mayonnaise is to acupuncture. Art has no rules. But on the other hand, craft is loaded with them. So, if your art employs any type of craft, it is wise to learn those rules, especially if you choose to eventually break them. For example, when I first got into poetry, I studied and learned the rules. And once I knew them, I ended up breaking just about every single one of them on a daily basis. In some ways, I think that one of the best paths to art is to enter on the road of craft, and once you know exactly where you are, take a series of unknown turns and lose yourself. At that point, you have the experience, and the knowledge, to know how to be lost effectively.

So how far do we go? That's up to each artist. How little is too little? There is no such number. How much is too much? The sky is the limit. Remember, it's art, there is no right or wrong.

As I said in a piece of mine called "Stream of Unconsciousness" (2009).

> There's spilled paint
> all over the ground
>
> Somebody should
> probably clean that
>
> But then again,
> maybe it's art
>
> Could be…
> after all,
> I've paid to see
> shittier stuff

New York / Pittsburgh, PA, January 2011

"I think as tarotists, we are in a constant state of studying life."

A conversation with STORM SCESTAVANI, tarot reader

From time to time I would get someone who says she has never, ever, had a reading done by a man. Have you encounteted that? Should we set ourselves above these differences? Can tarot readers claim to be the only men who understand women?

I do get that comment, but very rarely. In the United States, many noted readers (and I use this term to encompass all modalities) are male. I think male readers have become more accepted over time. I really don't know if we should set ourselves above anything. I think that the process of a reading should be to simply provide the clients with the information that they need rather than focusing on issues such as orientation, sexual anatomy, and identity. I think that we as tarot readers often get caught up in preconceived idealisms that really do not matter. To be effective, I feel that creating an atmosphere that is about the client and not about the readers is the REAL goal we should focus on. I asked God whether or not male tarot readers are the only men that understand women, and she said, "no!"

When was the last time you asked God something and he said "yes"?

The answer was factitious and with great humor. In reality, I really think that people in this day and age are interested in answers and are not so concerned with which body parts are attached to the oracle.

I cannot help but find that image fascinating: "which body parts are attached to the oracle". What attracted, or attached, you to the tarot in the first place?

I don't really know whether or not I was attracted to tarot or tarot was attracted to me. As a teenager, I was always in a state of questioning. I was looking for big gigantic answers to the universe, and felt that my purpose was larger (possibly because I am a Leo) than just studying and finding a profession to be in. One evening close to dusk, I was in my grandmother's attic questioning what I was going to do with my life. When it started to get too dark in the attic, I got up to leave and tripped over an old chest and landed up against a bookshelf. Two books flew out of the bookshelf and landed on the floor! One was *Archetypes of the Collective Unconscious* by Carl Jung and the other was *Saturn* by Liz Greene. I became fascinated with what would be metaphysics and psychology from that point.

Several months later, I decided to join an after school club. At one of the meetings, one of the other students had a deck of tarot cards (I do not remember which deck, but I believe it was the RWS), and I became fascinated with the images that were on the cards. I went that afternoon to the bookstore and purchased a deck of cards. Since I had an obsession already with Greek mythology, the *Mythic Tarot* was the most likely choice. I purchased the deck and it was off and running from there. My study of tarot became an absolute obsession and eventually I purchased several books, but my favorite has always been *Tarot for Yourself* by Mary Greer. I believe that being attracted to the tarot or the tarot being attracted to me was fate. Not the concept of having no choices or being predestined to something. It is my opinion that what we are fated to is being who we are, and tarot is very much a part of me.

These days I see 'fate' very much as I see 'luck'. In order to be able to respond to a lucky, or fateful, moment, one has to have done a big deal of preparation, which in some sense could simply be to pay attention to these things that truly resonate with us. A less attentive person could simply have put these books back on the shelf and walk away untouched by the happenstance. If I understand correctly, your relationship with the tarot started very early in your life. Which other disciplines informed that understanding of the cards? I know that in my case it was my background in the visual arts what gave structure to my approach to the tarot. But eventually, the tarot structured my understanding of poetry. How has your experience been? Which disciplines did you pour into the tarot, and which disciplines have been enriched by your work with the tarot?

My interest in tarot probably evolved out of my interest in literature and my interest in myths. I noticed from the very beginning that the cards told a story, and certain cards being next to each other brought forth many of the stories I had read. It became more amazing when I discovered that these stories made sense to the people that I would do readings for. Since I see tarot as a syncretic system, I have learned to use the cards in conjunction with astrology and psychology. I use them as tools of amplification to help me understand what is meaningful in the life of the querent at the time that I read for them. In return, astrology and psychology add to my understanding of the tarot. I've come to learn over the years that there are many ways to skin a fish, and I like having multiple layers to work with when I am working with my clients.

You mentioned myth, and I wonder: in your view, are there any constitutive, or fundamental, elements in the myths we consume that need to change, or has that changed from the ancient myths to the contemporary ones?

I think that we have to look at what a myth is. Many people believe that a myth is simply an untrue story, but I actually prefer another definition for myth which is a scheme or a plan. I think myths are myths because they describe archetypal experiences that we all go through regardless of our race, nationality, gender, or sexual identity. There is something about them (that seems to be organic and alive) that is relevant to all of us. I think that we attempt to retell these stories, much as the Greeks retold stories from other cultures, but the bare bones of the myth remain the same. Myths are part of the human condition, and although the human condition may progress I do not feel that it fundamentally changes. We may have better toys, but we are still concerned with the exact same issues that people were concerned with four thousand years ago.

I see myths as imaginary solutions. Blueprints, as you said, for potential dynamics. By saying that I am well aware of the fact that we tend to assign a negative value to whatever is 'imaginary', under the argument that imaginary things aren't 'true', when in fact, everything that exists that had been created by men started off as imaginary. To what extent do you see the things you tell to a client as 'real'?

I tend to tell clients very practical things that are usable to them. The good majority of my clients does not have the knowledge of mythology that I have, and it would be rather arrogant of me to take the reading to that level. On the other hand, I see mythic stories weaved through tarot spreads or astrological aspects that are more symbolic triggers to help me understand what the issues are that the client is going through at the time of the reading. It is my job to convey this information in a way that the client can understand. If I am doing a reading, and I have 6 different sword card in front of me then I know that there is much on the mind of the client. The client may have many decisions that they need to make (or have made), and some of these decisions might not be ones that are really desirable. In many ways, they are backed up against a wall and are experiencing anxiety and fear over their situation. The swords suit reminds me of the story of Orestes, and how he was forced to make decisions that were forced on him by forces much larger than himself. Now, I have not had a client that has come to me where he has had to kill his mother to avenge his fathers death; nor are they literally pursued by opposing deities. However, I do have clients that have sided with one family member against another and they are experiencing anxiety as a result of this decision. In this way, these symbols are very alive for them and ultimately they must find some resolution. In many ways, working with the figures gives the client a deeper understanding of the tapestry that is at work that allows them to understand their circumstances in a more meaningful way.

What you are saying is so interesting, and so useful, that I would like to probe you a little bit more: you are giving a very precise example of how you would use the meaning of the suit of swords to assess a client's situation and know what to say to her. Now, the association between swords and the intellect, albeit popular, is in itself an intellectual construct, a convention. By this I mean that, just as there is a tarot school that sees swords as representing the intellect, there are other schools that see swords as representing something else, and still, a reading done by following these other conventions will most likely be equally relevant for the client. So, in a sense, any meaning we attribute to the cards is an imaginary solution to the problem of crafting a narrative from the images. It is the contact between our narrative and the clients' own experience that gives these metaphors a literal value. In your opinion, when do your words become real? Is it when the client "sees" them in her mind? Is it when these things come to happen? Is it when they tap onto one of these archetypal myths?

I think the reading becomes real for all of the reasons you mention. I don't think you can sit down and create an algebraic formula that says that this is going to be where the client finds the situation to be "real". We could debate whether anything is real or simply a narcissistic figment of our imaginations. I think the value that is created is when the client can leave the reading and use the information she receives in a tangible way. This is why I avoid metaphysical language in my readings, because I don't really think that clients find value in it. They find value in understanding why their relationships are not working, why their finances are messed up, and why they are in job circumstances that are not to their liking. Where it becomes useful is when the client comes to you and has problems and you see an interwoven pattern within the spread or within a horoscope that reveals what might be "creating" this problem for them.

As far as your school of thought ideals, I do feel that we have to start somewhere. My particular understanding of symbols is from studying psychology, but other people may use a different set of symbols, and this is where the psychological process of transference and counter-transference begins to occur. I think we need to realize that this process can occur in the tarot setting as much as it can in the psychological setting. All we truly have is ourselves, our experiences, and our understanding of life and we are going to project that experience on everything outside of us – it becomes the lens through which we view everything. The alchemical process that occurs during a reading is the combination of my experiences with the clients' experience tossed into the alembic (fancy word for a cooking pot), and eventually (with enough patience) something positive and enduring will come out. I truly feel that as practitioners we have to be empirical in our sessions, and attempt to learn as much from them as the clients learn from us. Every consultation gives us more understanding of how these experiences occur and further information to ponder. Becoming a tarotist, (unlike many other professions) is an ongoing process because of its symbolic nature.

"Becoming a tarotist is an ongoing process because of its symbolic nature". That's a great phrase! Do you mind amplifying what do you mean by it?

If you make the choice to become an accountant, you go to college and get your degree and you start working with numbers. Those mathematical figures remain constant! The tools an accountant may use over time will be different, but the true essence of the profession remains the same. The same can be said about many professions. Where I think tarot and astrology (and the medical profession along with a few others) are different is that we are dealing with peoples' lives. They have problems, hurts, concerns, anxieties, and fears when they approach us. In many cases, the tarotist begins where conventional forms of counseling ends! Clients come to us when they feel they may not be understood by their family, their clergy, and their friends, and often with issues that will alienate or limit their relationships with others.

I feel that we are still concerned with the same issues we were concerned with thousands of years ago, but I feel that the way we approach them sometimes are different. For example, 60 years ago divorce might not have been the resolution to a relationship, because the needs of the family system were much more different than they are now. If a client drew the 5 of cups in 1955, would we offer her the same advice as we do today? I have no problem telling a client that if her relationship is not working then one of the options is ending the relationship – especially if she cannot find a solution to make the relationship better.

On another note, I remember when I was in high school that we were all encouraged to go into the technology fields because that is where the job security would be. The people (or culture) that were telling us to do this were people that went to work for the same job for their entire life. That was their experience, which was very real to them. You got a job, you worked hard, you retired at 60, collected a retirement check, bought an RV and traveled to a warm climate. Today, the average time at a job is under 5 years. It's a different experience!

I think as tarotists, we are in a constant state of studying life. Everything in our lives – media, the internet, culture, society is symbolic of the times. Even the most absurd (like the show *Jersey Shore*), has a symbolic element. We have to morph and shift with the collective consciousness to be effective. If we do not, and we continue to view life like it was viewed 60 years ago – and do not have some foresight into the future – we are offering the same thing that religion is offering. This is why I think it's a tough choice to become an "oracle", and the price that we pay for stealing fire (speaking the language of the Gods) can sadly be enormous.

In which way have you paid that price?

I have interests in other things besides Tarot. I have a huge interest in the equality movement, and I have a huge interest in politics. I think my making the choice (which I do not regret) to be a tarotist means that the larger social world, which may not appreciate or understand what we do may be turned off by it. If I decided to run for public office, you know that whoever is running against me is going to use it as a reason why someone should not vote for me. The same is true about relationships – it takes a very special person to be involved with us, and the reality is that my profession could limit (by association) my partners opportunities and options. The greater public does not take us seriously, and people tend to attack what they do not understand. There is a great unfairness in it, but unfairness is just as much a part of life as living is.

I ponder the Prometheus myth frequently, and I believe its deepest essence is a place where any oracle can find meaning. Prometheus stole fire (which you could translate into progress) from the Gods and gave it to mankind. He made a sacrifice, and he was punished for doing so. In many ways, we do the same thing! We steal the potential of possibility (and since I do predictive readings even more so) from the Gods, and as a result we give the client more choices and more options. They are still bound to their myths, but we provide them with the understanding that there is no myth that says they have to live life in a destructive way. In essence, we teach them how to be their own Gods! In order to do this, I think we sacrifice a lot. This is why I feel that tarot is a vocation, whose root in Latin means "to call". I think we all have a vocation in life, but I feel that many of us do not listen when the Gods knock at the door. I am glad I listened!

New York / New York, January 2011

"To limit Tarot reading to fortune-telling is like using a classic samurai sword for cutting bread."

A conversation with KATRINA WYNNE, tarot reader, psychotherapist

I am interested in understanding how the tarot, a tool that is commonly defined by superstitions, can be 'sanitized' and used in a therapeutic way, but I would also be interested on discussing if it does indeed need sanitizing.

To examine this question, I would need to break it down into some of its parts: superstition, therapy, and sanitization. "Superstition" tends to be a belief, often emotionally based, not backed by facts. Tarot readings also lack fact-based evidence, are mostly subjective, and relying greatly upon belief, either in the cards, the reader, and/or the client. Then there are the overriding beliefs, such as where the "information or guidance" is coming from: God, Goddess, Angels, the unconscious, etc. What might differentiate it from superstition? I would say it is the deeper, intuitive knowing and sensory-grounded confirmation that the client and the reader experience in the reading. This is the beginning of what I distinguish as Transformative Tarot Counseling™.

"Therapeutic" work implies that there is a treatment for illness. I have two points to make about this concept. The first is on ethics, while the other is philosophical. Ethically, tarot reading or interpretation is not meant as a treatment and certainly is not a substitute for professional help, especially when it comes to medical, psychological or financial matters, among others. For me this would constitute a "scope of practice" issue, and I encourage tarot readers to have a referral list for supporting their clients to seek such assistance. Second, I come from a different, more holistic, point of view in working with folks. I do not view people as sick, ill, lacking, suffering, evil, or negative. In fact, judgment is not a useful tool in my tarot work, or in my life. In addition to my background in Taoist philosophy, tarot has taught me a great deal about unitive values, seeing the wholeness of each person and people in general, as well as all of life and the universe.

"Sanitized" is a curious choice of words and I'd like to hear more about what you mean when you use this word.

Let me see if I can explain what I mean by 'sanitizing': There is a long tradition that links the tarot to divination, and more precisely, to fortunetelling. The first thing that comes to most people's minds when they hear the word 'tarot' is "telling the future". 'Therapy' (or the elicitation of some sort of transformative process in the client), seems to be – in the view of many readers I have spoken to – what is left if we take forecasting out if the tarot's equation. I am not saying that I am convinced that is true, nor that I believe the tarot is a form of therapy. In fact I agree with you in that readers should stay away from any therapeutic claim they cannot back up with the appropriate credentials.

Now, independently of where the reader stands (hardcore divination, counseling, projective tests, visual koans, etc.), this common link the tarot has with fortunetelling has given the word 'tarot' a stench. To say that you work with the tarot implies that you subscribe to a whole realm of beliefs, or superstitions, that many times have nothing to do with the tarot in itself: people would extend their hands assuming you also do palmistry, they would assume you believe in angels or UFOs, they would think you have a good aromatherapy recipe for growing a mustache or that you can cleanse their auras. This is why those who don't share these beliefs would flinch when they hear the word 'tarot' just as we flinch at the stench of rotten fish. I would submit that, although there's a market for these ideas, our society at large doesn't feel represented by them. In addition to that we have the fact that the tarot's public image has been defined by conmen and madmen. One understands that is not all the tarot is, or what the tarot could be, but one has to take that stench into account. To me, 'sanitizing' the tarot has to do with taking the stench off. (This, of course, assumes that one has to feel the stench in the first place!) I am very interested in talking to you because I have spoken with countless therapists who like the tarot and keep it private, out of fear. Some of those people have told me they can even get disbarred if they dare using the tarot within a therapeutic context. Then I have spoken with a few people, like you, who are proof of these fears not being totally founded. Maybe it takes courage, or conviction, or a certain personality to pull it off.

In any case, this all interests me because I wonder: what is the role of the tarot in the 21st century? Superstitions come in all shapes and forms. I suspect that feeling inadequate because you are 30 years old and single is based on superstitious thinking, just as believing that all you say in a tarot reading will be reversed if you hear a dog barking far away, or like assuming you are better 'suited' to get a job if you are wearing an Armani suit than if you are wearing a cheaper brand. But while we may not be able to overcome superstitious thinking, we may not even want to or need to do that, our culture keeps updating its superstitions. Aren't the superstitions surrounding the tarot dated? If so, what do we do? Should we update these superstitions? Can we get away without these superstitions being associated to the tarot?

What you call "stench" I would call a stereotype. Stereotypes tend to be promoted by mass media and gossip by putting huge concepts into comfortable little packages, yet are illusion, and mostly prejudice (pre-judgment) based on fear of the unknown. For me this goes back to what I was saying about my holistic view in contrast to a more one-sided view of life. If I'm interested in the whole person, I move away from pre-judgment and have no need for stereotypes. The stereotype might be a starting place for some people to open the door to experiencing what could be a totally new and unexpected awareness. This is at the heart of transformative work, to be able to step into and hopefully embrace some aspect of the unknown in such a fashion that we no longer experience our life in the same way.

You bring up the other end of the spectrum as well, when the reader or counselor is treated with prejudice due to the assumptions folks make about the nature of our work with tarot. Certainly it exists. I have experienced people turning away from me due to their preferences, prejudices, and the like, but should that change who I am and what is meaningful to me? No. This is where the spiritual practice of integrating the transformative message of the tarot is most helpful, for it is not only a tool for divination, but a profound book of divine wisdom. It is a guide for living one's life in beauty and balance, even if other people prefer a more one-sided existence. When people live in fear, they suppress themselves or overwhelm others with their power, for they actually feel weak. I have found that if I am congruent with my energy, power, and purpose, other people are not triggered by my presence and thus feel no need to manipulate me, for I have no need to manipulate them. I learn from my mistakes and continue to work on myself, my spiritual journey, the XIV Art / Temperance of life.

Although I still feel shy to pronounce this, it is a vision of mine to help people move past all fears, be it toward tarot cards, divination, the unknown, or otherness. Even among Tarot readers I've encountered fear of new ways of relating to the cards that expose them to the unknown. As humans, we often cling to the known, the familiar, routine. For readers, this appears as comfort in our typical reading style or knowledge of the cards. Sometimes I need to speak up and shake things up a bit. Isn't it card XV, The Devil who, like Lucifer, represents an obstruction on the road of life, whose intention is to wake us up to the message of God's light and love? Waking up to our attachments so we have more awareness of choices is my style in tarot reading, counseling, and living. As a trained psychotherapist, I have many tools in my magic bag for stirring the alchemical pot of life.

In the 21st Century, we humans have evolved as a species to the point where many are ready to transcend dependence on fear, attachment, or the known. In the spectrum of existence all of us are in various stages of development and maturity. I deeply believe in, have observed the evidence of, and have experienced the ultimate message in the tarot, that we have the potential to transcend duality to reunite with source, the Light, God/Goddess, the universe, the card XXI, The World. Not everyone chooses this path, but the pathway is illustrated by the tarot for us all to pursue whatever degree we wish to journey. There is something for everyone in the tarot to support each experience and stage of life. That is the beauty of this medium for offering support, guidance and reflection.

As readers, our preferred styles can be seen as signposts for where we are, our developmental stage on this journey of the Tarot. There are as many styles of tarot or reading cards as there are people. I find that the way a person approaches or uses tarot is very close to how they approach life. It is a reflection of who they are, their unique perspective, and perhaps their limitations as well. Here is where we might encounter "dated" or tried and true styles of working with the cards from some folks. We naturally attract clients and experiences that help us learn the lesson and essence of our chosen stage. As I always say, there is something for everyone when it comes to approaches with the cards as our tool. I value diversity for it represents the rainbow within tarot.

OK. What about "fortune-telling"? My response is to paraphrase my friend and fellow tarot enthusiast, Diane Toland, from her book, *Inner Pathways to the Divine.* To limit tarot reading to fortune-telling is like using a classic samurai sword for cutting bread. Cutting bread is a useful activity and feeds our basic need for sustenance, but there is so much more we can tap into and experience with the tarot.

I have been thinking that one of the most important things I have learned through the tarot is to appreciate, or understand, the true importance of Art. Most people find that unexpected or difficult to comprehend. The tarot has allowed me to experience, first hand, the power of images, words, and narrative, in a way that painting, or writing couldn't. At some point I understood how uncanny, how marvelous and even surreal is the fact that we, human beings, are these little two-footed mammals who can make images – visual, verbal, sound images – and these images can have us laughing, crying, feeling inspired or depleted. All arts are illusory and delusive at once, and man is that animal who can create a delusion and being changed by it, for real. I understood then that we carry within the power to change ourselves. We imagine the bridges that will have us crossing all the abysses we may find along our way, even when, sometimes, these bridges are, or must be, imaginary. But here I am talking about image-making as a craft that has us manipulating shapes, colors, forms, notes, to affect us both intellectually and emotionally. I am talking about art as a human event. I said that some people don't get it, or they are puzzled by this, because they would think that, yes, art is all that, but the tarot is different (which is a way of saying the tarot is not Art). It seems that a big part of these stereotypes you suggested have to do with assuming a link between the tarot and a certain set of paranormal beliefs. Do you think that a belief in the paranormal, or even the supernatural, is necessary to experience the tarot?

I would like to respond to the last question, first: No. Experiencing tarot does not require anything beyond the choice to participation on some level. There is neither necessity for belief, nor attachment to supernatural concepts. To explain, bottom line, tarot cards are technically just pieces of paper. As paper, they have no power other than what we imbue them with. Cards, as visual stimulus, can entertain, perplex, inform, trigger, or inspire the viewer into a variety of responses or reactions. The viewer can project beliefs, values, judgments, associations, and other cognitive-emotive connections from their personal experience upon the cards.

It can be said that individuals are also channels for the collective or the universe to connect through the relationship to the cards. But that is my belief which I bring to my relationship with tarot. And thus we have the beginnings of diversity in working with tarot images. Each person brings unique perceptions and experience to the mix, layering the personal, relational and universal levels of communication with one's style and preferences for perceiving and processing data. And from this mix emerges "meaning" for those who seek this conclusion.

This leads us to the heart of your question, the "Art" and visual language of tarot and its potential impact on us and what we find meaningful. To be touched by fine art is when we have been moved by an experience of the piece, otherwise we are neutral, with no connection, no engagement. What is it about tarot cards that command our attention, possibly triggering emotions or impacting us experientially? Dai Leon expresses it best in *Origins of the Tarot* (2009): "It is the goal of every Tarot deck designer to convey a remarkable appearance of beauty that reflects innate truth as much as possible." And further he says: "Plotinus recognized that the sensory experience of seeing an image translates smoothly into the recognition of a mental image resembling the physical one. The continuum then expands to include an intuited gestalt of the mind's image. This gestalt is based on the knowing and feeling intuition."

This "gestalt" refers to the whole being greater than merely the sum of its parts. Aristotle originated this concept, which has evolved into the art of creating a tarot card. By combining symbols, be they characters, props, numbers, words, implied movement or potential sound, a synthesis of possible meaning emerges in the form of archetypes, stories, and aspects of the mandala of life. Life as a mandala encompasses the totality of experience and expression, much like the tarot incorporates the holographic pieces of the total representation of life, albeit three-dimensional.

As "two-leggeds" we relate to storytelling. Just look at the popularity of TV, movies, books, history, etc. We look for a beginning, a middle, and an end, in order to better follow linear time, utilizing contrast (duality) to help us compare and observe differences, especially over time. I emphasize that duality is a tool, much like our two legs or two eyes are useful for balance or depth of perception. It allows us to raise our awareness of the opposing energies at work, which, ultimately, seek resolution. Let me illustrate what I mean. In theater, the classic template for the story is: 1) introduction of characters and setting, 2) conflict is established, 3) resolution is accomplished. This is also the basic concept inspired by ancient Greek philosophers, but most apparent in the work of German philosopher Hegel as he explored the triad of thesis, antithesis, and synthesis.

This is the manner in which the brain processes information, as well as the classic form of scientific inquiry with its hypothesis, test/results, and confirmed or new theory. Herein are the ingredients for a powerful tarot reading. By entering the gestalt of the energy or essence of the tarot card, while following the story in the querent, cards, and layout, we open ourselves to the possibility of a meaningful experience. This is terribly simplified, just the basic skeleton of the process, but I hope it helps to illustrate what is in the background laying the foundation for the "art" of reading and relating to the Tarot.

One of the quotes you shared brings up a question I often ask myself: what is the 'distance' between truth and beauty? I very much agree with the author in that images present us with a kind of beauty that, by becoming meaningful, feels true. So I wonder, is beauty the visible face of truth? Does beauty mirror truth? Are they one and the same thing? Are they different?

I.F. Stone, a maverick investigative journalist in 20th century America, reflecting upon himself in his renowned publication, *I. F. Stone's Weekly*, wrote: "I tried to dig the truth out of hearings, official transcripts and government documents, and to be as accurate as possible. I also sought to give the *Weekly* a personal flavor, to add humor, wit and good writing to the *Weekly* report. I felt that if one were able enough and had sufficient vision one could distill meaning, truth and even beauty from the swiftly flowing debris of the week's news." (*The Haunted Fifties*, from a collection of Stone's writings from 1963) When working with the Tarot, aren't we also investigators seeking to distill meaning, truth and possibly beauty from the chaos of existence? It is said, "Beauty is in the eyes of the beholder." In this sense, it is relative and subjective. Ancient Greek philosophers, such as Aristotle and Plato, posited: "Beauty is Truth, and Truth Beauty." Whereas Aristotle introduced the concept of the golden mean as the desirable middle between two extremes, Plato argued for objective values of truth, goodness and beauty, yet based on his own belief of wrongdoing and right. To measure something is to give it value. From this point of view, value is a dualistic tool for comparing and finding balance and meaning.

When I reflect on the tarot and where it teaches us about these values, I think of the three "virtue" cards: Balance (Justice or Adjustment), Strength (Lust) and Art (Temperance). I see all three of these as aspects of balance, respectively, mental, emotional, and spiritual balance.

However, in Dai Léon's masterpiece, *Origins of the Tarot*, he speaks of Truth and Beauty as essential non-dualistc aspects of life. I cannot completely represent his meaning, but this is what I understand from his writing and a couple of deep conversations we shared. As he states in his book, "Chaos and the changing world essentially exist to realize the Beauty of Goodness and the Goodness of Truth [...] For against all odds of chance, the cosmos does in Truth already exit in such a Beautiful and Good Way." I agree with Léon's premise that the Tarot is a "spiritual set of images", "a truly brilliant treasure of sacred knowledge" influenced by perennial wisdom of how "Unity of Being is wedded to the Myriad Becoming." They are designed to reveal and address ourselves as pure Being, radiant Consciousness, and absolute Bliss and Truth. Léon speaks of the fundamental principles of the universe as reflected in pairs of Triumphs of the Tarot, revealed as 10 nested levels of hierarchical evolution and integration. Each level brings us closer to the realization of Being, Consciousness, and Bliss.

Is there anything you wish to accomplish with your tarot practice that you haven't accomplished yet?

My "tarot practice" is more of a "Tarot Journey", a spiritual odyssey. Since 1971 I have studied Tarot as a book of wisdom. It wasn't until about 18 years ago that friends and others began to ask me to share my tarot knowledge and guidance. My "Tarot Counseling / Consulting" style naturally evolved from 23 years of psychotherapeutic training and service. As I was called by folks to teach tarot, I developed a program that incorporated the counseling skills and ethics of my counseling practice with the spiritual wisdom of Tarot. For more information on my unique program, see the "Transformative Tarot Counseling™ /Transformative Tarot Consulting™ Certification Program" (TTCCP) at TarotCounseling.org.

My tarot practice is a spiritual practice. At its heart, this is the wisdom I study, share, and hope to inspire in the world. I'd like to dispel the fear and superstition projected upon the cards. In fact, I'd like to help eliminate all fear. It may sound like a daunting task, but it is my path, my "lane" that guides my life.

This winter's goal was to establish a new website dedicated to Tarot Spirituality (TarotSpirituality.org). It is now up and open to comments, articles and links, with the hope of developing a global awareness of the profound potential of Tarot. So far there are topics such as "Tarot Cards as Tools" and "Tarot Spirituality™ as a

Legal Option?" with dynamic dialogues developing already. "Tarot Spirituality" is also a Facebook community with special discussions ready for comments.

It would be an honor to have you and your readers visit these Tarot Spirituality sites to share your wisdom on this topic. Thank you for the privilege of having my voice heard in conversation on Tarology.

New York – Yachats, Oregon, September 2010/March 2011

"Spending luxurious, contemplative time with the symbols and characters of the tarot would be enough to change us from the inside out."

A conversation with JAMES WELLS, tarot reader, consultant

How did it all begin?

Part of me wants to say that it all began when a hot and dense universe suddenly expanded. Another part of me wants to say that it all began when my mother and father got twinkles in their eyes. However, I'll assume that you mean how my involvement with the tarot began. My interest in what potentially makes people and life in general tick began as a child. Old Testament stories of parting waters to free people, Greek stories of gods and goddesses who have troubles and triumphs, Canadian First Nation's ways of being in harmony with the natural world, and a fascination with spirits, magick, and things beyond everyday knowing were on my mind. In some of my books, I came across references to tarot cards. When I was 12 years old, one book in particular – *Let ESP Work for You* by Patsy Ruth Welding – devoted a few pages to the tarot. Welding's short foray into the cards was so delicious that something stirred in me. So I set aside some money from lawn-cutting and paper delivery and took the bus to a games store where I had seen tarot decks. The only pack they had was the 1JJ Swiss Tarot, so I bought it. I winged it for a few years during my teens, just letting the pictures, lines, and designs bring things to mind. Looking back, I think I wanted to be psychic, special, cool, noticed for being different at that time. I practised on myself, a few friends, and some schoolteachers after school hours. Any time I found a book about tarot, it would be filled with such arcane references that I just put it down and didn't bother with it. When I bought Gail Fairfield's first book, *Choice Centered Tarot*, in my late teens, it was a revelation to me.

The whole notion of fate, predicting exact events, and trying to amaze people fell away and was replaced by living by choice, finding potentials in the moment, and being helpful rather than trying to wow people. It was a gateway into exploring tarot as a tool for personal insight, creativity, taking more responsibility for one's life, and being one's own best teacher. Through personal experimentation, taking workshops, and reading well thought-out texts, I continued (and still continue) the tarot path. Living with the tarot all these years has opened up other fields of interest in my life: circle process, goddess spirituality, dreamwork, archetypal psychology, various modes of healing, journal writing, and so much more. What I notice now is that the tarot is simply a tool; the processes with which I partner the cards are what count.

These days I have been enjoying some of Jerome Rothenberg's essays on the figure of the 'trickster' as a bridge between the shaman and the poet. Reading about the shaman's duty of sabotaging reality by using as his main tools ritual, trance and language hits very close to home in regards of the reasons why I do what I do. Reading about the role of the shaman as the gatekeeper of wonder I confirm once again how these traditional practices found their direct translation into our Western culture in the Art of the 20th century: Dada, Surrealism, Fluxus, Performance Art, Happenings, Conceptualism... From Contemporary Art as a system of superstitions based in the rules of sympathetic magic, the world (and work) of magic evolved into the grimoires of advertising, the rituals of fashion and the oracles of Wall Street. We live in a world full of magic: we get our charms from the fashion designer, our dreams from Hollywood, our symbols from artists and poets, our spells from the advertising agencies, our forecasts from the weatherman or the stock-broker, and our miracles from science. We tell our dreams to a therapist and get comic relief from our stand-up comedians. I can't help but wonder: did we miss the boat? Is our personal predilection for more traditional routes to wonder, such as the tarot, a liability when it comes to assess the role of what we do in the contemporary world? Have the traditional forms of magic become fringe simply because there are other, more elegant, forms of magic that are preferred by the mainstream?

The second sentence you said reminds my of Abraham Heschel's definition of a prophet as I heard it via radical theologian Matthew Fox. He said that a prophet is someone who interferes in history or who interferes with whatever interrupts authentic life. It's not about someone's random predictions regarding things that haven't happened yet, it's about being so present with what IS that one can notice the options in what is. The prophet or shaman or trickster pays attention to what's working and what's not working, what needs to remain and what needs to change. Then she or he communicates that observation to those who need to hear it. It's contemplation translated into action. In this sense, eco-activists are trickster-prophets, tarot consultants are trickster-prophets, poets are trickster-prophets, visual artists are trickster-prophets, stand-up comedians are trickster-prophets. Last Sunday, Kathy Griffin performed here in Toronto. Some may dismiss her work as potty-mouthed fluff, but she has a real sense of what's going on in our culture that's not humane. Her comedy points out what's ridiculous and often wrong. We laugh at her pronouncements as we realise, "She's spot on! That particular politician has no right to declare that people's ethnic origin or sexual orientation make them less than human."

Addressing your question about tarot in the contemporary world, I feel that tarot as a route to wonder, insight, and awakening is not a liablity in these times, but an asset. In many cultures, the shaman lives just outside the village, not quite among the people, not quite all the way in the wild. He or she dwells in the liminality between civilisation and wildness, the mandorla, the place of both-and. At the April, 2011 Readers Studio in New York, Caitlín Matthews said something that unexpectedly brought me to tears. She told us that those of us on the edge or fringe of society – tarot practitioners, shamans, undertakers, garbage collectors, agents of social change – are where we are so that when those who are in the middle of mainstream culture experience something that sends them running, they'll have somone on the edge waiting for them. Her words pierced me like lightning. It was a moment of prophecy. I heard her say that we who work, live, and play with tarot are on the fringe so as not to be as alloyed by the dominant culture's tendencies, so that when people come to us they really sense the tending, the holding of space in a different way, the possibility that what's in salons, malls, television shows, political rhetoric, and video games isn't all there is. Those who dwell on the perimeter offer alternatives, show another way of being that is more in harmony with what is life-sustaining. With or without tarot cards, that way of being is an act of interfering with what interrupts authentic life. For many, this is hopeful. It might not be glitzy or slick, but it's hopeful. Tarot, for me, *is* elegant, not in the fashion magazine sense, but rather in the way my Grade 10 mathematics teacher meant it when he referred to the elegant solution: simple and graceful.

"Interference" is a very useful word. The tarot seems to be a very apt tool to have life becoming its own détournement. It offers a possibility to interfere with the patterns of what we call "reasonable" once reason has run out of batteries. I am borrowing the word "détournement" from the situationists because their "interferences"

with reality had a political purpose. To what extent do you see these "interferences" we do as political gestures?

This question excites me, Enrique! I love to demystify the tarot in the sense that I like to dissolve the superstitons that have grown up around it. And I love to think of tarot consultations, tarot rituals, tarot contemplation, tarot journalling, tarot poetry, tarot decks, and any form of tarot interaction as countercultural, a swim against the current of the stream in which we live. To interfere with the dominant mindset as absorbed by ourselves and by the folks around us is no small feat. To really start dissolving the dominant paradigm, it helps to use images because they speak to the Deep Self, the unconscious, the True Self. Tarot images convey messages to us deeply. They're a fabulous antidote to the advertising industry's predatorial pictures. One of the ideas with which I'm currently living is that of primarily using tarot decks for myself and my clients that depict a countercultural way of being. For example, the *Gaian Tarot* and *Medicine Woman Tarot* show us humans and more-than-humans living in harmony. Their artwork and the philosophies in which they're rooted teach us how to exist sustainably and successfully. The images of the *Motherpeace* and *Daughters of the Moon* decks invite us to to honour feminine, relational ways of living. The *Tarot de Marseille,* in its various forms, calls us to tried-and-true virtues that help us retain our equilibrium. Even without doing readings/consultations, the tarot could inform us. Spending luxurious, contemplative time with the symbols and characters of the tarot would be enough to change us from the inside out. That, to my mind, is a simple and strong political gesture, subtle activism as some of my friends call it.

The other question that comes from these musings would be: where is the trickster in the tarot world? Isn't the figure of the trickster missing from the 'new-age shaman'? Aren't we too positive and 'reassuring' for our own good? Have we given up the potential for mischief as a restorative derailment shamans used to have?

I agree that there can be a fluffy-bunny aspect to tarot, indeed to any tool or process in self-help, human potential, or whatever you want to call it. There's a small handful of tarot practitioners, four or five, that I would trust with my desire to explore something because they work on a profound level and know how to take me out of my habitual patterns. They work *with* me rather than talk at me. On the whole, I don't get other people to read the tarot for me. If I hear, "Take up yoga" or "Just pray to such-and-such archangel" one more time, I'll shriek. Yoga and I don't get along and while I don't mind spiritual support, I'm not putting an entire situation into the hands of a being who may or may not exist without doing something proactive on my end. So, where is the trickster-shaman in the tarot world? The tarot itself is a great trickster. A counsellor in the form of a deck of cards? Ha! A map to self-realisation in a game? Silly! But true, at least for me. I'm amazed that this thing we call the tarot has endured for several centuries in various guises and for various purposes. It should take on Aleister Crowley's magickal name, Perdurabo, because it has endured and will continue to do so. Its capacity to adapt is fascinating.

If someone wants it to reflect Qabalah, it does. If another person feels that the tarot goes nicely with Celtic mythology, it does. Someone who identifies with post-modernism finds it in the cards. Perhaps this ability to shapeshift is one way in which the tarot is a trickster. It puts on a new costume and gets a new hairdo, yet its structure and essential concepts remain. Trump XV, the Devil card, is a lovely representation of the trickster. In certain circles, it is said that the Devil is merely the Divine as seen by the unwise. What I hear in that statement is that adversity contains wisdom if we really choose to look at it, that observation of an event brought before the imagination can open up our options. Awareness of our options can lead us to make choices. It's up to us whether these choices will be life-denying or life-affirming. Trump XV tricks us into liberation by binding us so we get to a point when we can no longer stand it and burst our bonds with the lightning bolt of the Tower. The Devil is a card that sticks out its tongue, blows us a raspberry, and taunts us with, "Victimhood is a state of mind. I'm really your own mind."

I adore your phrase "mischief as a restorative derailment"! When I work with the tarot, my own piece of mischief is to ask open-ended questions about observations made about a card. It doesn't matter if I'm exploring something in myself or with a client, the act of derailing someone's usual thought patterns by asking them to describe what they perceive in a tarot card then asking them a question based on their observation is a simple piece of play that opens up awareness. If someone pulls Trump XXI, the World, and says, "There's a person performing a striptease in the middle of a bunch of animals. She's naked before every species on the planet", I might ask the client, "In what way do you need to strip down naked before your fellow inhabitants of Earth?" This is certainly not something one is asked every day and it invites a more extraordinary response, perhaps a more primal and authentic response. Moments like that allow the trickster-shaman to shine.

Can you elaborate on the idea of asking "random" questions about what is seen in the cards as a way to interfere with... What?

Most often, a person and I work out a clear intention and a layout containing questions rooted in that intention. I rarely use a pre-fabricated spread, but prefer to explore a person's requirements with something custom-made, whether that person is a client or myself. The questions I ask from observations about a card are contextual. If our topic is a person's personal growth, I try to frame my questions around that. If the subject under exploration is right livelihood, I keep my questions in that context.

That said, a question that's a bit of a curveball can really get the creative juices flowing. What we're called to interfere with here is our habitual thoughts and well-worn strategies. I recall a client who drew a card to represent her next step in the process of creating her international business. She pulled the Hanged One, so I asked her, "How would you feel about doing sweet bugger-all?" The woman just about had a fit. She was so accustomed to doing, moving, and shaking things up that the Hanged One's question/message really challenged her. As we spoke, however, the client realised that at that point she had acted in every possible way and that the rest of the process was in the hands of those she had approached. To relax for a couple of weeks or so would be beneficial for her sleep life and her social life. She received a valuable teaching, for her, that non-action can be the right action.

Do you think often about your own mortality? If so, does this inform your tarot readings?

The simple responses to these are rarely and rarely. The more convoluted response is that I'm sure that life goes on after the change we call death, whether living on after death means my soul retaining a personality, my life-force being absorbed into the cosmos, or my body feeding the plants; however, as one octogenarian friend says, "I want to live until I die." I prefer to think of myself as a biophiliac rather than a necrophiliac. There's enough unnatural death-dealing in our culture without me contributing to it. If that viewpoint contributes anything to my tarot consultations (I almost never use the term "readings"), it's that I want the tarot and our interactions with it to be agents of sustaining life, both individual and planetary.

Last week a client of mine mentioned that I dress like a clown. I thanked her for noticing it. I derive lots of visual inspiration from clowns. I don't mean party clowns but people like Ricardo Bell or the Fratellini brothers, who had a very stylish sense of wonder. Nowadays the word clown is covered by a patina of shame. Same thing happens with words like 'magician' or 'fortuneteller'. A prolongated exposure to all kinds of formal and conceptual stultice had made it very difficult for someone to stand by any of these words. The reason why I bring this up has to do with your choice of the word "consultation" over "reading". I do the same thing. I do my best at referring to the trumps as "images", or even trumps, not as "cards", and I usually talk about "looking at the tarot". Instead of "getting a reading" a client would be invited to come "look at the tarot with me", or I will "look at the tarot for her". Back to the begining of our conversation, if there is something we have learned from the "bards" of marketing is to re-word things to make them new. I would like to know: what do you accomplish by using the word "consultation"? Do you feel this word brings the tarot closer to the therapy-model? If so, in which way do you feel this is beneficial?

Your sense of style, clown-like or otherwise, is appreciated. "Looking at the tarot with me" is a helpful way to put it, Enrique. It can dispel so many expecations, as can the term "consultation". Going back to the party clown image for a moment, there was a time when I would do tarot readings at people's parties – wedding showers, birthdays, TV show launches – in addition to doing the longer, in-depth private consultations. It felt like there was a split in me. One day, I asked myself, "Am I the tarot equivalent of a balloon-twisting clown or a counsellor? Am I the tarot equivalent of a D-list lounge singer or am I a someone who invites self-awareness through these splendid images?" The answer was simple, and I stopped doing parties. Addressing your question, I feel that by using terms such as tarot consultation, tarot experience, tarot conversation, tarot session, a look at the tarot cards with me, and so forth, we dispel the idea that the client/querent/seeker/friend/readee will be read to, or rather read at. We bring in the idea of with. It's a co-created and interactive experience. The participants are me, the other person, the tarot, the place, a topic, a series of questions rooted in that topic, curiosity, imagination, observation, and whatever someone believes their

Wisdom Source to be. For me, this does bring the tarot closer to the therapy or counselling model. I've just finished offering a four-week online course called Tarot Counselling for Self and Others, in which the cards were our chosen tool. It was the process that mattered in this class. We practised noticing what's happening in the moment, attentive listening, the art of asking open-ended questions based on what we notice, entering and exiting the session consciously, summarising what's been said, and helping the client (whether self or other) to come up with concrete, doable actions in the world based on whatever card strikes them as a visual representation of a way they'd like to be. Not a trace of, "This card means you'll have a good relationship and bad luck with money." Our focus was, and is, self-awareness and inviting constructive change. One benefit of working in this way is that the client generates his or her own primary insights and takes more responsibility for what's going on. This feels really good for the person, gives her or him a sense that s/he is wiser than s/he originally believed. This also benefits the practitioner in that s/he doesn't have to be "right", just a helpful guide.

There's a heck of a lot of work going on inside the tarot consultant: really noticing what's going on in the client's interaction with the cards, listening, formulating questions that create the potential for discovery. But the practitioner doesn't have to come up with all the answers. What a relief! There's nothing wrong, however, with a bit of commentary on the consultant's part. Sometimes things get stuck and a bit of tarot knowledge can get the session moving again: "For me, Cups can be about feelings, close relating, and emotional expression. And Threes can be about clarifying, defining, and getting ready for something. This makes me wonder what feelings you might need to clarify out loud with yourself or another." In other words, traditional information about the tarot doesn't necessarily conflict with tarot counselling, it can enhance it when employed judiciously. And if anyone uses tarot in a more psychic way, they can use that psychic sense in a tarot counselling session by sensing which questions might be more beneficial to ask the client. By the way, the verb "to counsel" comes from an old word that means "to consult", so if anyone is getting squeamish over the use of the term tarot counselling, it actually just means tarot consulting. To sum up, I feel that consulting instead of reading is empowering and far more interesting than us blathering on at someone for 60 or 90 minutes.

How do you think all will end?

If by "all" you mean the cosmos, I haven't a clue. My understanding is that creation is still happening. It didn't end when some folks decided to write a so-called holy book about how they thought the world was made, but rather life is still creating itself. The universe is still unfolding and humanity, a very young but bold species on this planet, is still figuring out what the heck it might become. I suppose it will all end when the organic process of everything's life is complete, when the universe (multiverse?) can expand and develop no more. How? Maybe the consciousness behind it all will finally take a nap. I'm shuffling my Camoin-Jodoroswky *Tarot de Marseille* and asking, "How will it all end?" Ha! The response is Trump XX, Le Jugement. This suggests to me that it will all end through someone's/something's final decision that all is ready to move into the next phase. It will occur via a great blast of celestial music and nakedly honest prayer. In a way, it contradicts my own thought about the universal consciousness taking a nap; this card suggests that it will all end by the universal consciousnessness finally waking up! However it ends, it'll be joyful.

New York - Toronto, Jun 2011

"Tarot was made by humans for humans."

A conversation with YVES REYNAUD, historian, collector, reconstructor

Is the tarot de Marseille a "tradition"? If so, why?

What is a tradition? The dictionary says a tradition is a transmission without any breaks of a cultural item through history. There is no need to know when the initial event happened. From latin, *traditio, tradere:* through and dare: to give, to pass to somebody else, to remit, trans-mit (trans-meet?). Tradition means a project AND memory. It is to remind first and to transmit after reminding. It is an obligation of transmission and an encouragement to enrich the initial item without betraying it. The aim of esotericism is to gather the common denominators among all cultures. In this sense Tarot is a tradition because it has a long history: Maybe seven centuries ago when paper cards made an appearance, maybe longer, if we consider other forms/materials: Wood, stones. It accrued many symbols that are more universal than just Occident myths and culture. Tarot and esotericism are in sympathy despite the fact that these pieces of paper are apparently made only for gaming/playing. For me Tarot is a tradition because it accumulated many signs, symbols and myths that became forged into a specific system. There is a structure, and order in a tarot deck that has the capacity to transmit its esoteric significance to another human. Tarot de Marseille means only a style pattern and not a specific place of manufacture of tarot: This designation is rather recent and has only a value for identifying this style. Tarot of Marseille Type I and Tarot de Marseille Type II are designations made by card historians to distinguish two substyles that co-existed in time. They are also extensions of clarification in time of two variants of it. TDM I and TDM II has existed in same moment of history without problem. They are not really a chronological distinction.

You undertook (along with Wilfred Houdouin) the restoration of Pierre Madenie Tarot de Marseille. Why this precise deck?

When we undertook restoration of Pierre Madenié deck, Wilfried Houdouin and I we were motivated by various reasons: Date of this deck: 1709 date make this deck being the oldest TDM Type II known. Type of this deck: A Tarot of Marseille

Type II shows the influence of Switzerland styles and conventions such as flower decorations, ribbons, and laces.

Location of creation of this deck: This deck was made in Dijon, a French city close to Lyon (175 km North Lyon), rather close to Switzerland (150 km East of Geneva), quite far from Marseille (450 km North Marseille), at 265 km West of Paris and 246 km South East of Strasbourg, (where Tarot of Besancon style pattern originally started), 140 km from Belfort (where a Tarot of Besancon style deck was also made). This city, Dijon, had a reputation for manufacture playing cards especially, Tarots decks. Dijon was a crossroad of influences and trades.

Quality of Pierre Madenié's engraving and colors: Up to now, I had never seen such superior quality in the details and engraving lines of the Pierre Madenié deck. Also the colors have been very well preserved, and all together it is the best preserved original deck that I ever seen.

Failure to recognize this deck by public: The Pierre Madenié deck was never reproduced up to now. Searchers had only black and white photocopies of it and b/w pictures in Stuart Kaplan Vol. II *Tarot Encyclopedia*. I was the first to request color high definition pictures of it from National Museum of Zurich/Switzerland who own it.

And, what did you learn about the tarot during this process that you didn't know before?

I learned that Nicolas Conver's deck is not the best example of an engraved Tarot of Marseille. I understood why and how "ghost traces" could have been printed on cards. Thanks also to Bertrand Saint-Guillain a "Scorpio" Tarot aficionado. The city of Marseille was important to tarot history because of the quantities of existent tarot decks but not for the quality of these decks. I learned how each detail is important but has to be understood after a large number of historical decks has been carefully identified and examined, comparatively. This close examination reveals the importance of sources and genealogy in Tarot research.

I learned the importance of working in network of collaborators such as Kenji Ishimatsu advising me to look after the Pierre Madenié deck and he deserves thanks and recognition for this prompting. Also Bertrand Saint-Guillain provided me some important materials for technical explanations on how cards were manufactured and alerted me to default technical sources.

Now, for the sake of completeness, could you briefly explain: what do you mean by "type I" and "type II" Marseille decks?

To answer this question, I prefer to use Thierry Depaulis' words as they were compiled by Ross Caldwell. I could not add anything except date 1730 I added for François Héri Tarot of Besancon Pattern deck. See below. What follows is a translation of part of Thierry Depaulis' review of Kaplan's *Encyclopedia of Tarot*, Vol. II ("Notes de lecture", L'As de Trèfle, Déc. 1986, p. 11), where he explains his insights regarding the two main branches of the TdM style. Square brackets ([...]) are additions of TD when Ross Caldwell sent this excerpt to me.

> Far from being tiresome, the multitude of tarots "de Marseille" which follow permits the distinguishing of two groups. The first is characterized by a Cupid without hair, going towards the left, eyes blindfolded (Atout no. VI, *l'Amoureux*); a Devil whose stomach has a human face on card no. XV; the Moon (no. XVIII) shows a face; on the World no. XXI, a feminine figure dressed in a loincloth and cape. [and the two figures on the Sun are an adult male and female, barely wearing a sort of loincloth, while in Type II they are two infants of indeterminable sex. Finally, the Fool is named LE FOL, while in Type II, he is named LE MAT.]

> The second type sees Cupid going to the right; he no longer has blindfolded eyes and his hair is curly. The Diable has a smooth belly, la Lune is in profile and the feminine figure is only clothed with a scarf and her left leg is bent.

> The first type has some chance of being older: the solitary card of the World from the Castello Sforzesco, which is dated to the 16th century, shows the same feminine figure; the tarots of Jean Noblet (c. 1650 [c. 1660]), Jean-Pierre Payen (1713), Jean Dodal (c. 1715 [c. 1705]), Jean Payen (1743) are clear examples of this type. More unexpectedly, those of Cosmo Antonio Toso (Genoa, c. 1770?) and even Gummpenberg (Milan, end of the 18th century, of 'Milanese' type then current [cf. also Mann 1990, no. 205] are witness to the permanence of the model.

> Finally, it becomes evident that the variant 'de Besançon', nearly to the smallest detail, comes from this Type I: the same *Amoureux*, the same *Lune* and the same *Monde*; on the other hand the *Diable* appears with a hairy body (Benoist and Carey at Strasbourg, Jerger and his successors at Besançon). It is interesting to compare the two tarots of François Heri, from Soleure, one undated (first half of 18th century 1730 probably), of Type I, but with Junon and Jupiter (it is certainly the first of the genre), the other, dated 1718, of Type II!

To this second Type belong the tarots of François Chosson (1672? [1762?]), Pierre Madenié (Dijon, 1709: finally recovered in its entirety), a number of Swiss tarots and classic tarots de Marseille (Conver, Bourlion, Tourcaty, etc.). Of course, there are those little pests who have mixed the two and with whom one finds a Lovers of Type II and a Devil of Type I... [see also D. Hoffmann, in Tarot, Tarock, Tarocchi, Leinfelden-Echterdingen, 1988, p. 11-12: 'Die Familie des Marseiller Tarock']

[Later addition]:

TdM Type I is represented earlier than Type II; it is found at Lyon, Grenoble, Avignon; it disappeared after 1750, not before having engendered the 'Lombard' and 'Besançon' tarots. Some variants of the TdM Type II exist: a mixed form, combining Type I and Type II (M-I/II), a Type II with the Fool named LE FOL (M-IIa) and a Type II 'Genoan' with the Pendu in profile.

Type II is only known after 1700; it is found at Dijon, Besançon, in Switzerland, then at Marseille in the second half of the 18th century; it survived alone, or nearly, after 1800. According to D. Hoffmann, the Piedmontese Tarot (cf. for example that by Lando) comes from the TdM Type II (Hoffmann/Dietrich 1988, p. 12). The TdM Type II seems to be a "calmed", "humanised" version of TdM Type I: the Devil is less frightening, the feminine figure of the World is more feminine, that is, more "sexy" in regards to her hips and breasts (whereas the the corresponding figure in Type I is more "austere", less feminine). Briefly, the TdM Type II appears to me to be a "modernisation" of TdM Type I. Is it the work of Lyonnais cardmaker? of a Dijonnais? And how to explain its success in Marseille?]

So according to this typology (which I find sensible):

Type I:

Noblet
J-P Payen
Dodal
J Payen
(and late 18th and 19th century Genoese and Milanese tarots)

Type II:

Chosson
Madenié
Conver
(some Swiss tarots and other tarots de Marseille)

Do you think that the "Marseille Tarot" denomination is still relevant, or useful?

This name "Marseille Tarot" was not created by Paul Marteau in 1930 when he produced his own version of the Tarot said to be Marseille. Papus (writer name of Doctor Gérard Encausse 1865-1916) created this designation in his book *Le Tarot des Bohémiens* published in 1889. When we read his book we can see images of Tarot of Marseille with Le Chariot clearly inspired by Nicolas Conver deck (Letters V.T in the shield). So to the question: "Is the Marseille Tarot a relevant or useful designation?" I say, yes, this style was manufactured in other cities, BUT as Tarot of Besancon style (surely engraved in Strasbourg) the designation, Marseille, surely enjoys a "trace in time". Facts may be facts but being from Marseille myself, I am happy to preserve this name. Really, ha! Marseille is a big city and port that attracted many cardmakers from other French regions such as Nicolas Conver and François Chosson. But that is another part of the Marseille Tarot story.

Now, I know that you have spent a serious amount of time compiling and comparing many of the Marseille tarots out there. What do you think these images have to offer to our contemporary world? Are not they too old, and outdated?

Our modern societies need their cultural roots for cultivating for each of us our individual "tree of knowledge". Symbols and archetypes portrayed in tarot lines, images and colors talk to our innate memory and psychology, regardless time past or present. The cards may be used to start a communication with our self. They are just (and may be more) a media for this aim. The cards' old fashioned style and the date of their creation is not an obstacle for most people. Of course, some may prefer a more modern version or even a completely futurist version: We are free to choose our medium as we are free to choose a specific doctor, psychologist, painter, food, music, drawing, book, author, tarologist, movie, partner and so on... If the medium talks to you, helps you, touches you, heals you, sounds good to you, gives you something positive, assists you to evaluate... Just do it! And choose it. Life is about choosing, life is a succession of choices and decisions. Just listen to your little voice inside you.

Modern tarot decks are useful for some people and I have nothing against this. Same for artistic tarots that are frequently divorced from tarot tradition. Art is art. We just need to remember that to know a subject in depth we MUST return to its roots; and study all ancient decks in their variety of versions, in the history of their stylistic and manufacture techniques, their dates, facts and even past economic and political contexts. So, is tarot outdated? Just see how it still feels alive and well seven centuries after its possible first appearance. Today, the Tarot of Marseille style is increasing its market share in Anglo Saxons areas (USA, GB) and in Japan. To me, this is not an accident.

Do you think that these changes from type I pattern to type II pattern have some esoteric significance?

Frankly I don't know yet. I have no intention to analyze many of these esoteric significances contrary to many other tarot authors or writers. Variations in style are important for Tarot changes and drawing and each period and place had its fashion or mix of fashions: More flowers and ribbons/laces decorate the cards in Switzerland for example; more classicism in France, more coloring in Spain. (It continues like this. See for example the recent Rhodes/Sanchez deck).

I understand Wilfred and you have planned more facsimile editions of several other Marseille decks. What do you expect to accomplish with this?

To allow tarot lovers to have a more clear picture and idea of variety and subtleties inherent in this Marseille Tarot pattern: To attract tarot lovers to fully appreciate the unknown images, the old and rich symbols of these decks. This quest is not for financial gain but rather personal vision based on my attraction to Marseilles style decks. (Don't forget I am first of all a collector and a researcher). I like to search, (my Scorpio part), share what I find (my Gemini part), and provide quality at top rank (my Leo part, I assume). My life numbers are in numerology 4/22, which means I take pleasure to think that, this Marseille style giving out is main part of my passage on Earth… In full simplicity I want to share the hidden life of Marseille decks past and future!

Could you tell me about the first time you saw tarot cards?

I was about 20 years old I suppose but can't remember exactly. As French it was common to discover tarot via Paul Marteau's 1930 book. This book is (and remains) the bestseller in France regarding tarot. This discovery was during late nineteen seventies. It was a reprint edition, of course, then. Later I did succeed to add the original 1930 edition to my little collection. I was recently told that this Paul Marteau deck (now slightly redrawn and colored yet) is still sold by France Cartes (who brought Grimaud House) on a 400,000 copies basis worldwide (100,000 copies in France).

Are you familiar with la langue des oiseaux? *If so, in which way do you think it relates to the Marseille tarot.*

I am familiar with *la langue des oiseaux* theory, yes, and it is for me a poetic possibility to decode tarot. But it's only a tool amongst others. I suppose that it may help and inspire a very intuitive tarot reader; but then, man is at the center of a tarot reading. At all times, and there is no exception for me. This *la langue des oiseaux* question caused me to remember an experience I had 25 years ago. I was about 30 (I was born on 13th June 1956) and during this time, I was fully involved (as usual) in one esoteric matter: Graphology. During course work home work we studied a particular case. We were given a page of handwritten signed material and… that's it! The question was: Give technical elements of graphology that will ground your typed analysis of inner character of this person. We all spent two weeks working on this exercise.

I found technical elements, made correlations between them, exploited the technical books and after some long nights (I was single then, luckily!) I typed my report decrypting the character of this person. The woman master graphologist tells our results one by one. At the end, she told me about my report: "Well now I have to tell you something about this report: Technical data that you based your report on is completely totally false. But your description about this character is exact! The best in the class! You must have strong insight and intuition since you succeeded to ignore the techniques and let your brain analyze and synthesize all you feel".

In your view, what is the future of the Marseille tarot?

The Marseille tarot will never end because it is so rich in materials, symbols and capacity to reveal human needs. Tarot was made by humans for humans. Life is cycles, and esoteric "sciences" cannot escape this universal law. Anglophone countries are not aware of its rich history and have poor knowledge regarding its variety and symbolic history. There are a few exceptions of real tarot lovers and seekers.

My aim is to spread knowledge of the subtlety of Marseille tarots West and East (USA and Japan) by publishing a collection of real facsimiles of Tarot of Marseille's decks. This is my contribution to tarot's circle of life during my own circle of life. When I feel something as evident, I am never wrong: This is my life experience. Regarding Tarot of Marseille I can say this deep feeling: No tarot pattern or style is at the level of Tarot of Marseille for various reasons.

One final thing: how many points has the word 'etoile'?

One point at the end of the word LESTOILLE. Like many other cards but not all. A particularity that could only be explained by knowing deeply what was the level of education, level of knowledge and real intentions of engravers and card-makers. Wilfried Houdouin explained well the etymology of word "l'étoile"/ The Star and how and when this old wording LESTOILLE slowly became *L'étoile*. See his book *Le Code sacré du Tarot*.

Strange question indeed...

But maybe you wanted my point of view regarding "codes" that some authors discuss and/or declare firmly as being implemented in cartridges for letters on tarot images? Bear in mind again that I make no pretension to explain this type of detail: I am not competent on this issue. Being myself on an ego trip with this facsimiles reproduction project, well, I suppose that I have also to respect the ego trips of others. This is a gift from my Scorpio side.

Luckily I am not presently floating on the back of a frog that I could not resist to prick with my venomous tail while crossing a river!

New York / Marseilles, 2012

"The Marseille Tarot, contrary to other types of decks, is multidimensional, in regard of both its structure and its symbolical language, so that any card is opened to multiple levels of interpretation, all being analogically correlated."

A conversation with WILFRIED HOUDOUIN, historian, deck restorer

Let's start with an unfair question: what is the tarot?

It would be far too long to fully present all the scope of what the Tarot actually is, so to cut a long story short, the Tarot is originally a symbological model of the Universe, being entirely derived from the very geometrical matrix of Creation, the universal blueprint known as the Metatron's cube, and structured as the analogue of DNA, the very code of all life on this planet. As a symbolical translator, it features the very universal archetypes at play in the game of life, or, as a *Quatrocento* deck close to the Tarot has been called, the "game of the government of the World" (to be related to the ancient Greek concept of the *arkhè*, the Tarot being indeed of Indo-Greek descent). As such, the Tarot is a universal symbolical translator, or decoder, serving as a universal instrument of knowledge, as the Ancient realized some limited principles rule all things, in their various states and degrees, or levels. Here it is essential to note that only the so called Marseille Tarot is entirely designed according to this archetypal structure. The (Marseille) Tarot, actually embodies the tree of Life, or universal logos (language-system in Greek, to be short). The name Tarot indeed derives from the antic word *taru*, which, in Sumerian means "return" (the wheel, or Ourobouros), and in Sanskrit "tree, plant, grass", the image of the tree applying here equally to the branched structure of the universe (fractal and cybernetics), seen as a whole, including that of the spoken language, or reason, itself. In a certain point of view, the Tarot is thus a program, or logiciel, made of cards. All these topics are discussed at length in my book *Le code sacré du Tarot – la redécouverte de la nature originelle du Tarot de Marseille (The sacred code of the Tarot – the rediscovery of the original nature of the Marseille tarot)*. As the great American linguist David Vine is presently working on some translations to make an offer to U.S. publishers, with luck the book shall be available in this language soon.

Is that DNA present in all tarots or is this a characteristic of what we call Tarot de Marseille?

The DNA analogue structure of the Tarot concerns the 78 cards decks only, historically designated as the "Venetian pack". The demonstration of this can be found in my book in the Note 13 of chapter VI, page 207-8. Now, only the Marseille Tarot type II, which is both structurally and graphically precisely designed according to the sacred geometry matrix, is actually analogous to DNA, as this last one is equally entirely "designed" according to sacred geometry. As it's been demonstrated by many scholars, its key numbers and geometry precisely match those of the Marseille Tarots as I also further demonstrate for the first time in my book, thanks to my rediscoveries. I believe the 56 cards deck and other types also derive from DNA, but to a lesser degree, both structurally and symbolically. The relation of the Marseille Tarot to DNA and evolution goes further, as it is not simply structurally and geometrically that the Marseille Tarot precisely matches DNA, but also arranged by its very archetypal symbols regarding evolution, both genetically, biologically, and spiritually. Indeed, for instance, the four suits of the Marseille Tarot relates graphically to the four majors species which first developed on Earth. They also analogically relate to the human body and to the four universal forces of physics. As a matter of fact, the relation of the deck of cards to DNA as a symbolical analogue model of the Universe justifies and gives the best explanation as to why humanity has always been fascinated by the cards, Tarot and ancient divinatory systems, such as the I-Ching for instance, whose relation to DNA has been demonstrated by scholars such as Fritjof Capra (*The Tao of Physics*). The whole extent of the relation between the Marseille Tarot and DNA is not discussed in my first book, but will, I hope, do it in a future publication. Again, with luck my book shall be published in English quite soon. If not, I shall translate myself my demonstration, and add it in the faq section of the website: http://tarot-de-marseille-millennium.com

I am a big fan of Jean-Pierre Brisset. In his book La Science de Dieu ou la création de l'homme (The science of God, or the creation of man) *he wrote:*

> J'ai un l'eau, je mans [I have the water, I ea(t)], which became j'ai un logement [I have a home], shows us that the first home was in water and that people ate there. L'eau j'ai, our ancestors were lodged (logé); l'auge j'ai = I have my auge (pig trough). The first trough was a pond (mare à boue [mud pond] or marabout [Moslem saint]), which became the first site for worship. A l'eau berge (at the water

bank; also, at the inn [à l'auberge]), on the bank of the waters; dans les eaux t'es (in the waters you are) =dans les hôtels (in the hotels)... Consequently, our ancestors lived in the waters, ponds, and marshes.

When you say that the word 'tarot' comes from the Sumerian word 'taru', are you using a homophonic argument, similar to those deployed by Brisset?

As a matter of fact, concerning the word *taru* as the true etymology of the word Tarot, I followed a thread, starting from the commonly accepted Arabic etymology, relating the word *turuq* (plural of *tarika*, "the method", "the path") to the Italian word *Tarocco*, and to the German *Tarock*. Indeed, as the Arabs are credited for having imported the cards into Europe, this relation makes sense. But following the thread relating the Tarot to the East, I discovered that *tarikawas*, in fact a Sanskrit word in the first place, which means "ferryman", in the sense of "savior" – the ferry boat of shuttle being besides the signification of the Sanskrit word *tari* – relates to the traditional symbolism of the shuttle, whose religious and cosmological symbolism is discussed at length in my book. But both *tarika* and *tari*, as well other related words such as *tarun* ("to stay young", as perpetually restored), *tara* (also "savior" "ferryman", or "ferrywoman", to be precise, "the shuttle"), *tarana* ("wave", "billow", "eddy"), all derive from the root *taru* ("tree", "plant", "grass") which is related to all the above significations by virtue of the analogic relation between the universal tree, and particularly its cosmological aspect, the loom as fabric of the Universe, the universal cosmic flow, etc. It would be too long to expand on this ancient symbolism, and quite complex to communicate it here, but again, it is presented at length in my book. The actual extraordinary cosmological knowledge of the ancients being conveyed through mythological allegories is fabulous. But the relation between Tarot and taru became obvious to me in light of my rediscoveries of the Tarot's original structure. The ultimate dynamic and multidimensional aspect of the matrix of the Tarot (for the Marseille Tarot is multidimensional, as I will demonstrate in the future) is the toroïdal vortex, which is actually the "real" tree of Life, as demonstrated in my book with much graphics and references to traditional symbolism and cosmology. Besides, the word *taru* pronounces *taroo*, so close to *taro* (the second t is additional, resulting from the full circle of the tetragram cross of the word *taro*) suggests that the relation between the two is simply undeniable. Besides, the word *taru* has complementary and coherent meanings in Sumerian ("return"), Thracian ("spear", made of wood, and symbol of the *axis mundi*), Maori ("plant", "seed"), Finnish ("legend", "myth"), Estonian ("hive", "honeycomb", relating to the hexagon, shape of the sacred geometry matrix), etc. Anyway, the relation between the Marseille Tarot and India (and Scytho-Greeks to be related to the mythology of Hyperborea) is obvious, and the symbolic and structural relation between the Tarot and the Tree of Life is also obvious, which makes me believe that the word *taru* is the true etymology of the word Tarot beyind any doubt.

From a purely poetic point of view what you are saying is beautiful. I see you are making use of analogical thinking, much as Brisset did, and I wonder to what extent you feel that such analogical thinking is present in the tarot. Is this Sacred Geometry something an image-maker would use to make "better" images, or is it something any person could use to build a "better" life? Is there an analogical connection between life an tarot?

Analogy is the very key of the knowledge the Ancient initiates possessed, to an extent we only now begin to understand. As we certainly can't know everything, yet, by means of analogy and symbolism, which is its very medium, we can somehow grasp and understand anything, precisely as to how differently it fits in and relates to the grand scheme of things, the very same universal principles underlying all things. What is so beautiful about analogical thinking is that it does not imply the intellect only, but also the intuition, the heart and the soul. The Ancients did understand that the microcosm and macrocosm are one and the same, Man being considered the very epitome of the Universe, standing at its centre as the "grand symbol of the Mysteries", as Manly P. Hall put it. Once these archetypal principles and their intricate articulations are codified, both structurally and graphically, a universal instrument of knowledge is provided. I discuss in my book how the Tarot actually came to existence, this sacred knowledge stemming from a very distant past having been defined partly by Pythagoras after he received it from the Druids and the Egyptian priests, by Plato, and then by the neo-pythagoreans and neo-platonists in Alexandria, where all the great minds of the age met coming from the four corners of the Earth, assimilating the ancient knowledge from the East thanks to Alexander the Great, and eventually defining the very basis of a unified intelligible model of the world. From these great advances, through a long and unbroken chain of initiates which received and transmitted this knowledge, down to the master cathedral builders of the XIth to XIVth century in Europe, the Marseille Tarot eventually came to existence, its "type II" version constituting the very last, and maybe most complete philosophical legacy of the Ancients. Now, sacred geometry is indeed the very key of it all, as the whole universe is determined or governed by its limited yet infinitely combined archetypes whose expressions encompass both the physical and the metaphysical sides of existence. It is very clear now that assimilating, or simply contemplating sacred geometry patterns does harmonize our lives on many different levels. Besides, it is very well known today that sacred geometrical blueprints allow us to produce the most exquisite designs, and that their use in art, such as painting, music, architecture, and also medicine, science, mechanics, etc., generate designs sustaining life and consciousness. Just look closely at a flower, take the time to smell it, and you'll realize how geometry, life, beauty and consciousness actually meet... As for the analogical relation between life and the Marseille Tarot, which can be considered as the very "game of life", as I have discussed in my second answer, it is absolute !

Analogical thinking seems to be at the foundation of most magical operations: the idea of Contagio contagium *and* Similia similibus curantur *can both be related to the tropes of metaphor and metonymy. You are mentioning something important: analogical thinking could bypass intellectual reasoning. I am very interested in this. The link between two objects that share some formal qualities becomes a form of "truth" and that truth can trump the products of reason; but the fact that we can map an analogy between two objects doesn't necessarily means that the connection is actually there. For example, nowadays we cherish Brisset's work as some sort of poetic pre-surrealism; but we see his actual conclusions as flawed. So, outside the poetical realm, how can we be certain that our analogies are correct? Isn't it a little risky to assume that they are absolute truths? At what level does that really matter?*

Actually, metaphor, metonymy and free associations of ideas, such as those of Jean-Pierre Brisset, must be distinguished from analogy in the philosophical sense of the term. In fact, analogy is generally referred to as regarding mere resemblances and comparisons, and to a certain extent, it relates to empiricism in a way. On the contrary, in traditional philosophy, analogy proceeds from metaphysics, relating things according to underlying universal principles or archetypes. So, analogy does not simply relate to associative thoughts, but to precise concepts. In the ancient Greek philosophy, analogy cannot be disassociated from initiation and teachings of universals. Once the metaphysic fundamentals are integrated, then imagination can bypass pure intellect, and reason can join poetry, freedom of thought and symbolism, still catching up with universal truths. It's just like music! Indeed, a good musician knows perfectly his scales, and the various rules, but by the way all these are effectively integrated (digested, assimilated), performing music turns into playing music, freely yet orderly and harmoniously, harmony being one of the signification of the word cosmos (with "order") according to Pythagoras. This type of analogic thinking thus relates dynamically to both hemispheres of the brain, the rational and the intuitive, but then again, intuition is guided by underlying rules. Here we touch the very core of it all, as this is precisely what the (Marseille) Tarot is all about! I often say, as I like to, that the Tarot is the Master, and that everything is embedded within it, so that from the very depth of our selves, our internal tree is reorganized, being in-formed by the Marseille Tarot's codified language, as pure logos. But to do so, reorganize our tree, as it were, we must realize and accept the Tarot, or any other traditional philosophical system, as a Master (which analogically, relates to the data encoding, decoding, and recording of our digital age, and more so, to the holographic matrix), understanding that this master is actually our higher self, the Tarot structure and articulation being that of ourselves. This is the beauty of it, of the whole Universe. Each card of the Marseille Tarot, analogically, relates equally to non-human aspects of the universal Manifestation rules, encompassing (see the cover of my book) both the macrocosm and the microcosm, as all being One, yet dynamic unity.

So, to answer your questions, we may say that casual or free-form analogy is fine, but whenever it is required to reach philosophical (scientific) heights, analogy cannot be severed from metaphysics and the traditional systems of knowledge attached to it, such as the Marseille Tarot, the I-Ching, the Runes, Astrology, the Hebrew alphabet, Geomancy, etc. Only then is our spirit safely guided, and do not stray away in vagueness and unreality, eventually vanishing away like puffe of fume with nothing left out of it. At this point, it is important to precisely define what analogy really is. Analogy is a Greek word which decomposes as *ana*: "from bottom to top", "from left to right", "backward and forward" (that is to say according to the 3D cross, the *axis mundi*), and *logos*: "language", "system", "reason", "discussion"... So the principle of analogy proceeds from a thorough consideration of objects on different levels and eventually different states, but always testing relations in regard of intelligible universal principles, as being related to a frame. So it relates to the universal Tree of Life again, as the *axis mundi*, frame and weft of the Universe, both physical and metaphysical, and it constitutes the very ruler of thoughts and reflections. Now, there are no such things as "absolute truths", as truths are always relative, and things are always considered and "realized" by means of projective, dynamic thinking. This implies that analogy actually operates on many different levels or degrees, from free-form imagination to philosophy and metaphysics as pure science, so that we can indeed consider poetic associative thinking as analogy, but operating at a definite level. Consequently, this implies that poetic analogy cannot be considered as inferior to philosophical analogy in the absolute sense, but only on the relative, keeping in mind that free imagination often catches up with truths from higher grounds !

You are touching on topics that are very dear to me, like etymology and visual or analogical thinking. Analogy certainly plays a fundamental role on the way visual representation becomes a form of creative thinking. One of the most striking examples of this is the story of how August Kekulé's insight on the circular shape of the benzene molecule came from a dream he had, in which he saw ouroboros, the snake eating it's tail. I am very interested in this connection between analogical thinking and visual language. The tarot seems an ideal tool to bypass our intellectual ways of reasoning, so we can arrive at unexpected insights by means of visual (analogical) arguments. Why don't you tell me more about your tarot. What did you do? In which way is your tarot of the Millennium an improvement on the already existing Marseille decks?

I know about August Kekulé's story, which is absolutely relevant to relate here, and it is true that one can gain unexpected insights by the means of the Marseille Tarot multidimensional graphics, as the sequences of cards are looked at according to definite situations and feelings. Now, I'm glad you asked these two questions, for indeed, in addition to my book, it is essential for me to explain and justify my work regarding the cards. To cut a long, long story short, the story begins when I decided to clear everything out about the Marseille Tarot after the Camoin/Jodorowsky Marseille Tarot was released in 1998. I was very disappointed and disturbed by this deck, which I would have never purchased had A. Jodorowsky not been associated with it – I loved him very much and have been following him and attended every week his "Cabaret Mystique" between 1993 and 1996. Indeed, just by looking at the deck, I realized that it was flawed. Yet I bought it, and got somehow used to it with time, as it "revealed" suposedly the lost design of the ancient Marseille Tarots. As a matter of fact, it provided a new impulse, but was troubling me at the same time as I was studying and using the Paul Marteau Marseille Tarot on an everyday basis since 1990. So, more than ever before, the question regarding the genuine Marseille Tarot canon was raised, and I could not ignore it any more. Since that time, as a professional infographist, I decided to do my own research, find out about the original canon, and make the correct cards myself, for I would not find rest as long as I wouldn't have a deck I could fully rely upon at last.

Then in the summer of 1999 I underwent to go alone camping out in Wiltshire England, to visit the sacred places of the area. I spent amazing time with great researchers as I planted my tent at the Barge Inn in Pewsey, half an hour from Avebury and Silbury Hill, which are some of the most powerful places I've ever visited. Then, with a group, we visited Stonehenge and made a group meditation on the evening of the total eclipse, on August 11. Amazing things happened. As I uttered the "Om", some sort of astounding vibration resounded within myself, and I had visions in the aether, among which geometric volumes like the star dodecahedron and the star tetrahedron. I was stunned and definitely restored by this experience, cleared out of many negative blocks, realizing that Stonehenge was a genuine ancient technology which, as a resonator, is a true "stargate". By the way, Stonehenge, as I found out many years after, was built on exactly the same blueprint as the Marseille Tarot, to the extent that it was originally surrounded by 56 stones, the hexagram defining the central part, this geometry being, as I demonstrate in my book, the very matrix of the number 22, so that you have, in the ancient Stonehenge configuration: 22 + 56 = 78. After I discussed my visions with a researcher friend of mine (June Mewhort, author of the *Spiritual Labyrinth*, 1992), she handed me an extraordinary book by Richard Dannelley (*Sedona: Beyond the Vortex*, 1995) which presents all the fundamentals regarding sacred geometry, among which, the Metatron's cube, popularized originally by Drunvalo Melchizedek. All this stirred me up in the deepest of my psyche. Then, later, sometimes in December 2000, I realized that the Metatron cube was actually the very matrix of the Marseille Tarot cards as well! At that time, I only realized it concerning the graphics of the cards, and it was later, step by step, that I discovered that this very matrix, that of the whole Universe, actually determined each and every aspect of the Marseille Tarot, both graphical, structural, and metaphysical. The complete demonstration of this can be found in my book. All the while I collected scans and photos of historical decks, and in 2007, I met Yves Reynaud (with whom I realized the Pierre Madenié 1709 facsimile) which underwent travels in order to complete this collection. Among all the decks Yves gathered stood out the Pierre Madenié 1709 (recommended by our Japanese friend Kenji Ishimatsu), which, I discovered progressively, was the very best source we had in regard to the original type II canon. The complete list of the decks which served as prototype models is in my book, as well as in the deck's booklet, which is both in French and in English, by the way. It was clear from that collection of historical decks that all these were more or less flawed, and were more or less decadent copies of older prototypes, unfortunately lost. Yet, enough was preserved to define the original type II canon satisfactorily, so that a restitution of this ancient canon was indeed possible, thanks to the deck carved by an unknown master, republished (with false colours) by Paul Marteau in 1930, this deck actually embedding geometrical markers, being besides stunningly accurate and pure geometrically (more in my book on that point). So I worked on that restoration for more that 7 years, and finished in 2009 (for the Pierre Madenié 1709's 300th anniversary!), after taking care to be as less personal as possible, and render a deck – the Tarot of Marseille Millennium edition – that could be relied upon as a sound model we can safely rely upon, at last!

Fortunately, Yves Reynaud, who visited me where I lived in Marseille on a weekly basis since 2007, can testify of the seriousness of my work, and how I started again when I realized I was mistaken. Besides the restitution of the Marseille Tarot type II original canon, the improvement of this deck relies upon the pure geometric regeneration of the cards, which I discovered were originally entirely designed by sacred geometry, to the point of observing that the graphics are actually fractals, generated by the sacred geometry matrix of the Metatron cube, which corresponds actually to the orthogonal projection of the hypercube, as proven by mathematical books. Additionally, by means of the geometry matrix too, I discovered that the card icons had been trimmed, or cut down by the scaling down of the frames, removing some of the original graphics on the borders. So, with much logic and a bit of imagination, and with some of the historical decks less altered in that regard (such as J. Viéville 1650 and F. Héri 1718), I regenerated the missing parts. Of course, I do not pretend to have regenerated the cards as they were originally done, but this is, I believe, the best and soundest rendition we have now, taking into account the best historical prototypes at hand. Besides, and most importantly, I discovered that two major Arcana (and one minor, the II of Disks) are actually mirrored in most of the type II historical decks known. These are VI LAMOVREVX [The Lovers], and XIII [Death]. This point is addressed in the faqs section of my website, and a complete demonstration that these three cards are reset in their original orientation in the Millennium Edition will be presented in my next book, or in a lecture to come if I'm asked about it. I can assure the readers that my demonstrations are sound, and that I would have never done this if I hadn't been absolutely sure about it. Now, this endeavour to retrieve the original canon of the Marseille Tarot is that, as a program, the deck is required to be accurate and "tuned" in order to work properly. Otherwise, you miss many things, and the analogy cannot fully operate, the harmonic resonances being impeded. For, remember that the very matrix and harmonics of the Marseille Tarots (along with the articulate structure) are those of life and that of our DNA! Obviously, it cannot fully operate, and we cannot fully relate with it if it is too much flawed on one level or another.

I would like to know about your reasons to choose a Marseille Type II pattern instead of the Type I pattern to work with.

As a matter of fact, the type II is simply the one in regard of the true nature of the Marseille Tarot, as this model, unlike the type I decks known, is precisely graphically designed in total respect of the sacred geometry matrix, which, again, underlies all the aspects of the Marseille Tarot. The problem with the type I Marseille Tarot, is that unfortunately, we only have very few decks left, and all, in my point of view, contrary to the type II copies, are heavily degraded copies of more ancient decks, the oldest prototype known of which being the Castello Sforzesco cards which have been found at the bottom of a well. Typical of the Renaissance (especially in regard of XXI, LE MONDE), this deck is definitely, in my understanding, a stylized adaptation of older prototypes. Indeed, I believe the main features of the type I decks certainly go back to the XII-XIIIth century, and the type II, as I demonstrate in the very introduction of my book and in the Millennium Edition's booklet, goes back to sometime around 1380, 1450 being the very latest period. Now, if the type I is not as archetypal as the type II, again, some of its features, such as XII, LE PENDV straitjacket, or the eyes on XV, LE DIABLE's bodies, relate certainly to the genuine ancient model. The frustrating part is that for now, we just don't know how the type I deck could have been in its early time, prior to the Renaissance era and its supposed subsequent iconographic degradation, which, it is important to stress, the type II has not suffered, or only very little for some decks (the Pierre Madenié 1709). So, again, the type II, though the known models may have lost some ancient features that could have been present in more ancient type I decks, is the most perfect, and so, effective as a philosophical instrument of knowledge. Besides, the type I decks aren't graphically and geometrically precise at all, and we can feel it lacks the iconic precision and integrity that the type II exhibits.

In regard of my rediscoveries regarding the original nature of the Marseille Tarot, the type II is definitely its very archetypal model, the most universal, and, as such, the only reliable model in regard to its original philosophical design. Now, if we consider the Marseille Tarot as a program, even if the type I, in its main features, pre-dates the type II, we can understand that the type II is best, as analogically, the first version of a program, or software, is never the most complete! So, the type II model can be considered as a perfected version in regard of what the Marseille Tarot truly is, that is to say, an archetypal instrument of knowledge. Now, again, it is possible that a type I style deck, accurate in regard of geometry and archetypality, did actually exist before the type II, but unfortunately, we may never know. So it is also possible that a former type II version, perfected as it is (the Pierre Madenié 1709 being the best model in regard of the iconographic canon), did feature originally the eyes on XV, LE DIABLE, and a face on its belly, though I doubt it.

However, I refused to create a hybrid deck (though I created an alternative version of XV, LE DIABLE with eyes and face on the belly, which I realized was not appropriate as it contradicts the type II symbolical encoding. The very face of the belly is, in transparency within the geometrical matrix, that of the central character of VI, LAMOVREVX, and that the belly design refers to the "mine" of the alchemist), and I decided to dedicate myself to produce a very accurate, as impersonal as possible, restitution of the type II Marseille Tarot canon, faithful to the historical prototypes, yet restoring some details and removing some parts. The only apparent exception to this is the "ribbon from Anjou" of XX, LE IVGEMENT which I have restored, but I demonstrate in the faq section of my website that this ribbon was without question there in the first place in that model. So it was essential to restore it, for its replacement with a vaporous thick cloud altered dramatically the original symbolical code of the deck.

By the way, I wish to say that this conversation is a pleasure for me, Enrique. I'm indeed very pleased and much honoured to contribute to your fantastic collection of interviews with some of the most prominent tarologers of our time. I believe you're doing a great service to the community, and I especially think of the future generations that will benefit greatly from these conversations. If we had such interviews on the subject of great figures of the past, such as Court de Gebelin, Eliphas Lévi, Papus, Oswald Wirth, Joseph Maxwell, etc., that would simply be amazing.

Jean-Claude Flornoy used to say that we don´t work on the images, but the images work on us. I recently came across that very same idea in a documentary about painter Gerhard Richter: it is not the painter the one who "makes" the painting, but the making of a painting builds the painter up. Jean-Claude said he understood the tarot by copying it. This is something I always found beautiful, as I always felt he was talking about a tradition in image-making that could only be understood through craftsmanship. Curiously, when he did so, he actually copied a Marseille Type II pattern, the Nicolás Conver tarot. But when he decided to restore some historical decks, he chose to work on the Noblet and the Dodal decks, which happen to be examples of the Marseille Type I pattern. In fact, he thought something had been lost in the transition between Type I and Type II patterns.

I don't want you to feel in need to debate Jean-Claude's ideas, but here is what I would like to know: lets say that I look at your tarot of the Millennium instead of, lets say, the Jean Noblet. What would be different in terms of my experience? Your work seems to be about precision. Would it be possible for you to tell me in which precise way my experience of the tarot will be enhanced by your deck? In which way would these images "build me up"?

First, regarding the Type I vs. Type II Marseille decks, there is in fact northing lost in a transition, as these two types (among others) did coexist at a later time. As a matter of fact, the Jean Dodal 1701 and the Jean-Pierre Payen 1713, categorized in the Type I category, are clearly of a later Italian origin XVIth-XVIIth century, whereas the type II is mainly Germanic and French (and early Venetian), and dates back from the XIVth to mid-XVth century. There is in reality no continuity or discontinuity between these. Indeed, obviously only certain features of these cards may date back to XIIth-XIIIth century (as prototypes, in the true sense of the word, have certainly existed prior the perfected version known as the "type

II" Marseille Tarot), and have been preserved up to the XVIth-XVIIth. As for the Jean Noblet Tarot, in my understanding, its canon relates to a secondary, rather profane and unlearned, lineage in regard of Tarot's esoteric tradition, and being well implanted in its time, contrary to the type II model which is somehow "out of time". But Jean-Claude Flornoy was absolutely right in saying that the images do work on us, and build the artist up, and by saying so, he echoed what Tchalaï Unger (one of the women to which my book is dedicated) also said in a fantastic booklet for the Grimaud's Paul Marteau's deck published from 1981 to mid-1990s, regarding the very icons of the type II Marseille Tarot.

This leads us to the present question, for indeed the Marseille Tarot "type II" (quotes added because this classification is arbitrary and illusory), informs us in the very logical sense of the word, each card featuring the universal archetypes at play in the "game of life". I invite the reader to see my book and visit the website, presenting a couple of pages displaying Marseille Tarot cards within the sacred geometry matrix, and presenting the very cosmological nature of the Marseilles Tarot "type II". Here there is something at work which goes beyond the images themselves that relates to the whole of the deck as a conscious and precisely elaborate metaphysical construct, echoing the universal logos itself. So, when you apprehend the cards, especially that of the Millennium Edition deck because of its restored traditional canon and because of its geometric purity – (created in pure fractal geometry with Adobe Illustrator, a vector graphics program – an historical deck from the XVIIIth century demonstrating besides that the icons were indeed designed that way in the first place) – one is being actually harmonically and analogically interacting with the very construct and articulation of one's being, reconnecting oneself to the higher intelligence at play in the universe, granting a new awareness for one's own sake.

The ancient concept of participation (in the universal order) is essential here. Harmonically, the Marseille Tarot "type II" re-harmonizes ourselves as it reconnects us to the very universal Tree of Life, the cards featuring the very archetypal facets of human (and universal) experience and evolution. So, the Marseille Tarot type II definitely proceeds from an "intelligent design", not in the theological religious sense of the word though, the Marseilles Tarot being, as I like to say, transcultural and meta-religious. Again, the Marseille Tarot ("type II" from now on) is a Master, which does instruct us, but only if we pay close attention, and listen to our inner voice, and decide to work it out in order to receive its teachings, as we decide to play its game!

I understand you decided to preserve the "old" trump names, where the V replaces the U and the I replaces the J, among other particularities. To what extent is etymology important to your work? To what extent could we say that naming an image alters it?

The names of the cards of the Marseille Tarot have indeed been precisely defined, with a definite orthography and lettering which all the historical Marseille Tarot, having preserved a coherent canon, do share. It is only from the midst of the 18th century that, according to the humanist fashion, the letters V and I were actually replaced by the U and the J, respectively. Only VI LAMOVREVX and XVI LA MAISON DIEV have preserved, for reasons unknown, their exact lettering. We have certain researchers believe in the existence of a digital code for these two cards only, leading them to many speculations which rest, unfortunately, upon erroneous bases. The Tarot of Marseille Millennium Edition, for its part, has restored integrally, besides the structural and iconographic canon, the traditional naming of all the cards. Thus, creative combinations of both the names and the numbers of the cards can actually occur. These allow for multiple levels of interpretation due to homonymy (linguistically, words having a similar pronunciation and/or a written form identical to another, but of a different meaning), paronymy (linguistically, a word presenting, in regard to another, a certain phonetical analogy, but having a different meaning), or by paronomasis (in rhetoric, a process consisting of using two or more paronyms). Moreover, and it is very relevant to point this out here, through heteroglossia (linguistically, the plurality of meanings that a specific statement can have), it is possible to read the words using phonetical transposition from one language into another. For instance, the Arcanum LE MAT (commonly named the Fool in English), is characteristic of this. Indeed, the word "mat" means "dead" in Persian; "entangle", "plait", "dull", or "braid" in English; "food" in Swedish; "good" in Breton; "feeble" in German; "dull" and "twilight" in Vietnamese; "dull", "mast" and "tree" in French, etc. A single word or a part of name can so form a meaning close to several others, allowing multiple levels of understanding, according to the specific approach of the card sequences at the time of the reading. For example, the last part of the name X LA ROVE DE FORTVNE can be read as Oud for tune, the oud being an Arabic type of guitar, the sphinx of this card being akin to a Djinn, or Arabic Genii, and some wheels being sometimes used as part of some music instruments. By these infinite possibilities, the absence of apostrophes, and sometimes even the separation between the name and its article (LIMPERATRISE, LECHARIOR, LESTOILLE), finds all its justification. In consequence, foreign editions of the Tarot of Marseille which translate each card's original name into another language is a grave mistake, which simply ruins the original encoding and integrity of the cards, these being downgraded to a single and definite rationalized signification. Indeed, the Marseille Tarot, contrary to other types of decks, is multidimensional, in regard of both its structure and its symbolical language, so that any card is opened to multiple levels of interpretation, all being analogically correlated. One perfect example of this is the Arcanum XVI LA MAISON DIEV (The Tower in English, which more accurately would be translated as "The God House"). Indeed, on the exoteric level (popular symbolic), the flaming ball is actually a comet. But, by passing in front of the tower, the Tarot shows that it is, on the esoteric level, something else as well, such as a flaming sword, for instance. As this card also relates to the fall of Atlantis at the bottom of the sea (the coloured floating circles then corresponding to the dissolved colours of the tower), it is also possible to see in it as a jellyfish, which is not a foolish idea, as this creature, being translucent and gracefully floating as in the aether, relates symbolically to the spirit world, to which the comet and the sword symbolically relates too, as the left character's clothes evokes a fish with its tail… So we come full circle, with an infinite array of analogic relations, each card figuring an archetype which does express itself "the real world" within infinite, yet correlated, conditions and levels. With the Marseille Tarot, we're dealing with pure traditional science, and not with something produced out of fancy.

To return to the names of the cards, the infinite combinatorial relation existing between them thus produces phonetic plays with multiple levels of meaning. To give an example, VII LE CHARIOR became VII LE CHARIOT, altering the card's integrity considerably, for indeed, according to the "Language of the birds", VII LE CHARIOR can be heard as [VII LE]CHARIE OR, or charrie de l'or("transport some gold", as a ploughshare chariot). This is actually relevant for this card is indeed symbolically related to the constellation of the Plough, nowadays known as the Ursa Minor, composed of 7 stars, and revolving around the Pole Star which is assimilated to the "eighth sphere" considered to be the the centre of the celestial wheel, abode of the divine (to which Gold is associated), and that of the King of the World, which, in India, is the chakravarti, the One who turns the wheel of the universal Manifestation, while standing still at the centre. Another example is XVII LESTOILLE, which became XVII L'ETOILE. Here the original name is of paramount importance, not only to really understand the traditional symbolism of this cards, but also because this very name is one of the elements which gives a hint regarding the origin of the Marseille Tarot and the time period in which it has been originally designed. Indeed, according to *The Historical Dictionary of the French Language* (prepared under the direction of Alain Rey, Ed. le Robert, 2006) this ancient word is Provençal, and was in colloquial use precisely between 1380 and the end of the 15th century, the standard French word étoile having entirely supplanted it by the beginning of the 16th century. In addition, this Provençal word signifies, at one and the same time, "star", "star of the sea" and "pupil of the eye". As a matter of fact, these definitions relate precisely to the sacred geometry, specifically to the Pentagram with its Golden Ratio, and to the "Solomon's Seal" (which, set within the Flower of Life, reveals the "Eye of God"), or hexagram, the very ideogram of the matrix of Creation, which, as you all know now, is the very matrix of the Marseille Tarot. More informations regarding the traditional naming of the Marseille Tarot arcana and their alterations through time is provided in the Tarot of Marseille Millennium Edition's booklet (both in French and English), and in *The sacred code of the Tarot – the rediscovery of the true nature of the Marseilles Tarot,* which is only in French today, but probably soon in English, and which, I've just been infomed, will be published in Brazil by fall 2012 or early 2013.

One final question: what don you make of this phrase?

> "le Tarot contient de 22 lames ses leçons "
>
> "le Tarot qu'on tient, devin de lames, c'est le son"

I think you've got it. Free is the wind, as are the breath and chimes of the Spirit. With the Tarot as guide and instrument, let us play with the divine Language of Creation, opening doors to never ending Mysteries and wonders. So, as food for the soul, body and spirit, I would say : "Le Tarot contient de vin de l'âme sel et son".

New York – France, April, 2012

"It is very interesting to see and to experience all that wordplay, so we can play with all these seemingly failed acts. But I mean serious play, in the widest sense of the word, with the same commitment a child puts on a game."

A conversation with PABLO ROBLEDO, deck restorer

While working on your own rendition of the Jean Dodal tarot you went deep into the old craft of the image-makers. You spent almost two years working on this project. I understand this was due to your passion for the Marseille tarot. So, I wonder, in your view, what is going to happen to the Marseille tarot tradition? Where is it heading?

It is hard for me to answer that question because my mind works in the same way I read the tarot: I don't see the future. I can see facts, and tendencies. Based on what I can see happening at the moment with the Marseille tarot, it seems clear that it is becoming more popular. More and more people are willing to read with it and to study it in depth. The Marseille tarot is heading toward a path of discovery, its value is being re-assessed. Jodorowsky had given it a nice face-lift (not only to the Marseille tarot but to the tarot in general); and now there are many wonderful people doing a very serious job at researching its history. That will help us understand its evolution. We could say that the Marseille tarot is heading towards truth.

What are the main features of the Marseille tarot tradition? Is it really a tradition?

The Marseille tarot represents a huge chapter, perhaps the richest and most beautiful, within the tarot's tradition. More precisely, we are talking about a style. The name itself is a convention we have gotten used to, although the oldest cards come from other French cities. The term "Marseille tarot" describes a huge variety of packs developed over a particular period of time. They all share the same pattern and style, in some cases the results are more accomplished and complex than in others. We can confidently call that a "tradition" since it includes myths, signs, and symbols that can be found, or are latent, within the structure of the system. The tarot is a tradition in itself. It contains several sub-traditions, just as the Marseille tradition contains several sub-styles.

What aspects of that tradition needs to be, or must be, preserved?

I am not sure. I don't see myself as a keeper of this tradition's purest form. I rather think I am at an "experimental" level, always within the parameters of the tradition. Jean-Claude Flornoy did an excellent job at leaving us a simple, pure and honest legacy. I started restoring the Dodal in that interval of time between the publication of Flornoy's artisanal and industrial versions of this deck. I launched myself in this crazy adventure because, even when his versions are immensely beautiful, I didn't agree with some small details, like the characters' eyes. I had a huge desire to read with this whole deck and sadly, the Duserre-Dodal is almost impossible to find. I was half-way into my version when Flornoy published his industrial version of the Dodal, but I kept working. It was a great adventure to swim for a year and a half deep into the images of such a beautiful and rich tarot as the Dodal is. Our versions are at once very similar and very different. For example, Flornoy colored the cup at the center of the 7 of Cups and I didn't. I followed the two surviving versions of the deck that are kept in the Biblioteque National of France and the British Museum. These are small details, almost imperceptible, that could alter the message or meaning of an image. It is my speculation that this precise detail in that specific card served as inspiration to its equivalent in the Rider Waite Smith pack. We could say that the important thing here is the richness of the images, and their direct colors.

Paul Marteau, or more precisely the Camoin House, simplified these colors to conform to the industrial change in printing colorization. Marteau followed this erroneous direction creating a sub-style that even today has a very strong presence in the decks on the market. These many forgotten colors were resurrected by Jodorowsky and Philippe Camoin in their deck. In my opinion, they made the colors too exaggerated. The Marseille tarot is way simpler, and that is in turn what makes it complex. We can rest assured about the fact that the tarot can take care of itself.

Why is that the French word "rêves" (dreams) and the Spanish word "revés" (reverse) are almost identical?

How curious and beautiful! Somehow our dreams show us the reverse of our Self, of our soul, in such a way that when we get back to our "reversed" state of vigil we can understand what we were telling ourselves.

Recently I had a symmetrical day. It started with an extroverted woman who started to choke as soon as she pulled LA LVNE; and it ended with an introverted woman who couldn't stop talking after she pulled LE SOLEIL. How do you think these things happen? Are they mere chance or something else?

Those were coincidences. Hmmm... To me those seemingly a-causal events we experience while working with the tarot operate in the same way Jung's synchronicity operates. The tarot has been in my life for a long time. I tried to study it many times, but it was only after reading Richard Wilhem's translation of the I Ching that I finally found some congeniality between me and the tarot. It is amazing how these images become alive and meaningful in different ways for every person. For some time now, in my readings, I have taken a stance about keeping myself more and more "distant" from the querent, as to allow the person to look at the images and discover on her own what the images have to offer her. The fact the way images become operative in a reading usually surprises me. Ha! Ha! Ha! After some time people usually come back saying things like: "Yes, Pablo. You were totally right in all you told me". These are things I don't even remember telling them. It is funny but, yes, it also works like that sometimes. These images work on us on many levels.

Do you consider images to be information or experiences?

Now we are getting into the mechanics! In terms of the images' operative quality, in the course of a reading the image is a little bit of both: we process the information, we absorb it, and we digest it based on these experiences we already had, or the ones we want to have. This takes place in the form of a constant motion inside our heads. This is what could allow us to say that the images are "alive". Often the images act like warning signals. Based on our experiences the information that is being transmitted by the images may help us avoid recalling, or reenacting, painful experience.

I work with packs whose names are written in French, basically because I consider them to be more pure; but the way they have been named and numbered is only useful to me on a personal level, for my own study, to achieve a closer relationship with the images and what they could mean. The people I work with do not speak French, so, all that information has very little to do with them. The study of the language of the birds loses all its value once I translate all these names into Spanish. The study of all that information serves me as an experience, so I can experiment with that playful way in which the cards interact. This is, in a sense, what makes me prefer the TdM II pattern over the TdM I pattern.

In the 9 of cups, for example, the information contained in the cards belonging to different patterns propose different experiences.

TdM I Dodal-Robledo 2010   TdM II Robledo 2011

In the 9 of cups from the TdM I pattern we see 3 vertical rows of cups, 3 cups to our left, 3 cups to our right and 3 cups that seem to have been captured by the floral ornaments in the card. The image feels quite aggressive, as if there is no way out and some issues are hurting us.

There is a similar organization in the 9 of cups from the TdM II pattern, but also some differences. You could see the cups creating three horizontal rows, with the top and middle row very close to each other. The cups in the bottom row are flanked by withered flowers. The same crisis we observed in the 9 of cups from the TdM I pattern is now confined to these 3 cups at the bottom of the card. If we were to release that conflict we would end up with the 6 of cups, which represents the pleasure of feeling the things we like.

As part of a system, the cards are information but they also contain experiences. Many people (me included) use the tarot as a way to know themselves, as a source of wisdom, or as a path toward evolution. The meaning of the cards doesn't remain fixed all along our lives. As our consciousness gets expanded, the information in the cards gets expanded too. The same thing applies to the dynamic of a game of tarot. The more we play with the cards the more experience we gain and the more we know how to use all these experiences in our advantage.

We are both outsiders to a tradition that links the very existence of the cards to the French language. The French style of word-play is in some way unique to French poesis and does not have direct analogs in other languages, but Spanish and English also have poetic idioms that can be equally amusing. Perhaps because of that I have come to understand the language of the birds as a way to use wordplay rather than narratives to deploy the potential of language (any language, not only French). What the language of the birds has given me is awareness about the fact that all texts (the tarot is a text) have the potentiality to be read in ways that transcend their original intention.

Yes, it is very interesting to see and to experience all that wordplay, so we can play with all these seemingly failed acts. But I mean serious play, in the widest sense of the word, with the same commitment a child puts into a game.

Now, what purpose does it serve to read the pips?

The minors... I could say they are what I love the most about the tarot. They seem to be simpler, humbler. Historically speaking they are the less understood. They are the cause of the schism between the Marseille tradition and all the other tarots. The minors are useful giving us nuances and layers in a reading, enriching it. The minors tell us about the way all the different energies move or how they are blocked. They speak of quotidian energies that are closer to us and therefore easier to grasp. The minors tell us how that energy mutates and lives. Once we learn to listen to their mute voices there is a revolution, and the majors reveal themselves to us in a renewed, wider, way. That way the mandala is completed and the wheel/ROTA starts spinning.

New York / Río Cuarto, Argentina, 2012

"Tarot is first of all a work of art. This does not mean you cannot speak about it as magic. Art and magic have an age-old relationship."

A conversation with YOAV BEN-DOV, philosopher, physicist, deck restorer

You created the CDB tarot de Marseille. I guess I could start the interview by asking: why follow the Marseille tradition instead of making your own deck?

In my first years as a Tarot reader and teacher I was using the Rider-Waite deck. But then I was lucky enough to learn Tarot from a real master, Alejandro Jodorowsky. I could see how deep and powerful his readings were, using just a few cards from the traditional Tarot de Marseille. Then I understood that the power of the Tarot is in the images. It is a living work of art that evolves for many centuries, and undergoes transformations and natural selection through countless hands and eyes. The result is a set of images that has a very mysterious power over people – you look at them, and they bring up in your mind contents that can change your life. Now Tarot is a very flexible system. You can re-draw it in many different styles and the magic still works. This is what makes possible the new versions. But the power is diluted when you leave the original path. People using Tarot de Marseille often experience this: once you get used to them, new versions look flat and lifeless in comparison. I can understand why this is so. How can a single person, as talented as he or she could be, compete with 600 years of a living and evolving tradition, and with the hands and eyes of so many masters?

Indeed. People often obsess about finding a secret behind the images, when in fact, the images ARE the secret. Yesterday I saw a woman reduced to tears by noticing how the fire in La Maison Diev was flesh colored, like La Papesse's book. (I was looking at the Jean Noblet tarot). It is very hard for someone outside the tradition to understand the magic of these images that consists of bringing us back to the modesty of experience.

Now, while talking to all these authors connected to the Marseille tradition I have noticed a pattern: they all coincide, loosely, in a general narrative: the tarot the Marseille is the repository of the knowledge of the image makers, this is, the same knowledge one would find in a cathedral, a mosque, a tanka painting... A knowl-

edge that is based in the ability of use forms to lift us up. But the coincidences end there. No two authors agree on the details of that story. They even contradict themselves. I believe the problem resides in our need for absolutes. To me that story seems to be a myth, a "deep truth", which works better at a poetic level than as a historical fact. What do you think?

I agree. Even if we believe that some mystical, esoteric group in the 14th century (or whatever) has put its teachings into the cards, this does not explain the magic of the tarot. There are so many mystical groups from previous periods that we don't take as a guide for our life today. Why should we treat this one differently, just because it put its ideas in picture form? The power of the cards for me is not in their origin, but in their evolution. For some reason, people feel the desire to preserve and develop this set of images. Why did they do so? I believe that the power of the images themselves was working on them and motivating them. And in their turn, they were modifying and adapting the images so as to have a stronger impact on people's minds. And this went on for centuries. So, when someone feels he can see a repository of ancient knowledge in the cards, I take it as just another example of their impact. They make people project on them their ideal of ancient sublime knowledge, whatever this idea is: ancient Egypt, Cabbala, medieval or Renaissance secret societies... I can learn a lot from these projections. They tell me what intelligent and learned people can see in the cards. But I don't take them as real history.

I agree with you in the sense that, on one hand, I find rather silly the romantic notion of all "ancient wisdom" being inherently superior than our own innate wisdom. On the other hand, when I say that the secret in the images is the images themselves, I am alluding to a tradition of image-making in a literal sense: draftsmen, painters, stone-carvers (but also musicians and poets)... They all knew how to move our souls by means of the manipulation of materials and forms. That is the craft of the image-maker. Since the tarot is a set of images, it obviously inherited these qualities. To me the bottom line is this: the experience of the tarot is the experience of art. Looking at the tarot de Marseille images and letting them speak accomplishes the same thing as the experience of art accomplishes. Now, these 22 images we see in the Marseille tarot are especially apt. We live now in an age of image-making in which anybody can snap pictures, rework them and share them with the world in a manner of seconds. But, in consequence, these images are only good for a few seconds. The 22 trumps of the Marseille tarot have survived for centuries.

Anybody can make up a new tarot pack. But the moment you change The World card into whatever image tickles your fancy, you lose the possibility to see the mandorla (MANDORLA = ALMOND = LA MOND = LEMONDE) as an eye, or a vagina, womb, wound, or the Anima Mundi. The moment you change the images, you render their range of significance, their language, mute.

Yes, I agree – tarot is first of all a work of art. This does not mean you cannot speak about it as magic. Art and magic have an age-old relationship. But also it is a very special form of art. It is not like a painting that, once finished, is framed and put on a wall and that's it, you can admire it but not touch or modify it. Tarot is a living and evolving work of art. It exists in the hands of people. It undergoes natural selection: somebody invents a new feature, which could be for any arbitrary reason (like a random mutation) – for example, to show the moon in profile and not full face as it was until the 17th century. Either the modification catches on and people accept and propagate it, or it gets rejected and does not appear in later decks. In this sense the evolution of tarot resembles the slow adaptation process of a living species. Or, if you want, a meme system. Like a living system, it is always on the brink of extinction: It could be enough that one generation would reject the set of images for the chain to be broken. Tarot as we know it would disappear and be replaced by a different card game. So, tarot had to prove itself continuously for each generation.

How do you see the relationship between the tarot and language? In which way do you think the names in the cards affect the images, or vice versa?

Originally the texts were not part of the printed cards. But once integrated into it, they become part of the language. You can go into the text of each card and find meanings for it, but like the image, there is not a fixed interpretation. Considering the captions in general, in Conver's version you can see that they are archaic-looking, inconsistent and with many anomalies, compared to 18th century standards (when there was already a standard orthography, for instance, a clear distinction between U and V).

Some examples of these anomalies:

- Inconsistency in the use of U and V.
- Sometimes an apostrophe appears where it should not be (L'A ROVE DE FORTVNE), sometime the opposite (LETOILLE).

- Irregularity in breaking up or joining of words, unclear use of points or periods between words and groups of small vertical lines.
- Three court cards are spelled BATON, one (the Queen) BASTON.
- Three suits have number cards with numerals written on them, but not the coins.
- 15 court cards have captions below, and one (Valet de Deniers) on the side.
- And, of course, LE MAT without a number but with a blank band, XIII without name and without blank band.

What is the function of these anomalies? Perhaps one function is to give the cards an archaic feeling (compared to the time of printing in 1760). But perhaps there is a deeper reason: the balance between order and chaos, which is also expressed in other card features like broken symmetries in many card details. In my view this is something very important. Any well-trained artist knows to balance between regularity and irregularity. Also in modern terms of complexity theory, "edge of chaos" is the permanent state of living and evolving systems. So, these irregularities are an important feature which makes the cards come alive.

You have said that you retraced the Marseille tarot while aiming at making it contemporary. What do you mean by that?

Since the tarot is an evolving system, when I restored the CBD Tarot I was not looking for the oldest original deck. It is like saying that "the real Einstein" is who he was as a newborn baby. Instead, I tried to catch the magic of the tarot from the most potent deck, which has proved its power and influence over people's minds by becoming the most influential deck in Tarot history. Clearly, this is the Conver (1760) deck. So I tried to reproduce it as faithfully as possible. A major factor in the visual impact of a Tarot deck is the quality of the lines. Today it is not practical to reproduce the woodprint technique of the original Conver cards. But I still wanted the lines to be handmade, not computer-generated. So I took an illustrator who traced the lines with ink on paper, working by the eye. I then scanned the drawing, had it cleaned, and re-shaped the lines by hand using high-quality scans of the original Conver cards. It was important for me to preserve the fine details of the original, up to a single line resolution.

Still, I was not interested in making a museum restoration. Rather I wanted to produce a deck usable for people today. It is not possible to reproduce exactly the techniques, the coloring materials and the quality of the paper used for the original cards of 1760. And even if I could imitate them with artificial means, the visual impression on the observer would be totally different, as our present-day eyes are accustomed to a completely different world of images and graphic materials. Due to these differences I had to introduce some adaptations in various places, such as to soften an "abnormal" detail which would stand out too much with the modern means of printing. I made especially significant changes to the facial expressions, since an exact copy would have made them too gloomy and depressive to a modern observer, although I tried to preserve the general facial traits. In addition, since there is no way to reproduce the original shades of color pigments and the impression they made at the time, I had to rebuild the scale of shades of the various colors. This means that a red surface in Conver's cards would still be a red surface in the CBD Tarot de Marseille, but I had to decide which shade of red to use.

Speaking of color, where, in your view, does the images' emotional impact reside? Is it in the color, the shape?

I think there are many factors which together create the magical impact of the tarot. The colors and shapes are part of it. But they are not like the deck structure, or the symbols, which represent a long established tradition. Instead, what we see here is the art of the particular deck creator. This is what made me really excited about when I was working on the CBD deck. Suddenly I could see what this person, Nicholas Conver, was doing, how he was composing the cards with the colored surfaces, so as to give each card a different structure of movement and harmony. Now these compositions were there in the original Conver cards, but you could not see them clearly because of the fading and the wear of old age, and with the imperfect quality of the original printing materials. I suppose that the last time they were really clear to see was in Conver's original designs on paper, which he must have made before starting to cut the wood. So it was very exciting for me to see these compositions appear again on my computer screen after 250 years, once I copied the exact shapes and filled them with fresh colors. Especially that I was not looking for them in advance, because I was not thinking of this aspect of the cards and nobody else mentions it. For example:

- How the colored shapes are arranged so as to give a feeling of anticlockwise motion in the wheel of fortune.
- The dynamic tension in the temperance card aroused by a bow-and-arrow composition.
- How the observer's eye is drawn by the shapes and the colored surfaces towards the focusing points in the hermit and the queen of coins cards.
- The integration of the staring lines of the figures' eyes into the compositions.
- And then there are some crazy things, like the Picasso-style play with surfaces in the valet of clubs, so that the hands detach from the body and become one object with the stick.

This is why I think that Conver was first of all an artistic genius.[1]

What do you make of la langue des oiseaux and/or gay savoir? Do you see any relationship between these notions and the Marseille tarot?

I suppose by that you mean the ideas of Fulcanelli from about 100 years ago, that were adapted by Jean-Claude Flornoy in recent years: there is a historical connection between the cathedral builders, Templar knights, compagnions, troubadours, a secret initiate language, and the tarot de Marseille. As a historical thesis, there is no solid evidence for any of these links. Also, I don't see that the examples given for "the true meaning" of the cards based on this theory are so enlightening. Still, there are two points in Flornoy's text that I find interesting. One is the idea that you should try to understand tarot images by direct intuition, not by rational reasoning. I agree with that. It reminds me of Chinese Taoism, for example the story of Chuang Tzu and the happy fish in the Hao river: you are not a fish, how can you know that the fish are happy? Well, you cannot know how you know, but you know that the fish are happy when you look at them. In a similar way, you "know" the meaning of the card when you see it while reading. It is not a rational process that you do by the book.

---

[1] You can see some examples in the video on the art and composition of the cards here: http://bendov.info/tarot/cbd/cbd_video.html

The second is the idea of deconstructing words like in puns and word games. I think the same is true with surfaces in the tarot de Marseille images: you can play with deconstructing and reconstructing them into new forms and objects. You can also do it with the texts: Jodorowsky reads "Le Jugement", the Judgment card, as "le juge ment" – the judge is lying. Also you can read "Letoille" as the star, but also as the tissue (both slightly misspelled), and understand it as an irony on her nakedness. This kind of word games is done in Cabalistic writings and also in Lacanian psychoanalysis. Now Cabala and tarot is not a new link, but I think there are interesting things to understand on the tarot from a Lacanian point of view.

New York / Israel, 2012

EN RUNE QUIZ ERE QI: THE LANGUAGE OF THE BIRDS IN MANHATTAN: TOWARD THE HOW AND WHY ENRIQUE ENRIQUEZ READS THE MARSEILLE TAROT

A collaborative interview with PAUL NAGY

Enrique Enriquez resides in Manhattan and is well known for his appreciation of historic tarot decks. His fresh and disciplined approach to the interpretation of this antique imagery bears only a superficial resemblance to the more synthetic ways tarot is usually read. Because of this distinctive approach to tarot reading, Paul thought an investigative interview designed to explain Enrique's suppositions would make clear to the tarot reading community what he does when he reads.

Paul Nagy is a professional tarot reader with a background in anthropology and the study of religions. He has been reading tarot infrequently for nearly 40 years. He has a special interest in how the iconic images of the tarot create communities of discourse and meaning.

PAUL: The purpose of this interview is to ask you to show other tarot readers how and why you read the tarot the way you do. Let us begin with some direct examples of how you approach reading the Marseille tarot.

ENRIQUE: Let me point out one main characteristic to a reading: an emphasis on the concrete as a source of unexpected swerves. Instead of moving from the cards to a place where I want to go, I move towards the cards, hoping they will take me to an unexpected place. In principle, I hope to stay at the descriptive level. Instead of attempting to decode a symbolic system, I create an opportunity for me and others to contemplate the tarot as an object: its materiality, visual organization, temporal placement, its patterns and overall design. This way of reading is strictly about the material qualities of the tarot, not about its meaning.

A first level of reading tackles the whole image. The card 'Judgement' may be described as "an angel blows a trumpet and a man wakes up", or even as "a noise wakes up a person". The Fool may be described as "a man walking" or as "a man leaving". You put these two cards together and you have "get up and leave". This makes it possible for anybody to address the tarot, and for the tarot to address anybody. It rules out a need for any type of special 'knowledge', occult or otherwise. It also rules out any need to possess some sort of psychic or 'intuitive' gift to look at the cards. In other words, one does not need to believe in some external agency working in the cards, but rather merely look at the reality of cardboard, ink and pictures.

Within this first level of reading, and depending on the situation, one may respond to the imagistic analogies present in the cards. Every card offers an image that can be described by more than one word or sound. Death can be the Grim Reaper, or a gardener. Temperance can be a moral virtue or a bartender. Usually, it is the client's question that anchors these analogies to one sense or another. What I would try to avoid is to project my subjectivity onto the images. If we can see a bartender in Temperance it is because the image of temperance and a bartender share some concrete qualities. That would be very different from seeing a seagull in Temperance's dress, for example. I do my best to avoid seeing Elvis on a toasted bread slice. The tarot is not a Rorschach test. At another level, a homophony [the quality of having the same pronunciation as one or more other words with a different origin and meaning], can be found in the way one or more cards, together, spell something. Perhaps it becomes a pun as: The Sun/ the son.

- The Fool spells "full".
- The Fool next to The Wheel of Fortune spells "fooling around".
- The Wheel of Fortune spells "the will of fortune" and "four tunes".
- The Wheel of Fortune next to The World spells "around the world".
- Judgement next to The Hanged Man spells "blow your noose/nose".
- The Star next to Justice spells "wash/watch the scales".
- The Tower alone spells "Fall" alluding either to the act of falling down or to the autumn season.
- The Sun spells "the son".
- Next to The Empress, The Tower spells "her fall/fault" and also "hair falls". Hour to impress!
- La Papesse is a nun, so, she spells both "none" and "noon".

As long as you look for exceptions instead of rules, the game is endless.

A second level of descriptive, or literal, reading may focus on the relationship between the elements of two or more cards that are somehow similar. This is looking for homologies such as colors, animals, articles of apparel, body gestures, gaze, direction of movement. When you place two cards next to each other, the eyes start bouncing between patterns. The eyes look without knowing, until they know. Let us say we have two cards: Strength and The Fool. The characters in these two cards look towards the right. The woman in Strength stands still and struggles with a big blue creature in front of her, a lion.

A first level of reading would present us with a woman standing, seeing how a man walks away. We could 'spell' that as "forced to leave". We could also see it as a woman who is struggling at the fact that this man is leaving. I would present all of these observations as layers of the same reading, without favoring any of them, unless there is a question in the air raised by the client that derails my observations in one precise direction. A second level of reading shows how the man in The Fool walks forward, while ignoring a small blue creature that is behind him, a cat. Since both cards show a person and both cards show a blue creature, I will take the two persons to be one and the same, just as the blue creatures are one and the same.

Now, is this what you mean by similarity? What about variety such as a hand on a walking stick or her hand over/in the mouth of lion?

That is part of the set of similarities, of course. From a bodily point of view, you can map similarities between the heads of the characters (facing left, center or right), the bodies of the characters (sitting, standing, walking), and whatever the character's hands are doing. Having two or more characters showing a 'turn' of the head, from left (past) to right (future) is a story in itself. The same thing applies with hands struggling with something and then holding a cane. There is a whole narrative process going on there.

We may perceive this similarity as a key to a possible narrative. To make these visual rhymes obvious to myself and to shape what I may say I follow two simple rules, both based on the idea of treating the tarot's images as language (we will discuss the poets who inspire this image-to-language approach later):

- All elements showing similar shapes refer to the same idea.

- Elements from different cards that occupy the same position within the surface of the card (i.e. "center", "upper left corner", etc) are related.

If we look again at Strength and The Fool, we see how my initial observations follow these two rules. Rule number one connects the blue creatures as representing one single idea: the same big thing we struggle with in the first card is the small one we leave behind in the second card. Rule number two accounts for the relationship between the two human figures: the person who stands in the first card and the person who walks away in the second card are one and the same. Understanding this is instantaneous. It only takes a glance. I like to think this is akin to "thinking" with our eyes.

I like to think that, if we stay at the level of concrete images, without venturing any definitive significance to these visual connections, we are enacting beautiful thinking. The Greek word for 'beautiful thinking' is *eunoia*. This is the shortest word in English that contains all five vowels. The shortest word in French containing the five vowels is *oiseau* ('bird'). The word *eunoia* is used in medicine to define a normal, healthy, mind. I like the connection between a bird flying from tree to tree, and therefore connecting these trees as if it were outlining some sort of invisible drawing, and the idea of a healthy mind that draws connections between apparently distant ideas.

A healthy mind flies like a bird.

At the center of the whole image-to-language translation lies a poetics of erasures. Not only are we erasing all the cultural baggage that comes with the cards, but more importantly, when you notice a common element in two or more cards, the rest of the details in these cards vanish.

Do different elements vanish in different readings?

It is only by placing two or more cards together that you see which elements these cards have in common. It is only by noticing what these cards have in common that you will know what to vanquish. This is similar to making anagrams: the same elements arrange in several different ways to show, and conceal, several different things. In our example, as soon as we 'lock in' the lion-cat rhyme, the rest of the elements in these two cards become more or less irrelevant. The beauty of it is how the second card is the one telling us how to read (or what to see in) the first card. Each card re-contextualizes the previous ones. I like how that outlines the fact that the Marseille tarot follows the logistics of a language: the context gives meaning to its units. Things get really exciting when we work with the pips. Let us say we have the IIII of Swords followed by the Queen of Coins and the V of Cups.

Following the first rule we notice how the flower in the IIII of Swords looks similar to the blue vines in the V of Cups. That yellow flower also looks similar to the golden coin held by the Queen of Coins.

Look at the center of these cards: if we follow the second rule, we see a flower in the IIII of Swords, a hand holding a scepter in the Queen of Coins, and a cup in the V of Cups. If we look at the upper left corner of these three cards, we see how the IIII of Swords shows the tip of two scimitars and a little flower bud, the Queen of Coins shows a hand holding a coin and the V of Cups shows a cup.

The fact that these elements can be linked to each other has intrinsic narrative qualities. I can simply point that out, and it will be meaningful. I like the idea of the reading being an object I toss to the other person. The act of meaning-making becomes a matter of how that person catches the object.

Is that because the object stays concrete? It is sort of like a physical pun? "Anna logical is an oxy moron, because met a four adore I need to open." "Analogical is an oxymoron because metaphor [is] a door I need to open."

Exactly. We can only get to the pun, or to the swerve, if we address the image's concrete nature. I try to stay at the concrete level to leave the interpretative aspects to my client. Projecting my own subjectivity into the cards serves no useful purpose. It is the client's subjectivity that counts the connections.

I am also aware of the fact that any description is in itself a form of interpretation. At times, describing these visual rhymes could be fascinating enough. I like to think that the rhythm we see in the cards may somehow find their match in the spoken rhythms we create when we describe these cards. So, here is where I am now: I am looking for a visual-oral cadence that can help me thread these visual correspondences into a consistent sound pattern. Perhaps I was inspired to do this by René Guenón's definition of the language of the birds as "the science of rhythm". If there is rhythm in the cards, then there should be rhythm in the voice that describes the cards.

I believe in 'retrospective inspiration'. Sometimes I am working on something and after the fact I discover that someone else did the same thing before I did, so, that person inspires me to have my own idea again. That can be humbling, sobering, crushing, or inspiring. But I have discovered it can help me make sense of what I am doing on a whole new level. I like the idea of seeing these elements turning into each other, because the notion of transformation also has inherent narrative qualities. Anne Tardos says that life consists of "trying to preserve a certain form", but I suspect it is the other way around: Life is the narration of how our forms are constantly changing. It wasn't until I saw Richard Serra talking about how, at the beginning of his career, he created his sculptures by using verbs to have an effect on industrial materials that it hit me: a reading consists of using words to have an effect on the cards.

Now you are really moving into an exciting way of generating tarot readings, and I hope others are following along with you at this important level of transition; it seems to be two things at once. It is the image, and it is the suggestive transformative verb; the words and sentences suggested by the images. The verb is the nerve of a sentence. It is of the soul of utterance. Yet here the utterance is the formal quality, an isolated image held together by a homology, by likeness, thereby difference.

Yes. 'Verb' here is understood both as part of the sentence, technically speaking, and as the soul of the cards, the utterance that gives them life. I started by working with the verb 'turn', in a very simple matrix:

_____ TURNS INTO _____

My choice of this verb comes from the actual experience or reading a sequence of cards in a narrative fashion. When I read the tarot I assume that the characters and elements in the first card become the characters and elements in the second card. Their transformations account for the pass of time and the actual action in the whole sequence. Spring turns into summer. Night turns into day. Childhood turns into adolescence. We are all familiar with such ways of mapping the narrative of life. If we 'fill in' this matrix with the rhymes we saw above, we get:

A flower TURNS INTO a hand, a hand TURNS INTO a cup.

Two scimitars TURN INTO a coin, a coin TURNS INTO a cup.

By this repetition of the matrix verb and the individual elements, we obtain an automatic cadence that is both pleasing and intriguing to the ear. This pattern also has an inherently narrative quality. Anybody can do this. It does not have anything to do with being 'intuitive', 'gifted', or touched by lightning. Rather it is adhering to the constraints of the rules and the transformation of elements of the cards' images into words in a disciplined way. Just as Serra made a list of verbs to use, I thought I could use other verbs besides 'turn'. But I struggled to find a coherent way of choosing these verbs. The tarot follows a specific logic based on chance operations. It seemed to me that simply choosing verbs at will wasn't consistent with that logic.

I like your economy of choice. Sure, any old verb will do, but will it be true to the natural integrity of the tarot? Even with the quaint innovations in Jodorowsky's reading of the Marseille tarot, he attempts to stay within the natural economy of the cards.

I agree. You can't cut an apple with a tennis ball. The material should dictate the way you play with it. Then I realized that if you borrow the structure of a sentence, subject-verb-object, and impose on to a three-card sequence, you are automatically turning any middle card into a verb. As I was walking in the street I named three random cards aloud and noticed that I actually was spelling a sentence: "Temperance coins the Chariot". This is almost like treating the three-card sequence as a rebus (a sentence made of pictures whose names spell syllables or words), or a visual pun. I got lucky because, by chance, the first time I thought of this I got coins as my second card. See what happens there? The word 'coin' can function both as a noun and as a verb. This made the fact that the second card may function as a verb even more obvious to me. But at that point I realized you do not need an actual verb in the middle place. You can use any element as a verb. The idea of turning cups, swords or wands into verbs fills me with wonder.

Nouns become verbs when names are allowed to act as well as designate.

Beautiful, yes, and words inspire in me a desire to take a second look at the image-words, and let them open up to phases and new turns of nouns and verbs. I assume that a person comes for a tarot reading because she ran out of reasonable options. I feel it is my duty as a tarot reader to present her with signs and sounds she may not have considered, and the card images, following the constraints, seem to suggest in the words.

Back to our example, IIII of swords followed by the queen of coins and the V of cups becomes:

swords turn into cups · swords queen cups

a flower turns into a hand · a flower queens a hand

a hand turns into a cup · a hand queens a cup

two scimitars turn into a hand · two scimitars queen a hand

a hand turns into a cup · a hand queens a cup

Read aloud it gives rhythm to the card-image transformations. Now we have music! I like to think that the end result becomes a score for a performance piece, not so much as performed by me, but by the person hearing this reading. A reading like that should take them right to that point in space where they are reading it. They are seeing and hearing it.

If I understand what you are saying so far, there does not seem to be a serious solicitation of the needs or the wants of the client as preamble to the reading: such as asking if they have a purpose for the reading or a question. I agree with you in practice that a tarot reader's discipline is to read the cards and not attempt to psych the client, but sometimes having a sense of the client's concerns helps shape the reading. Do you follow any rules of thumb here?

A person needs to have a very particular kind of intelligence to engage with images (any kind of images) in a useful way. The whole enterprise of art is based on the fact that we, human beings, possess such intelligence, but it is also commonly assumed that art is not for everybody. At the moment I can't honestly subscribe to any bombastic claim about the purpose of tarot readings. The tarot may not be for everybody. Tarot readings won't accomplish the same things for everybody. So far I have been talking about the performance of tarot, which may or may not be the same thing as the performance of a reading for a client. On top of having empathy with the images, a reading asks for creating rapport with another human being. So far I have been discussing my quest to find the tarot's crank, or its pedals; that contraption which, once located, guarantees that I may get some sound out of the cards. I simply hope to be the monkey grinding the organ. I seek for beauty in the performance of the tarot, by a notion that, if such beauty is brought forth, the client will in turn make beauty into meaning for them. By the same token, I would not betray the simplicity of the Marseille tarot. It only takes a glance to get a direct answer from the cards. If a person just has a question, I am happy to answer it, so long as the person leaves right away! I never know what can be accomplished in a reading until the reading is over.

That is better than me, I will often do a reading and have no idea what it is about, but, the client seems to know and that seems good enough.

That would be my ideal approach, in that it is the best way to make room for extraordinary happenstances.

II

Enrique, can you say how you became aware of tarot? And then how you became a tarot reader? Provide us with some autobiographical context?

I was that child you find in every classroom: the one who can draw better than the other kids. I remember my kindergarten classmates teasing me. It was the 70s and there was this idea that aliens were coming to take all the talented people. I was the only kid in my class who could draw a horse with four legs; not four sticks, but actual legs with hooves and everything. So, my classmates thought I was doomed. I had to be on the aliens' list! But the aliens never came. Not for me at least. Perhaps I wasn't that talented! I am thankful to drawing because drawing made me who I am. Drawing is not art, but a practice, like language is a practice, or like tarot is a practice. It builds us up. Drawing is a form of thinking and a way we have to interrogate the world. The tarot is drawing made language.

Drawing is re-seeing?

In terms of 'seeing' drawing helps me apprehend the shape of objects, and more importantly, I learn to see their relationship in space. It is interesting how close drawing and metaphor are. Both share the notion of bringing things from one realm into another realm. The word 'draw' includes the act to marking the surface of the paper with a pencil, the act of mapping an analogy, and the act of bringing something out. I understand drawing as all of these things at once. In terms of 'doing' drawing, this is a very similar process to spelling: the body contorts to create forms that weren't there before, forms whose language can be meaningful to others. Here, 'spelling' should be taken both as speaking and as exorcizing. We 'spell' out words or images ejected from the body into the world. When we point out the visual relationships between two or more elements in the cards, or in space, either by gestures or with our voice, we are drawing. When we map the connection between two objects with our eyes, we are drawing. The actual making of the drawing amounts to a bureaucratic task that I am not interested in anymore. That holds nothing for me.

If I had an artist's gift of rendition, confronted with Marseille tarot deck's images, I might study the images for their vocabulary of design, but as a designer, I would be tempted to redesign the images to bring out what I see and what is not seen because of visual drift.

That is the route Jean-Claude Flornoy followed. He understood the Marseille tarot by re-drawing it. I don't mean re-interpreting it or by making it his own deck, but by copying the existing ones. That was also the advice Jean Auguste

Dominique Ingres gave to his students: "the secret of the masters was to be humble, to copy everything dumbly". Jean-Claude Flornoy left us with two great reconstituted decks: the Jean Noblet and the Jean Dodal. I use them both. The Noblet is crasser, and even so, it is more elegant. The Dodal is clumsier, but it is full of details the Noblet is lacking; details that the Marseille tarot folklore regards as relevant: Death has no name; there is a black bird in The Star; one of the kids in The Sun is blind… Jean-Claude taught me that you do not work with the images, but the images work you. Images affect you, change you. To me that links the experience of the tarot to the experience of art, not to divination.

I personally have experienced the possibilities of drawing as a repository of memories in the most absolute primal sense: whatever I was thinking, hearing or experiencing while I made a drawing, anything, even if it wasn't related to the drawing in itself, can be retrieved back by me when I look at the drawing again. For example, when I was 18 I did some drawings in my grandfather's house. I would be drawing while he was in the next room watching TV. I would look at these drawings a week or two weeks after I made them and recall bits of the shows he was watching. It wasn't the whole drawing that elicited these memories, but specific lines, or sections of the drawing, as if one line could contain the memories of an auditory experience. This happened only at a personal, subjective, level. I could not make another person hear the jingle I was hearing just by looking at my drawing. I think Jean-Claude believed he could connect with the original card-makers by copying the cards.

This is an intriguing observation. Of course there are many approaches to learning tarot where the tarot reader is enjoined to copy his own deck for reading. I crudely render tarot card images all the time. I also discover in the process of copying I see things by tracing and concentrating on parts, and the way an image inheres strikes me as if I have never seen it before.

That experience of encoding a sound in a line, in a way that can be replayed by another person, is something I have only achieved through the tarot.

You seem to not want to redraw the deck to your own ability, but rather you seem to want to re-see, envision the crude images in their suggestive but also occulted complexity.

The fact that I can draw doesn't mean I have to show my drawings. The fact that I can draw doesn't even mean I have to make drawings! Rather, I "talk drawing" with other people, through the Marseille tarot, by using my eyes and not my 'I'. There is a notion I have borrowed from Conceptual Writing that I find useful to explain how I approach the tarot: "source text". The writer takes any found text, a text she did not write, and applies a set of constraints to it, creating a new text. For example, poet Jen Bervin took several of Shakespeare's sonnets and picked only a few words in them to create new poems. The position of the words in the page remains the same as in the original sonnet, but by eliminating most of the words, the ones remaining draw new relationships among themselves. Or we have poet Michael Stewart, who only kept the words "and" in Magdalena Tulli's "Dreams and Stones" while eliminating all the other words on the page. You could do this right now with this interview: change every single word to white except for the word "tarot" and you will find what Stewart found: the repeated word, scattered on the page, creating constellations like the ones we see up there in the sky.

Yep, I am already anchoring myths to those patterns...

I like to see the Marseille tarot as a "source text". I don't want to make new images. There is nothing wrong or incomplete in the ones already existing. I want to make these images new by re-telling them while following some specific constraint I have previously defined by looking at the cards themselves. Sometimes I would read them by paying attention only to the direction of the character's gaze. Some other times I would read them by describing these things that two or more cards have in common. Or I would read them by looking only at what the character's hands are doing; or by describing the next card in sequence to the one I am seeing: or by paying attention only to the shapes taken by the color blue as I demonstrated above in the tarot reading example. The cards tell me how to read them. They dictate which constraint I should use.

This claim is made by Camion and Jodorowsky, among others, that the cards themselves are sufficient to significance. The importation of other systems of signification is not necessary to the oracular voice of the deck. The art in tarot, once the deck is created, is not so much in the deck as it is in the tarot reader who reads the deck toward uniqueness, because the cards' images themselves are mass produced and mechanically alike.

Yes, the art of the tarot is in the performance of the tarot. As I do it now: I translate pieces of tarot images into words and sentences following the constraints suggested by the deck in itself. We have seen in the last fifty years much thought and work devoted to the visual aspect of the tarot, but very little in regards to its aural level (the eye-in-the-ear, so to speak). Usually most tarot readings seem to have a "default" sound defined by the social purpose given to the reading: a reading would sound like a weather forecast if the reader is a fortuneteller, like a therapy session if the reader is a therapist, or like a fairy tale, etc. I am interested in reworking the sound of readings. That may include the reverberations of forecasting or therapy, but it should open up to other sounds that would make the reading interesting in itself.

Seeing-to-hear and looking-to-tongue-or-voice is often how we catch ourselves in space and naturally extend our self a bit beyond the surface of our body. So you also bring forth what you see by drawing. It becomes your drawing by telling the visual language of tarot.

I discovered the tarot when I was 18 and went to study graphic design. What we were taught there was precisely that, a visual language, or the ability to communicate visually. I never had any intention to work as a graphic designer, and I never did. Back in Caracas, at that time, all the art schools were in the government's hands and all of them were quite mediocre. So, whoever wanted to become an artist had to get into this small private school modeled after the Bauhaus. You couldn't say you wanted to be an artist, of course. You had to put on a face that says "I don't want to express myself, I want to communicate to the masses!" and cheat the system. In order to be accepted you had to endure a two-week long test, 8 hours a day, and you were competing with hundreds of other applicants for 20 spots. I got in. I don't remember much of these two weeks. I only remember those two weeks made me allergic to gin. I also remember a self-portrait made by this beautiful girl from Sweden who was also taking the test: she drew herself standing in front of a tree that had a bird-headed man hanging from it by the neck. "Who is that?" I asked her. She said he was a friend.

In retrospect, I might relate that bird-headed man to The Hanged Man, but I had no knowledge of the tarot at the time. There was a great library at this institute. I remember seeing tarot cards, for the first time in my life, in a book about the history of printing. There were some knights, queens, a devil, a tower. Medieval-looking, crude, images that I found very intriguing. I didn't find them intriguing because of what they meant. I didn't know their meaning. I found them intriguing because of what they were: basic, solid images lacking artifice and therefore being primal, primitive, truthful, like the German Expressionist woodcuts are truthful in that they lack any affectation. They were pure. It would be tempting to do a reading on these cards I saw in the book, but I never apply the cards to my own life. I think about the cards and that makes my life better, not because any message or meaning the cards may have, but because the beauty of the visual connections I draw between them is uplifting.

Likewise I rarely read the cards for myself. If I have an issue I want to consult an oracle about, I go to another reader because I am too aware of self-deception. However, I read cards very often about the meaning of cards.

There is something else I remember from those times: there was an art history teacher who decided to hate me as soon as he laid eyes on me. I was never in his class, nor did I ever speak to him, but he hated me anyway. He was a tarot reader! It seems that having a reading with him was some sort of secret privilege. A girl told me he would see you at his apartment, and read the tarot to you for an entire afternoon. Since most of the students at that institute were quite gorgeous women, I always thought he had something great going on.

Is tarot a trope for seduction as well as suspect persuasion? Given how often the query is about a serious love or soul mate?

I would quote Prophet Muhammad: "avoid ye rhyming prose of the soothsayers or diviners". I personally love that quote because my aim is to achieve in my readings what Muhammad is reproving: a sound-sense of rhyming prose. The quote points out that a reading is always an act of seduction, even if not necessarily sexual seduction. A tarot reader is selling a story. Selling is an act of seduction.

The persuasion of the sing-song rhyme subverts our reason by lulling us into trance.

I am convinced that readings operate through hypnotic patterns. This is both exciting and terrifying. Outside the tarot world, where people tend to be compassionate, and we have several authors giving serious thought to what we do, the tarot inhabits a world of ignorance: ignorant people looking for lottery numbers going to see ignorant people possessed by the fictions of their own 'gifts'. Ignorance fueled by the power of seduction adds up to a nightmarish landscape.

Thank goodness I know no such devious tarot readers! The worst I see is people who cannot see beyond their own projections, and since I can make no claim to privileged knowledge and am as gullible as any when it comes to my blind spots, at least perhaps, I can amuse a client with an entertaining tarot reading.

There is a key element in the art experience that has been eradicated from tarot readings: pleasure. For the enthusiast the tarot is a source of pleasure; but I would go as far as saying that pleasure is the last thing the average client looks for in a tarot reading. They come for practical purposes. They want to know how things are going to play out. They want answers, insights, and solutions to their problems. I tend to find that a little terrifying. We can get straightforward practical advice from the tarot if we use the images as traffic signals: The Fool suggests "go for it." La Papesse directs us to "sit down and wait," etc. But putting our blind faith in the cards that way would be a form of madness, unless we are consciously taking these instructions as constraints we accept with certain playfulness. Such playfulness is the underlying principle of any kind of art.

Michel Foucault said something like "madness is life without art". When you take the pleasure off the equation, you are left with madness. I eventually left the institute to focus on my painting, and I forgot about the tarot. (Well, that is not true. My wife recalls that the day we met, at an art show where I had one piece, that piece was a tarot deck. I basically re-painted the Marseille trumps onto oversized wooden plates, creating a clumsy, heavy deck that could not be shuffled).

'Botánicas', the shops where people linked to spiritism and Afro-Cuban religions went for their materials, interested me. Those were the only places where you would find tarot cards, and the only tarot you would find there was the Marseille. I was fascinated by the imagery of these shops, where you could buy an armadillo tail or a stone that came from the place where a lightning bolt touched the earth. You want to travel more? Tie up a toy airplane to your bed. Do you want to break up a couple? Put two figurines representing them in your refrigerator. In a sense, a tarot reading is no different: we affect people's minds with symbols. Now I understand that what these shops really sold were metaphors.

Yes that is what magic is: concrete analogies, metaphors, where something is itself and something other. Much like language: it is speech sounds that are another thing, what the speech sounds represent. Though supposedly a complex idea built out of many analogies and metaphors, symbols are actually the seed for the analytics or particular additive or subtractive functions of analogy and metaphor. This is the echo of our theory of mind: The shift of what makes humans speak.

Magic symbols do not live exclusively in old grimoires anymore, but in art, advertising and fashion, so, even when I started out as a painter, I soon moved onto the idea of using mass-media as my art material. I took any intervention I could make in the media as my artwork. That included interviews, articles I wrote, projects I designed for posters, billboards, magazines or radio stations, and any gesture that would turn the artist's practice into a media event. That certainly taps into the idea of the artist-as-trickster but without the spiritual overtones of the artist as shaman. I wasn't trying to 'heal' the world, but to sabotage it.

There is a word in Spanish *bochinche* that perfectly summons up my philosophy at the time. It means something like a "playful sabotage", a derailment from the established order taken for amusement purposes. I won't waste too much time talking about the things I did before becoming a tarot reader. Suffice to say that I had enough notoriety to get away with many shenanigans. (I still think that is a good definition for 'happiness,' by the way). But whatever I was doing was derivative and of little consequence for the world at large. At some point someone offered me the possibility to move to New York to work in animation. I jumped at it, but it did not last. I became a tarot reader because there was nothing else I wanted to be, or perhaps, because there was nothing else this city was willing to accept from me. I am happy enough to be called a "tarot reader"; although these days I feel the word "fortuneteller" is more beautiful. I love conjoined words.

So does James Joyce! Soothsayer is soothing, wouldn't you agree?

Absolutely! Although I cannot help but seeing the 'tooth' in soothsaying, which to me suggests that the word is made of xilocaine. My work as tarot reader is informed by many of these ideas I borrow from the arts, but I do not think I can make art more interesting than it is. I think the tarot can be made more interesting than what people think it is.

This seems to be crucial. You stay with the image as the processes of thinking to speaking, and these cards for you become the vocabulary of the speech act as the process of discovery and invention.

The cards are my source text to create unlimited texts. Here, we can go back to the idea of drawing as a repository of memories: the words I said while pointing at a card become attached to their recollection of the cards. By recalling the images my listeners recall my words, just like when I looked at the drawings I made at my grandfather's house and recalled the sounds of the TV shows he was watching.

Also, how has the culture of New York City aided you in reading the cards?

I believe in the idea of living a 'beautiful life'; a life in which you wake up every day and go do something you love in a context where you can experience and create beauty. New York is a place where you can find the most diverse range of people and personal stories. Every person I see on the street is a landscape I want to travel in. I need a bridge. I have years of experience using drawing to think about reality. I have been flirting with the tarot images for years. It seems natural to start "speaking tarot". I found a coffee shop, sat in there once a week to read tarot for free, and became part of this city, part of its many landscapes. (There is that other version of why I became a tarot reader that I have told before, about a "tall, dark, stranger" telling me that I inherited the 'gift' from my great-grandmother. That's a true story and it may be a better tale, but it is not one I believe. I made myself a tarot reader because I needed to survive. I don't mean making money. I needed to relocate myself within the world of images, a world outside of which I don't know how to live).

Reading the Marseille tarot is a creation of beauty! How so?

Traditionally, we see the creation of beauty as mainly consisting of putting together some pleasing arrangement: a painting, a sculpture, a symphony, an outfit, a meal, or a bouquet. I am interested in how our ability to map connections between things is pleasing in itself. In other words, crafting a pattern, as in making a drawing, a poem, or a song, can create beauty, and that beauty will give us pleasure; but detecting a pattern is also a pleasing act derived from its inherent beauty. I don't mean only the beauty of the pattern, but the beauty of seeing the pattern. Detecting a pattern is creating a pattern. To be able to see is a kind of beauty in itself. There is also beauty in sharing that ability to see, not as one final, finished product (a drawing), but as an experience. I can turn my eyes into birds and have them flying from one object to another, but it is way more memorable if I also turn your eyes into birds and you can fly with me.

Here perhaps we are at the crux of your practice! Drawing is a way for you to think about how things can become.

Exactly! I draw with my eyes by using only straight lines. My sight travels on a straight line to the moon. Then, it travels on a straight line to a hole in a curtain. Perhaps my finger follows that gesture by drawing an actual straight line in the air. That straight line is just a reminder of the fact that I have drawn two things together: the moon and a hole in a black curtain. After I draw that straight line, I know more about the moon, the sky, a curtain, and a hole than I knew before.

The Marseille tarot images have captivated you for some years. Given the primitive, visually simplified, stylized tarot images, what were the elements that caused you to see in new ways these simple images when set in relation to each other during random selections?

Every material brings its own ideas. The ideas you would have while dealing with a piano are not the same ideas you would have while cutting a woman's hair. I want to stress the fact that the possibility of seeing the Marseille tarot as a visual language is contained in its own forms. I didn't make it up. If it weren't for the Marseille tarot I wouldn't have had these ideas and we wouldn't be having this conversation. There is an actual consistency in the Marseille tarot's images that manifests through homomorphism and visual rhyme; and there is a folklore risen up during the last century around the Marseille tarot that suggests this approach. You can find these ideas hinted at by Paul Marteau, outlined by Tchalai Unger, exploited by Philippe Camoin, and echoed by several other readers and authors, like Jean-Claude Flornoy or Alejandro Jodorowsky. I am simply following that tradition while trying to expand on it by drawing a connection between that visual language and certain poetic traditions based on wordplay and punning. The distance I see between me and those tarot authors I mentioned has to do with the fact that I don't go around talking about secret codes, but I keep repeating: Look! That way of reading the tarot is identical to the way poets play with words!

III

How would you succinctly sum up your tarot practice?

My practice is focused on the performative aspects of the Marseille tarot, which include, but are not limited to, tarot readings. I focus on the experience of the Marseille tarot as a concrete object in space (pieces of cardboard with images printed on them), an object whose poetics can be narrated. I would make a distinction between the poetics of the tarot's images and the mythologies surrounding the tarot. Thinking in terms of how La Papesse's crown is The Tower's crown has little to do with the meaning assigned to these two images. I am becoming increasingly interested in the narrative of how the object works, and less concerned with the narrative of what the object means in its possible historic or mythic contexts.

There are other ways of approaching the tarot different from readings for people, such as the tarot as a poetic artifact, as in the whole *tarocchi appropriati* tradition. *Tarocchi appropriati* was a poetic game consisting of using the tarot's trumps to describe a person in an amusing, poetic, way. It seems that almost from the moment people started playing with tarot card trumps in games, they also started using the tarot for poetry. A big part of what interests me deals with the sound patterns of tarot readings; that aural layer of the cards I mentioned before, which cannot be reduced to voice alone: a gasp is part of it, crying or laughter are parts of it. The sounds of gambling are also part of the tarot's sounds.

There is the tarot as the score of a performance, as in Calvino's *Castle of Crossed Destinies*, which I have reenacted a few times. Calvino laid the whole deck on a table and wrote the stories he saw both in the horizontal and vertical rows these cards created. Calvino was a member of OuLiPo (*Ouvroir de Littérature Potentielle*, or, workshop for potential literature'), a literary group whose main mission was to create 'writing machines', literary devices that could help writers create texts. These writing procedures hoped to function as substitutes for inspiration. Following Calvino I have improvised stories for an audience, starting with the full deck face down and asking some participants to turn several cards over. Calvino uses very direct descriptions for the cards. For example: "a man attacked in the woods (The Hanged Man) is found by a woman who licks his wounds like a lioness would do (Strength)." It is powerful to see the power of the voice at re-contextualizing these images. His treatment of the pips is also very direct: coins are money, cups describe a party, wands describe the woods and swords describe battles. *The Castle of Crossed Destinies* is all one needs to read to understand what to do with the Marseille tarot.

I have been working on a series of *situations* in which a tarot card could instigate a poetic subversion of reality, such as when I stopped the subway commute by trying to use the Chariot card as my metro card and acted as if I wasn't aware of the absurdity of it. Overall, there is the idea of how all these visual and verbal connections in the Marseille tarot are a tool for beautiful thinking. The tarot is an object whose poetics can be narrated, and such narration can be a means in itself, a way to achieve stasis, a point of equilibrium in which we confuse the inner logic of a game with an outer truth about life.

When I hear you say what the objective means in the narrative, it seems to me you are alluding to the exegesis (interpretation based upon the subjective experience and bias of the reader or client). In theory one may court an objective meaning to the image that is only the appearance of the image and does not allude to learned discourse on medieval social customs and outmoded theological minutiae. That theory is an exegesis (interpretation based upon the objective card and image itself and the cultural-historical contexts that produced it), but in practice let us discover what is to be gained?

I try to make my description as literal as possible because I trust my client will turn all these literal accounts into metaphorical statements about his/her situation. The fact that we are meaning-seeking machines becomes especially true in the context of a reading. We use what we know to understand what we don't know. That's the basis of metaphorical thinking. That's why tarot readings work If at any point I allude to the tarot's iconography "The Hanged Man is an image derived from Italian Shame Paintings, depicting the way traitors were punished" or folklore, "Justice carries around her neck the rope to hang The Hanged Man", I would present that information as something that has been said about the cards, not as something I say. In other words, such information becomes part of my description of the tarot as an artifact, not my own opinion. I can't help it if the object, through the narration of its poetics, becomes an allegory for something else; but I do not see the crafting of a discourse about another person's life, or her problems, as my ultimate goal; and I am not interested in elaborating a discourse about my 'abilities'. Where the market expects for the reader to promote his/her own uniqueness, I divert all the focus away from myself and into the tarot.

It seems to me now that you are practicing a form of learned amnesia? Forgetting the arsenal of historic, cultural, and psychological associations these cards accumulate with past readings and study, you let the at-hand letters and images and perhaps fragments of images recombine among each other in an anagrammatic dance of new possibilities with little deliberate recall.

It has been said that all the words we use are anagrams for 'abcdefghijklmnopqrstuvwxyz'. We don't really know what these letters in that sequence mean, but that doesn't prevent us from understanding the meaning of any of the words we find by anagramming it. In the same fashion, we don't need to know the original meaning of the whole trump series (if there was any) to understand the meaning of any sub-sequence we find by anagramming it. Any reading of the tarot, any tarot, we do will be defined by some constraints we impose on it. Assuming a kabalistic approach is a type of constraint that would render a very specific kind of reading. Opting for an astrological approach would signify another type of constraint whose end result would be a very specific type of reading, different from working with a 'four elements' constraint, or a numerological constraint, or a combination of all these constrains, or a "go with your gut" constraint. I have simply chosen a type of constraint based on the way the Marseille tarot's visual language has created a folklore that in turn created the Marseille tarot's visual language.

Does this practice have a process you follow?

There seems to be poetry in these cards. I would like to bring it out. You look at the cards and you discover that they are linked to each other through (visual) rhyme and pattern. You read their names and find puns in them. (The folklore says that La Maison Diev sounds at once like "the house of god" and "the soul and its god"; but let us not forget that The Sun is blue in the face, or that The Fool doesn't have where to hang up his spoon). I play with the aural description of the cards, with layers of sounds on top of the images, and I get all kinds of weird correspondences between them. (L'Empereur is anagram for 'merle pure' (pure blackbird), like the one we see in Le Toille. The woman in Le Toille/le toilette is watering herself. To water oneself, 'eaux soi', is anagram for 'oiseaux' the French word for birds). The French call that word play "la langue des oiseaux" ("the language of the birds"). I pay attention to the work of any author that plays with this language in one way or another. I read lots of poetry, and more precisely, wordplay-based poetry mostly written by French authors because French is the Marseille tarot's language.

You privilege French because the Marseille tarot is generally a French artifact?

Yes. By this I simply mean that these tarots were made in France; their images are inhabited by the French language. The French language has it, as almost everything sounds like something else. Think of the example on how Robert Desnos wrote an entire poem using phrases that are homophones to its title, Rose Sélavy: Rose aisselle a vit/Rr'ose, essaiea lá, vit/Rots et sel á vie/Rose S, L, have I... or how the OuLiPo group wrote 32 homophonic sentences to "le tramway de Strasbourg" to be placed in 32 respective train stops. It is hard to think in any other language where you can take one sentence and find 32 other sentences that sound the same but mean something else. Similarly, in the Marseille tarot everything also looks like something else. Both are languages full of swerves: you think you know where they are going, and they end up taking you elsewhere. It makes sense then to have some folklore around the Marseille tarot suggesting it can be 'played' (as in 'performed') as the French play with their own language:

> *Le Tarot contient de 22 lames ses leçons/Le Tarot qu'on tient, devin de lames, c'est le son.*
>
> (Roughly: the tarot contains its lessons in 22 cards/the tarot the diviner holds is made of sound.)

I haven't been able to pin point the actual origin of that phrase, which is an example of what the French call *rime riche* or *rich rhyme*; where several words with different meaning are pronounced identically. That phrase is both defining and exemplifying of how to play with the Marseille tarot. I brush my teeth with it every morning. Raymond Roussel was a master of *rime riche*. Here is his classical example:

> *les lettres du blanc sur les bandes du vieux billard*
>
> (the white letters on the sides of the old billiard table)

les lettres du blanc sur les bandes du vieux pillard
(the white man's letters about the old pillager's band)

Roussel wrote that, for him, writing a novel consisted of setting one of these sentences as his starting point and writing his way towards the second sentence. Writing becomes the act of reflecting on the unexpected connections between two dissimilar ideas brought together by an accidental similarity in shape. (Roussel biographers suggest that he was quite familiar with the *têtes de carton,* huge *papier maché* effigies of politicians and prominent people that would carry humorous, pun-based captions on their heads. For example, the effigy of a bald man would carry a sign saying "Je suis chauve, hein!" *chauve* means 'bald' but "chauve, hein" sounds like "chau-vin", this is, a chauvinist).

The Marseille tarot's design also allows for a visual version of *rime riche,* where several elements in the cards have similar shapes but represent totally different things. The World card and the II of Swords are the same image made from different elements. The mandorla (that blue floral ornament in The World card) resembles the elliptical shape of the two scimitars we see in the II of Swords. They share the same shape but differ in meaning. Thinking with our eyes we draw a straight line from the mandorla to the scimitars. By doing so we trace all kinds of connections between the idea of swords and what they represent, and the mandorla and what it represents, very much in the way Roussel did in his writings.

 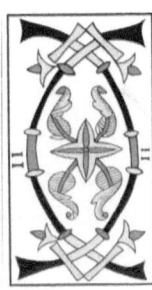

The woman in The World takes the shape of a flower in the II of Swords. A flower blossoming inside the clash of two swords gets visually and conceptually paired to a woman inhabiting a garland of blue leaves. Reading the Marseille tarot becomes an act of reflecting on the unexpected connections between these two things. What French wordplay allows and what the Marseille tarot allows are one and the same thing: their forms take us where we weren't going in an accidental way that, once it becomes evident, doesn't seems that accidental. All over the Marseille tarot's images we see a similarity of forms drawing connections between dissimilar objects. The working principle in rime riche is homophony: a similar sound draws two different words together. The visual version of this would be homomorphism: a similar shape draws two different things together. That is the Marseille tarot's visual language active principle.

I don't see any real evidence of a secret code embedded in the Marseille tarot. To me, redrawing the images would be a futile exercise. I did it when I was twenty, and I accomplished nothing. Even so, there are plenty of authors swearing they possess the only key to the Marseille tarot's 'decoding'. So, if there is something to be discovered there, I am sure there are other people more suited to find it than myself. I am not interested in the tarot because it is the repository of ancient knowledge, but because some of its performative aspects are the result of misreading a simple game of chance into an oracle. This is as wonderfully absurd as convincing a lady that her left shoe is a French poodle, and as such, it is full of poetic possibilities. I am fascinated by the potential of such swerves, even if I don't care for the direction a particular swerve has taken us so far.

I see more continuity between oracles and games of chance, divination and gambling, so the absurdity is not that her shoe is mistaken as a French poodle but that she wants to wear shoes that resemble a dog.

I agree with you about oracles and games, but wearing shoes that look like dogs will not take you out of your narrative. Petting a shoe as if it were a dog will. That's the gesture I am pursuing.

The Camoin-Jodorowsky reconstruction of the Marseille tarot is an example of accepting the limitation of the image while also inventing a consistency of a detailing and coloring that one would be hard pressed to prove was in the previous versions of the Marseille tarot.

Their tarot is an extraordinary extension of the Marseille tradition. They truly brought the deck to the 21st century. It was literally as if they blew the dust off the cards! Sadly they presented it as a restoration of the 'original' Marseille tarot. I understand how clever this marketing ploy is, but I feel it betrays Jodorowsky's accomplishment at bringing shamanism to a contemporary audience. No one has done what he has done. The idea that something can only be meaningful if it has an 'ancient' origin is one of the biggest conceptual limitations of the new age world.

Personally I like your approaches to wordplay that derive from your reading Francophone poets and artists. The Dadaists and Surrealists among others are rife with astounding metaphors derived from mechanical happenstance and found images.

Here is a cool conjunction: by the time Paul Marteau reinstated the Marseille tarot in the 1930s, the Surrealist movement was the main cultural force in Paris. Bretón and his cohort had rediscovered the work of authors like Roussel, or Jean-Pierre Brisset, who wrote: "All ideas uttered with similar sounds have the same origin and all refer, in principle, to the same object"; or Alfred Jarry, who wrote: "the alliterations, the rhymes and the assonances reveal these deep kinships between words". Jarry used to play a game he called *Les Propos des Assassins* in which the participants would say words aloud, looking for homophonic associations, either by saying these words forward or backwards. Eventually, dadaists and surrealists would repeat these games.

Those were authors who made an extraordinary use of homophony, wordplay, puns, constrained writing, etc. Jarry stated that through such humorous wordplay and association one would find the truth at every detour "On retrouve la verité à tous les detours". In his view, wordplay could take us to a more accurate, truthful representation of the world "les jeux de mots ne sont pas un jeu"("wordplay is not just a game"). If we move forward 30 years or so, we find an echo of such ideas in Michael Leiris words: "By dissecting the words we like, without bothering about conforming either to their etymologies or to their accepted significations, we discover their most hidden qualities and the secret ramifications that are propagated through the whole language, channeled by associations of sounds, forms and ideas. Then language changes into an oracle, and there we have a thread (however slender it may be) to guide us through the babel of our minds".

Jarry is especially relevant because he is the creator of 'pataphysics, a science of exceptions and imaginary solutions. As charming as the Marseille folklore is, nothing in it amounts to a whole coherent system or 'code'. What we have is the regularization of exceptions, which is an eminently 'pataphysical gesture.

'Pataphysics does not aim at unveiling that what is invisible, but to derail it. That pretty much sums up what I personally expect from tarot readings. Through 'pataphysics I arrived at the work of other, more contemporary, authors, like bp Nichol, Christian Bök, or the OuLiPo group. I read their poetry, I read about their poetics. All these authors shared a desire to play with language, either by means of free association or severe constraints, hoping that language would then take them to a place where they were not going.

Eventually, Bretón wrote *Arcane 17*, a whole book inspired by Lestoille (The Star) card. If you read that book expecting to find the 'meaning' of The Star in the way a tarot enthusiast is used to think of 'meaning' you will be lost. The book is an extraordinary example of analogy as thought-process. *In Arcane 17*, the morning star becomes a promise of a new day. That new day is brought by a woman's hand operating through/on nature. The 17th trump becomes an analogy for the recovery of Europe after World War II by means of ecology and feminism.

> ...the star found here again is the early morning star, which tended to eclipse the other heavenly bodies in the window. It surrenders to me the secret of its structure, explains to me why it numbers twice as many points as they, why its points are fiery red and yellow, as if it were two overlapping stars with alternating rays. It is the product of the actual unity of these two mysteries: love summoned to rebirth from the loss of the love object and only then rising to its full consciousness, to its complete dignity; liberty vowing to really know itself well and to become dynamic since its own loss is at stake. In the nocturnal image that was my guide, the resolution of this double contradiction takes place under the protection of the tree that encloses the remnants of dead wisdom, through exchanges between the butterfly and the flower and by virtue of the principle of the uninterrupted expansion of fluids, connected to the certainty of eternal renewal.

For Bretón, the morning star suggested the unavoidability of a new day, a new life. After La Maison Dieu comes Lestoille. After the fire from the Heavens overthrows the Devil, the maid comes to heal the world.

Just as I read all that poetry, I make as many attempts as I can at playing with language in the way they did, not to write poems, but to develop a way of thinking about the tarot based on the poetics of wordplay. That is what I call my 'tongue exercises'. I don't consider the things I write to be poems. They are my shared thoughts. It is my view that, if you follow my tongue exercises, you will learn tarot. I don't mean that every single tongue exercise needs to be applied to the cards. It is the persistence of their gestures that could have you thinking in terms that follow the Marseille tarot's logic.

Perhaps you can offer a few selected examples of your tongue exercises here with explanations of constraints or rules of transformation?

My favorite tongue exercise is this one:

Y L

WY EL

/waɪ//ɛl/

VOYELLE

It interests me because it shows, step by step, the process of turning an image into sound in such a way that the sound takes us to a whole different direction from the one the image was going to. The act of voicing YL aloud takes us to a detour in which two consonants pronounced in English are turned into the French word for vowels. I love when a simple gesture presents us with more than one layer of significance. At one level we have an image: Y L which turns into two different phonemes when you read it aloud: WY EL. At another level we have the notion of consonants being the body of a word (con-sonant, to sound with, the consonant is the physical resistance that the tongue, teeth and lips make to the air passing through the mouth) and vowels being the soul of words (a breath from the bowels, the most primal sign of life). But a breath is a bowel movement, a 'soul' created by the physicality of breathing. That notion is reflected by the fact that, in the exercise, two consonants create 'vowels'.

Analogously I am reminded of the number odd-even rule: Two odds (consonants) equal one even (vowel), One odd plus one even equals one odd. One even plus one even equals one even. Vowels are open sounds, consonants are closed sounds. Two closed sounds open. One closed and one open sound equals one closed sound. One even sound plus another even sound equals a diphthong!

Beautiful! The body against itself equals one soul. There is also that other level where the whole thing becomes an allusion to the fact that our experience of the tarot is embodied: we only understand what the characters in the cards are doing because we have experienced these actions ourselves. At one level the exercise is saying: "pay attention to the swerve that occurs when you describe a card aloud. Follow it!" At another level, the exercise reinstates the embodied nature of the tarot experience.

Another tongue exercise I especially like is this one:

a b c d e f g h i j k l m n o p q r s t u v w x y z

    b   i j   o   u   x

I made this tongue exercise after meeting Vito Acconci. It was Acconci who made me aware of the fact that words hide words in them; just like a sequence of tarot cards hide visual rhymes. I was curious of what kind of words could be concealed in the alphabet itself. What I found was an epiphany. Finding the word 'bijoux' (jewel) hidden in the alphabet is a way to exemplify the search for patterns within a sequence of cards. At some point you find a group of elements within the whole image that says something coherent and allows you to 'erase' the rest. What makes this tongue exercise especially relevant for me is the revelation of the 'hidden gem' in the alphabet. The gesture literally shows that the alphabet hides treasures. By extension, this tongue exercise shows that there are always hidden gems in any word or image, waiting for us to uncover them.

"I was a hidden treasure who loved to be known; therefore, I created the universes so that I might be known," is the sacred Sufi saying (hadith) of Mohammad speaking in the divine voice indicating the ultimate motivation for the creation.

Aha! We go back to the idea of pleasure. We look at other people's creations because it gives us pleasure. We create, not only out of necessity, but out of pleasure.

Here is another tongue exercise I like:

    ow, ow
    slowdown
    woo, woo
    swoon woods
    ow, ow
    lowdown

ow, ow

owl snow

woo, woo

wools woos

.wo, wo

wow won

This is a very simple exercise that proposes the recognition of a pattern: ow ow. The exercise also proposes the recognition of a mirror pattern: wo wo (the mirroring gesture is hinted at by the dot in front of the 'w' in the second to last line). The pattern is 'hidden' in the words of the text. In the same way, all kinds of patterns are hidden in the tarot. For example, there is a pattern of wings hidden in a sequence of cards like Temperance, The Lover, Judgement. There is also a pattern of two small characters being topped by a huge character in many of the cards. We see a sword–flower–sword pattern in the suit of swords, and so on.

All these patterns give a distinctive visual sense to a sequence. At the same time, repetitions of visual patterns translate into repetitions of sound-patterns. The tongue exercise makes this evident: the sound "ow wo" gets repeated in every single line of the text. We would get a similar sound-sense by describing the patterns we find in any sequence of cards: a pattern of wings, wings, wings; a pattern of crowns, crowns, crowns, a pattern of thrones, thrones, thrones, etc.

I did a variation of that exercise in which the hidden pattern was oo, o o:

oo, o o

soon, solo

There are two letters 'o' in the first word and in the second word, but while in the first word they are together, in the second word they are separated by another letter. There is a difference between 'oo' and 'o o', just as there is a difference between seeing Temperance's vases in Justice's scale and seeing Temperance's vases in The Chariot's horses.

The main intention behind all tongue exercises is to instill a spirit of playfulness in the way we deal with any language. Any language can be used in ways that transcend everyday communication. The non-standard use of any language opens up unexpected ideas. The only caveat is that all these ideas arise from taking any the signs of language for what they are, at a concrete level, while leaving aside their traditional meaning. Someone said that "poetry is evidence of inquiry". I like that. I use that. I use poetic thinking to inquire on the formal aspects of tarot because I don't think that prose is the most useful way of thinking about it.

Your observation causes me to be reminded of how mind numbing even some of the best guidebooks to the tarot can feel after one becomes absorbed in the mystery of card readings. Perhaps we need to encourage our tarot interpreters to return to poetry and be sparing with prose. Who knows the world is awash in too much self-confident, self-deceiving prose!

Most of the prose you read in books regarding the meaning of the tarot is the author's creative response to the images. That creative response is embellished, or informed, by the author's personal tastes: those who find beauty in numerology would respond to the images with a numerological-informed kind of prose. The same thing goes for those who find beauty in astrology, the kabala, or the Holly Grail. It can be said that I am also responding to my personal preference for poetry, except for the fact that I never cared for poetry before I started contemplating the Marseille tarot. It was the Marseille tarot's own visual logic what lead me to poetry, and to the work of all these authors we discussed, plus many others like Richard Kostelanetz, Victor Coleman, Charles Bernstein, Caroline Bergvall, Vanessa Place, or Kenneth Goldsmith.

I hope that the Marseille tarot in itself would dictate the constraints I would use to craft my creative response to it. Poetry provided the resources to accomplish this. It was as if the tarot wes telling me: *'learn about rhyme, rhythm, homophony, and wordplay and you will get what I am saying.'* When you realize that the 'ear' is concealed in the 'pearl' you start seeing the cards differently. You start thinking with your eyes, and you realize that the yellow sprout in the Ace of Baston rhymes with the fire in La Maison Diev; the fire in La Maison Diev rhymes with the water stream in Temperance; Temperance's vases rhyme with Le Toille's vase; Le Toille's black bird rhymes with Lemperevur's black eagle; Lemperevur's crossed legs rhyme with Le Pandu's crossed legs, and so on. Just as the Marseille tarot demands a style of readings that emerges from its own forms, I hope these forms will eventually point out an organic way of performing the tarot in which readings may only play a part.

How so?

There are people who inspire me without even trying, or knowing it. I spent "Sword-Swallower's Day" keeping company with Harley Newman, a performer of fantastic, death-defying, stunts. He told me something that was a revelation to me: "the same thing I accomplish by swallowing a sword or hanging upside-down in a straitjacket, you accomplish by changing a letter in a word. We throw people off-balance so they find themselves outside of what they thought was possible." I have thought long and hard about that. I am fascinated by the subversive power of the smallest gestures.

I have been thinking a lot of Aram Saroyan's *Lighght* poem. Saroyan added an extra 'gh' to the word 'light' so the word cannot be pronounced anymore, only experienced. Some people swear that this poem IS the actual experience of light. Saroyan's gesture takes us back to Alfred Jarry, who opened his play *Ubu Roi* by adding an extra 'r' to the French word for shit: *merde*. Saroyan's 'Lighght' and Jarry's 'merdre' speak of how a small gesture, such as adding a letter to a word can have us stepping out of the world, out of the way we use language. Incidentally, both Jarry and Saroyan raised riots with these small gestures.

'Reality' is a big word. I see the tarot as the extra letter that can turn 'reality' into a whole different experience. I just need to figure out where exactly I should slip that extra letter, for the whole wor[l]d to topple over? I am working on it. I try to stay open to all these games I play with images and words, so the tarot can become a source of signs and sounds, a source for pleasure. I don't necessarily know where I will go with all this. I only know that, after every twist and turn, I always go back to the simplicity of the Marseille tarot, and to the visual coherence of its images, as a source of inspiration. I go wherever the Marseille tarot takes me, and I always come back to it for more.

I'll keep my eyes open and my ears alert and perhaps I'll catch a whiff of what you are working on! Thank you, Enrique!

Thank you, Paul!

www.ingramcontent.com/pod-product-compliance
Lightning Source LLC
Chambersburg PA
CBHW030403250426
43670CB00049B/128